THE OPINIONATED UNIVERSITY

The Opinionated University

ACADEMIC FREEDOM, DIVERSITY, AND THE MYTH OF NEUTRALITY IN AMERICAN HIGHER EDUCATION

+ + + + + + + + + + + + + + + + + + + +

BRIAN SOUCEK

THE UNIVERSITY OF CHICAGO PRESS
CHICAGO AND LONDON

The University of Chicago Press, Chicago 60637
The University of Chicago Press, Ltd., London

Published 2026
Printed in the United States of America

35 34 33 32 31 30 29 28 27 26   1 2 3 4 5

ISBN-13: 978-0-226-83965-3 (cloth)
ISBN-13: 978-0-226-84615-6 (paper)
ISBN-13: 978-0-226-84614-9 (ebook)
DOI: https://doi.org/10.7208/chicago/9780226846149.001.0001

Library of Congress Cataloging-in-Publication Data

Names: Soucek, Brian, author.
Title: The opinionated university : academic freedom, diversity, and the myth of neutrality in American higher education / Brian Soucek.
Other titles: Academic freedom, diversity, and the myth of neutrality in American higher education
Description: Chicago ; London : The University of Chicago Press, 2026. | Includes bibliographical references and index.
Identifiers: LCCN 2025021934 | ISBN 9780226839653 (cloth) | ISBN 9780226846156 (paperback) | ISBN 9780226846149 (ebook)
Subjects: LCSH: Academic freedom—United States. | Freedom of speech—United States. | Education, Higher--United States.
Classification: LCC LC72.2 .S68 2026 | DDC 378.1/2130973—dc23/eng/20250605
LC record available at https://lccn.loc.gov/2025021934

∞ This paper meets the requirements of ANSI/NISO Z39.48-1992 (Permanence of Paper).

Authorized Representative for EU General Product Safety Regulation (GPSR) queries: **Easy Access System Europe**—Mustamäe tee 50, 10621 Tallinn, Estonia, gpsr.requests@easproject.com
Any other queries: https://press.uchicago.edu/press/contact.html

Contents

Introduction
The Myth of Neutrality

By the time the presidents of Harvard, MIT, and Penn appeared before Congress in December 2023, their universities were already in crisis because of what they had said—or not said—about Hamas's October attack on Israel and the counterattacks that followed. Statements had been too slow to come out, critics said, or failed to condemn the right atrocities or to distance the university from student groups or faculty seen as endorsing violence.

But few on the House Committee on Education and the Workforce, where the three presidents testified, wanted to parse the statements Claudine Gay, Sally Kornbluth, and Liz Magill had made on their universities' behalf.[1] The exchange that would soon cost two of the three presidents their jobs focused on a different issue: student speech codes. Representative Elise Stefanik, Republican of New York, wanted to know whether calls for genocide against Jewish people would violate school rules. In answers that quickly went viral, the three presidents each repeated the legally correct claim that calling for genocide *might* be prohibited, "depending on the context." Representative Stefanik responded with disgust: "The answer is yes, and this is why you should resign." At least the first half of Stefanik's response soon gained bipartisan support. A White House spokesperson, the Democratic governor of Pennsylvania, and Democratic representatives from Massachusetts all suggested that it shouldn't have been hard to condemn genocide. Few seemed to notice that President Gay had repeatedly characterized calls for genocide as "personally abhorrent" and "at odds with the values of Harvard."[2]

Many in the House, and later in the press, converged on a single culprit both for the presidents' perceived failures at the hearings and for antisemitism on college campuses: "DEI." University initiatives to advance diversity, equity, and inclusion, one congressman suggested, were directly linked to "Marxist centered groups like BLM, Antifa, and pro-Hamas."[3] "Harvard Chooses DEI Over Academics," the *National Review* titled its summary of the hearings, treating then-president Gay's "glib performance" as the predictable result of a rushed hiring process that put "ideological objectives over and above, you know, academics."[4] The article's barely concealed subtext, which major donors were saying outright at the time, was that Harvard's first Black president was academically unqualified for the job. "Rather, her ascension to Harvard's president represented the culmination of the Diversity, Equity, and Inclusion (DEI) agenda," the *National Review* concluded.[5]

Where some blamed DEI efforts, others drew a different lesson from the hearings. One headline summed it up: "Now is the time for administrators to embrace neutrality. The Israel-Hamas war might finally show colleges the virtues of the Kalven Report."[6] The report in question, a policy at the University of Chicago dating back to 1967, imposes a "heavy presumption" against a university "expressing opinions on the political and social issues of the day." To speak out as an institution, the Kalven Report claims, is to endanger the academic freedom of the institution's members; making collective statements comes "at the price of censuring any minority who do not agree with the view adopted."[7]

If keeping quiet might have kept the presidents out of hot water, as some said, it might also have led to charges of inconsistency, even antisemitism—since schools like Harvard had a long history of speaking out on other world events, even flying the Ukrainian flag over Harvard Yard after Russia's invasion. But committing to neutrality could at least set a less divisive precedent going forward. That's what many of the country's leading campus speech organizations argued, and pushing universities to commit to institutional neutrality soon became a central and successful focus of their advocacy.[8] New policies and even state laws requiring universities to stay neutral have been multiplying ever since.[9]

Universities are mistaken, though, if they think neutrality pledges are going to solve their current problems. For as this book aims to show, the promise of neutrality is just an illusion.

: : :

Linking institutional statements, DEI initiatives, and campus speech codes seemed original when I started writing this book. I worried that readers would need help seeing connections among what might have appeared to be unrelated controversies. Little did I know that all three would soon appear together on the front page of the newspaper. But, in fact, choices about what universities say, what they prize in faculty hiring and advancement, and what speech they allow on campus all amount to much the same thing. They all express a university's views about how its values—whether they be freedom of expression, scholarly expertise, academic freedom, or diversity and equitable inclusion—should best be understood and balanced. They all say something about how a university views its mission.

To see that universities express their commitments as much through what they do as what they say is to see calls for neutrality in a different light. To put it bluntly, it is to see institutional neutrality as a myth. Universities are unavoidably opinionated. That is this book's central claim.

The congressional hearings help make the point. Staying silent may seem wise, may even *be* wise, when the topic is something like the two-state solution in the Middle East. "The University of Wisconsin does not have a foreign policy," its provost smartly declared in 2003, when the invasion of Iraq was the controversy of the day.[10] But a college president's principled neutrality would have done nothing to avoid Representative Stefanik's attack. *Will* students be subjected to investigation or discipline if they chant "from the river to the sea" on a campus quad? Even if the answer depends on context, as the presidents told Congress, it will ultimately be either a yes or a no in each particular case. The pro-Palestinian encampments that filled university quads in spring 2024—including at the loudly "neutral" University of Chicago—showed how unavoidable these decisions are. A university *necessarily* makes choices about what kinds of speech it allows and what kinds of harms it protects against. And when faced with those choices, no option counts as neutral.[11]

Fine, neutrality hawks might respond. That just goes to show that there are some things a university can or must opine about (like the bounds of permissible speech on campus) and others (like Israel's borders) on which it should or even must not express views. Even the University of Chicago's Kalven Report—with its presumption in favor of neutrality, which has since become a model for other schools—allows for exceptions. It accepts that a university must be able to defend against threats to its "very mission . . . and its values of free inquiry." But necessary as this exception is, just look where it leads. The presumption is no longer that universities should refrain from expressing opinions on controversial issues—a nonstarter in our hyper-politicized nation—or on issues that can be characterized as political, a category that has increasingly come to include basic scientific and historical facts. The claim has come to this: A university should stay silent on anything that doesn't threaten its mission.

Calls for neutrality thus reduce to arguments over the scope of a university's mission. We might easily agree that certain opinions are external to the mission and that others are at its center. Endorsing a candidate for president is no business of a university. It would be illegal at many public schools and a danger to the tax-exempt status of the rest. By contrast, when a successful presidential candidate goes on to ban the teaching of certain "divisive concepts,"[12] the impact on core university operations might provoke an institutional response even from die-hard Kalvenists.

There are endless examples lying between these, however. Sure, institutional endorsement of political candidates is impermissible, but what about the statement signed by most US law school deans denouncing the January 6th rioters and the Big Lie as a threat to the rule of law?[13] Yes, a ban on teaching critical race theory directly affects speech on campus, but what about abortion restrictions or bans on gender-affirming health care for minors? Does the answer turn on whether universities in the states passing these bans have a hospital or medical school, where faculty and students would be forced to teach and learn something other than evidence-based standards of care? Is that what would turn these bans into threats to the university's mission, or are their effects on some students' and faculty's ability to engage in the work of the university enough to merit a statement?

What would count as a *neutral* answer to questions like these? Even if a university commits to the principles of the Kalven Report, it needs to decide what values it harmonizes within its mission before it can decide what issues count as sufficiently mission threatening to justify an institutional statement. The so-called neutrality debate really amounts to a debate over how a university defines its mission—a question that, again, can't be given a neutral answer.

If fights about institutional statements turn out to be proxy wars over universities' missions, so, too, do the other two issues this book explores: the increasingly controversial requirements that faculty report their contributions to diversity, equity, and inclusion, and ever-recurring debates surrounding hostile speech on campus. These are also contests over the mission of a university, the values it should endorse, and the way those values should be balanced.

Contrary to arguments I'll be confronting throughout this book, no single mission is essential for an institution to count as a genuine university. I talk of *a* university's mission to emphasize that different schools—public or private, religious or secular, global or local, progressive or tradition based, HBCUs or women's colleges, those oriented more toward cutting-edge research, civic engagement, or social mobility—might each balance different values in different ways without thereby becoming something other than a true university.[14] And that point goes for departments and other units within a university as well.

When I talk about a university's mission, I mean something deeper than its "mission statement." In keeping with this book's claim that universities' actions can be as expressive as their words, I understand a university's mission to emerge not just from policies that explicitly state its aims, but also from those that define, protect, or advance values like freedom of expression, academic freedom, academic merit, and diversity, equity, and inclusion. A university's mission is reflected in the kinds of students and faculty it works to attract. It can be seen in a school's curricular requirements and the strengths of its faculty. It's found in the details of an institution's budget and investment decisions.[15] And a school's mission, as we'll see, can sometimes be gleaned from the public statements its leaders choose to make.

But how much do universities' missions actually vary? Stanford may care about different things than Smith, and Salve Regina is a very different place than Southern University. But surely universities all exist to foster some mix of research and teaching, both of which require some measure of academic freedom. At least within different categories of schools, we might wonder if universities' missions are different enough to matter. Isn't one big research university engaged in more or less the same business as the next?

Pluralism about universities' missions certainly doesn't require us to deny the commonalities. As Stanley Fish has rightly observed, "A university would still be one if all it contained were classrooms, a library, and facilities for research. A university would not be one if all it contained was a quad with some tables on it, a student union with a food court, an auditorium and a bowling alley, a gymnasium with a swimming pool and some climbing walls."[16] Even the commonalities can hide important variation, however. The pages that follow describe deep differences in the ways crucial values like academic freedom are understood, in the specific ways they are protected—say, by insisting on institutional neutrality but not on shared governance, or vice versa—and in how they are balanced with potentially competing values.

Or consider curricular requirements. Three times in my life I've taken or taught a required set of classes based around the so-called Great Books. The books themselves were pretty much the same at all three places, but the point of reading them was wildly different. At Boston College, a Jesuit school, the goal was to help students develop morally and spiritually, to consider what makes for a life worth living. At Columbia, the humanities core was developed during World War I to help students understand the democratic values they'd be fighting for. And at the University of Chicago, the Great Books were taught largely because of their greatness. They were seen as the texts most worth the intellectual effort, the ones a truly educated person needs to know. What from a certain distance may have looked like a shared curriculum was, at closer range, really three different educational projects reflective of three institutions with importantly different conceptions of themselves—which is to say, three different missions.[17]

Universities, like all of us, face unavoidable choices about what they value and what they want to be. Calling on universities to stop expressing opinions is a distraction that masks the necessity of these choices. This book refuses to pretend that neutrality is an option. In doing so, it forces us to ask just what universities' commitments should be—and who should (and shouldn't) be forming them.

: : :

This book puts the conversation around institutional statements alongside two other debates currently roiling universities (and the country as a whole): whether to reward DEI contributions, and how to regulate harmful speech. Looking at institutional neutrality in the broader context of universities' expressive actions helps to reveal how unavoidably opinionated universities really are. This is the argument that spans and structures this book.

But each of these three topics is difficult and important in its own right too. Fights over mandatory diversity statements, institutional speech by universities and their departments, and the regulation of hostile expression on campus each count among the biggest controversies in American higher education right now. They are the subject of faculty meetings, lawsuits, legislation, and, more recently, front-page news—even presidential politics. I was already on the losing end of each of these fights even before the 2024 election. Since then, the second Trump administration quickly began using executive orders, federal funding, and the litigation power of the Department of Justice as tools to end DEI efforts, which it views as discrimination against white students and faculty. It is leveraging charges of antisemitism to escalate the crackdown on campus protest that began in response to the encampments of 2024. And it is doing all of this in a world where an increasing number of universities have pledged (or been told) to speak out less often, if at all.

The Trump administration's attempts to reshape American higher education are just another reminder that there is no neutral ground in these fights. In the current context, what's called "neutrality" is often nothing but quietism in the face of value-laden attacks. The unprecedented breadth of these attacks makes it even more important to understand the values that are at stake. This book aims to clarify and provide guidance on controversies surrounding diversity, academic freedom, and freedom of expression, even as it uses them to build an overarching claim against the misleading rhetoric around university neutrality.

Chapters 1, 3, and 5 are devoted, respectively, to debates over diversity statements, institutional speech, and the regulation of speech on campus. In between, chapters 2 and 4 bridge the primary topics, suggesting connections between conversations that have often been seen as separate. The underappreciated—or hypocritically ignored—academic freedom threats presented by student teaching evaluations and college rankings are the topic of chapter 2, while chapter 4 explores the potential use of institutional speech as an alternative to the direct regulation of student and faculty expression.

To give a preview of how it all fits together:

Chapter 1 focuses on requirements—which were growing more common until they started getting banned—that faculty seeking jobs or promotions submit statements describing what they have done to promote diversity, equity, and inclusion in their professional lives.[18] These mandatory "diversity statements," as they're often called, have been condemned as modern-day loyalty oaths, akin to the anti-Communist pledges of the McCarthy era. Critics say they give rise to unconstitutional viewpoint discrimination and threaten faculty's academic freedom.

I've been a vocal defender of diversity statements,[19] but I take seriously the charges that have been made against their use. In some ways, I take the charges more seriously than many of those making them, often in op-eds, blog posts, and tweets that give short shrift to the complicated free speech law and academic freedom principles that their arguments invoke. Untangling and explaining academic freedom and freedom of expression, as chapter 1 does, provides necessary background for all the chapters that follow. And it's especially necessary in order to understand why critics see diversity statements as such a profound threat to higher education.

Taking these threats seriously, however, also allows us to see how they can be avoided. Chapter 1 points the way. In using DEI statements, universities need to focus on *plans and actions* rather than *beliefs*; these plans and actions should address identified DEI shortcomings *within* a particular discipline; and like all other evaluations of faculty merit, judgments about the value of DEI contributions should be made by *experts in that discipline* rather than being imposed from above, or simply presumed.

All too often, critics of diversity statements beg the question of what counts as an academic contribution. They simply assume a notion of academic merit that excludes DEI contributions as extraneous. (A report on DEI statements from the American Enterprise Institute is actually titled *Other Than Merit*.[20]) But why assume that the work (some) faculty do to help a diverse set of students flourish, or to produce research that meets the needs of diverse communities, isn't part of a job done well? To assume that this work is something "other than merit" is to see the university's aim of discovering and disseminating knowledge as somehow abstracted from questions about who benefits from that knowledge.

When we stop begging the question of what counts as academic achievement, we're forced to think more deeply about what a particular university's purpose should be. The controversy over diversity statements thus turns out to be, at heart, a debate over the scope of a university's mission—this book's running theme.

The attention, even fury, that diversity statements have attracted is especially striking when placed next to more dire threats to academic freedom that receive little public attention at all. Chapter 2 looks at universities' reliance on student teaching evaluations and their shameless pandering to *U.S. News* rankings—two of the greatest and least-discussed threats to academic freedom in American higher education today. Congress isn't holding hearings to ask college presidents about these things. State legislatures aren't rushing out corrective legislation, editorial boards aren't calling for change, and advocates for campus speech and academic freedom aren't trumpeting these threats in their press releases (and fundraising emails). Why the different treatment, compared to DEI policies? Is it because the well-established disparate impacts of student evaluations and *U.S. News* rankings affect different groups than those who feel disadvantaged by mandated diversity statements?

In looking at academic freedom distractions and hypocrisies, chapter 2 connects chapter 1's discussion of diversity statements—that's the distraction—to chapter 3's discussion of institutional neutrality as a requisite for academic freedom, a position now most closely associated with the University of Chicago. That's the hypocrisy. Academic freedom, after all, rests on the idea that academic judgments must be made by disciplinary experts, not outsiders like administrators, trustees, donors, legislators, or the general public—much less students brand-new to a field, or to a digital media company like *U.S. News & World Report*. And yet certain universities have built a brand around academic freedom even as they've allowed arbitrary rankings criteria to shape some of their most central academic decisions.

However consistent its commitment, the University of Chicago is undeniably perceived—not least by itself—as a national leader on academic freedom.[21] Its heralded and now widely adopted Kalven Report treats institutional neutrality as a necessary condition for academic freedom; by extension, that means institutional neutrality is necessary for a school to be a genuine university. Chapter 3 questions whether neutrality really is necessary, or even possible. Universities are unavoidably opinionated when making decisions about what to do. That is this book's overarching argument. Chapter 3 shows that decisions about what to *say* are no less value-laden. And this is true even by the lights of the Kalven Report itself. Since the report permits institutional speech to counter threats to "the very mission of the university," faithful Kalvenists will end up expressing a view on the scope of a university's mission every time the university is called upon to speak. None of this is neutral.

And just as this is true of speech by universities, so too is it true about statements by units *within* the university. A central topic and, hopefully, contribution of chapter 3 is its discussion of speech by departments, schools, and centers within a university—or by their chairs, deans, directors, or collective faculty. The costs and benefits of departmental speech are different from that of speech by the institution as a whole, and they are surprisingly underexplored, especially given all the controversy that certain statements by departments have provoked in recent years.

Chapter 4 builds another bridge, using the notion of institutional counterspeech to link two topics: institutional speech (the focus of chapter 3) and an institution's *restrictions* on the speech of its members (the topic of chapter 5). One of the main reasons a university might want to speak is to counteract a harm that the university itself has caused. Sometimes universities are forced or pressured, often by law, to do something that runs counter to their values. Their only recourse might be to do so under protest—to speak out against the law or in support of people the law is hurting.

Chapter 4 develops this point through examples of institutional speech countering discrimination based on gender identity and sexual orientation, in contexts as visible as military hiring and as under the radar as campus blood drives. The time when institutional counterspeech is most often needed, though, is in response to hostile speech on campus. Hate speech often can't be regulated by the university, but that doesn't mean it should be left unanswered. If, as we're often told, the best answer to offensive speech is more speech,[22] universities can provide an important part of that answer. Chapter 4 explores how institutional speech can help counterbalance institutional action, or inaction, that causes harm, thereby lessening the need for direct regulation of speech.

Chapter 5's focus on speech regulations brings up an issue that every generation seems to face anew. Sixty years ago, the tumult of the Vietnam War era gave us the free speech movement and the Kalven Report. Thirty years ago, "political correctness" played the role "cancel culture" does now, "multiculturalism" was the "wokeness" of the day, and lawsuits striking down bans on hate speech foreshadowed the suits against bias response teams today.[23] Then, as now, university antidiscrimination policies faced legal threats. Universities were sometimes losing and, to a shocking extent, they were settling the cases brought against them. The same is happening now.

Each of these moments has seen universities grappling with how to meet their competing duties to protect speech and prevent discrimination. Then, as now, universities were deciding how to balance robust expression with more equitable inclusion of an increasingly diverse population. And courts were refusing to defer to some universities' views on these questions, putting their own finger on the constitutional scale.

What is different, from then to now, is the particular balance that free speech advocates and, increasingly, courts have been pushing universities to strike. Chapter 5 looks at two important lines of cases, one challenging attempts to curb racially and sexually hostile student speech, the other alleging an academic freedom right for faculty to misgender their students. By pairing student speech—largely in non-academic spaces like quads, dining halls, and dormitories—with faculty speech rights in the classroom, chapter 5 shows the importance of distinguishing general free speech protections from academic freedom. Expanding the former can actually undermine the latter. Different spaces and activities on campus require different rules.

Free speech advocates, reporters and commentators, and even courts often flatten out these distinctions. They fail to see how universities' conflicting values should be balanced differently in different spaces across campus. As a result, courts sometimes end up replacing the balance a university would choose with a judgment of their own. They limit universities' ability to express their particular mission through the balance they strike between speech and other values.

This brings us to the book's coda, which asks more broadly who should get to do this kind of balancing. If universities are unavoidably opinionated, as this book argues, how should their opinions be formed? And insofar as the controversies discussed in this book turn out to be fights over the mission of a university, who ultimately gets to decide what a given university's mission is to be?

No one has understood the stakes of these questions better than the red state governors and legislators who have recently banned DEI initiatives (including diversity statements), required institutional neutrality at public universities, and pushed against anti-harassment rules meant to promote sex and racial equality on campus. (Attempts to prevent religious discrimination on campus have received a less consistent response, blurring some of the usual partisan lines.) The havoc these interventions have caused at what were once great colleges and universities shows the dangers of letting state officials, or wealthy donors, simply dictate what a school's mission should be.[24] But someone has to make these decisions. There is no neutral fallback position when debates over a university's mission are underway. And as the following pages aim to show, these fights are always, unavoidably underway.

So who should be making the decisions? The rich tradition of *shared governance* within the modern university provides the best model. But shared governance is under threat. Too many legislators, trustees, donors, and administrators have shown little interest in working with faculty to shape their university's mission. And shared governance gets too little support from some of our most vocal defenders of academic freedom, whose focus on individual rights comes at the expense of the collective action that higher education currently needs.

Truly shared governance requires both material commitment from a university and genuine bravery from its faculty. To bust the myth of neutrality—to accept that universities can't help but express opinions about their values and their mission—is to recognize that if faculty don't do their part to shape those opinions, others surely will.

1 *Diversity Statements*
A Performance Evaluation, Not a Litmus Test

"If Albert Einstein applied for a professorship at UCLA today, would he be hired?" In 2018 the answer was no longer clear to Heather Mac Donald, a conservative commentator writing in the *Los Angeles Times*, because UCLA had begun requiring that all new hires "document their contributions to 'equity, diversity, and inclusion.'" According to Mac Donald, "UCLA's infatuation with diversity is a costly diversion from its true mission." The Einsteins of the world should be left to do science, she argued, instead of "also being tasked with a 'social justice' mission."[1]

Fast-forward five years to 2023, and the Manhattan Institute, where Mac Donald was and remains a fellow, was releasing model legislation that would *prohibit* public universities from requiring diversity statements in faculty hiring or promotion. Under its proposed law, universities would be barred from asking faculty and faculty applicants about their experience and views surrounding not just DEI, but also "marginalized groups; anti-racism; social justice; intersectionality; confessing one's race-based privilege; or related concepts."[2] The draft legislation was written by Christopher Rufo—famous for his attacks on critical race theory (or something he gave that name), his coup at New College of Florida, and his successful campaign against Harvard president Claudine Gay[3]—as well as Ilya Shapiro, formerly of the Cato Institute and then Georgetown Law School, where he ignited a firestorm for a tweet about President Biden bypassing Shapiro's preferred Supreme Court nominee for a "lesser black woman" who "will always have an asterisk attached."[4]

Within a year or so, Iowa, Texas, and Utah had turned the Manhattan Institute's draft legislation into actual state law, and six other states had banned DEI statements at their public universities as well, using different language.[5] During that time, similar bills were introduced in sixteen other states, and the House of Representatives considered a bill that would have stripped universities of federal funding if they required diversity statements, defined just as the Manhattan Institute had suggested. Meanwhile, MIT made headlines for announcing that it would no longer use diversity statements, which its president, Sally Kornbluth, said "impinge on freedom of expression, and . . . don't work."[6] Harvard's Faculty of Arts and Sciences soon followed suit, leading the *New York Times* to ask, "Is This the End for Mandatory D.E.I. Statements?"[7]

How have a couple required pages in a personnel file attracted the attention of state legislatures and the country's leading newspapers? It can't just be that some people think diversity statements "don't work," as President Kornbluth said. As the next chapter shows, our main way of evaluating faculty teaching—through student evaluations—has been exhaustively shown not to work, and to be racist and sexist to boot, but the editorial boards of national papers aren't weighing in on that, and politicians are hardly making it a priority.

The other half of President Kornbluth's statement gets closer to at least the official reason for all the hubbub: she says diversity statements "impinge on freedom of expression." The Academic Freedom Alliance—an advocacy organization formed in part to fight diversity statements—has put it more pointedly: "The demand for diversity statements enlists academics into a political movement." It imposes a "suffocating orthodoxy" that is "inimical to fundamental values that should govern academic life."[8] The AFA is just one of many intersecting, well-funded organizations that have pushed the claim that DEI statements pose an uncommonly dire threat to some of our universities' most cherished and necessary values.[9]

The importance of the values involved in this debate is beyond question. One of this chapter's goals is to explain and disentangle the academic freedom and broader free speech principles that are at stake here, setting the stage for the following chapters as well. What's questionable is whether diversity statements necessarily pose a *threat* to those values. The main aim of this chapter is to show how DEI statements can be used in ways that avoid the dangers that are so often alleged.

Hardly any of the arguments now being made against diversity statements are new. As far back as 2001, one of the country's most prominent campus speech advocacy organizations—FIRE, then the Foundation for Individual Rights in Education, now the Foundation for Individual Rights and Expression—was pushing a public community college in Pennsylvania to stop asking job applicants how their "commitment to diversity" was demonstrated in their work. "Your inquisition into private views of 'diversity' would force potential hires to confess both by word and by act their faith in the opinion that 'diversity' was essential to their teaching and academic life," FIRE wrote at the time. "This is a politically correct equivalent of a loyalty oath, as objectionable as a 1950s question asking for a statement from an applicant about his or her 'commitment to patriotism.'"[10] As FIRE and friends have often asked proponents of diversity statements in the years since: How would you feel if faculty had to demonstrate their "love of country" or their belief in "empiricism, biological determinism, or creationism?"[11]

This wasn't FIRE's only challenge. Already in 2001, FIRE was accusing Bucks County Community College of violating both its "constitutional obligation to content neutrality" and principles of academic freedom, developed by the American Association of University Professors (AAUP) in a series of policies dating back to 1915. According to FIRE, Bucks was forcing its professors "to introduce into their teaching controversial matter which has no relation to their subject."[12] FIRE succeeded in getting Bucks County Community College to drop its diversity statement requirement. But more importantly, FIRE succeeded in setting the terms of the debate going forward. In the two decades or more since, critics have seldom strayed from FIRE's three original lines of argument.

First, diversity statements are *loyalty oaths* or *political litmus tests*.[13] FIRE's claim finds echoes today in Florida's ban on "political loyalty test[s] as a condition of employment" at its public universities and Texas's "prohibitions regarding ideological oaths or statements," the title of the legislation it passed to ban diversity statements.[14] Model legislation proposed by the James G. Martin Center and Goldwater Institute in 2022, which the Manhattan Institute credited in its own anti-DEI proposal, is titled the "End Political Litmus Tests in Education Act."[15]

Some scholars have recently claimed that mandatory diversity statements are even *worse* than the loyalty oaths of the past. Northwestern

University law professor John McGinnis compares current requirements unfavorably to the Anglican creeds once required at Oxford and Cambridge, since those compelled statements of belief without requiring professors to actually *do* anything.[16] For Professor Richard Epstein, DEI statements are worse than the anti-Communist oaths of the McCarthy era because those at least were aimed at national security, a governmental interest Epstein views as more important than the educational benefits of diversity.[17]

Second among FIRE's arguments is the claim that universities engage in *unconstitutional viewpoint discrimination* when they use diversity statements in faculty hiring and promotion. Technically, this argument (like the first one) applies only to public universities, since the First Amendment applies to governmental entities, not private ones. But many private schools commit themselves to First Amendment principles, either in aspirational policy or in binding contracts like faculty or student handbooks, so the viewpoint discrimination argument often hits home there too.

Brian Leiter, a philosopher at the University of Chicago Law School and a prominent commentator on higher education, has argued that viewpoint discrimination is "the real moral and legal problem" with diversity statements. Leiter claims that "government cannot, excluding a few exceptions such as political appointments, base a hiring decision on the speaker's political viewpoint." Yet universities, he says, have started requiring "allegiance to a controversial set of moral and political views that have little or no relationship to a faculty member's pedagogical and scholarly duties."[18] On his blog, Professor Leiter repeatedly encouraged his readers to sue the University of California over diversity statements,[19] and in 2023, when a lawsuit finally appeared, a viewpoint discrimination claim was at its heart. J. D. Haltigan, a psychologist "committed to colorblind inclusivity," alleged in his suit that applying to UC Santa Cruz would have been a waste of time, since it uses DEI statements to "screen and penalize applicants" who don't endorse ideologies like anti-racism or concepts like intersectionality: the idea that race, gender, and other identities interact to shape distinct experiences of discrimination. (This was a somewhat surprising objection coming from Haltigan, given that he has described his work as studying "different stylistic ways of talking about early life attachment experiences among

African American pregnant women"—an intersectional identity if ever there was one.)[20]

The third line of attack from FIRE and its followers centers on *academic freedom*. Jeffrey Flier, former dean of Harvard Medical School, made headlines in late 2019 when he tweeted that requiring diversity statements "is an affront to academic freedom, and diminishes the true value of diversity, equity of inclusion by trivializing it."[21] (He added that he would never have been able to say such a thing as dean.) Flier wrote this while forwarding a statement from FIRE where it distinguished two ways that diversity statements threaten academic freedom. Mandates at places like UCLA were coming from administrators, not faculty, FIRE's then-president Robert Shibley wrote. And they endanger scholars' credibility with the general public, which depends on a perception that their research is motivated not by ideology or self-interest, but—to quote the AAUP's *1915 Declaration of Principles on Academic Freedom*—only by "their own scientific conscience and a desire for the respect of their fellow experts."[22]

When the Academic Freedom Alliance was launched in March 2021, the "right to be unburdened by ideological tests, affirmations, and oaths" was one of the academic freedoms it vowed to protect.[23] In case there was any doubt that this was code for diversity statements, the group's founder, Keith Whittington, spoke to the press on the day the AFA was announced, warning of a "growing movement today to use a new set of required affirmations to filter out potential faculty . . . who might not share certain orthodoxies regarding social justice or inclusivity."[24] The following year, the AFA officially called on universities to "desist from demanding 'diversity statements,'" which it said were spreading "with far too little attentiveness to obvious threats to academic freedom."[25]

A fourth argument sometimes also gets made against diversity statements, but it comes from a different place than the first three. It's an argument about equality rather than free speech, so it's not one you tend to hear from organizations like FIRE or the AFA. The claim is that diversity statements are just thinly veiled attempts by universities to increase the racial diversity of their faculty, especially in places like California, where taking account of race in hiring is prohibited by the state constitution. On this argument, diversity statements are nothing but a ruse to get around the color-blindness that is increasingly equated with nondiscrimination in American equality law.

All four of these critiques are serious, but that's not to say they're unanswerable. In fact, one way I differ from nearly all of my opponents in this debate is that I don't think abandoning DEI statements is the only possible response to the criticisms. Proponents of diversity statements—like me—do need to take steps to ensure that we're avoiding the problems critics raise. Let me put that more strongly: If a school is doing some of the things critics allege, it needs to stop. The problems DEI critics have identified implicate some of universities' most important and deeply held values: academic freedom, freedom of speech, diversity, and what some have called "inclusive excellence."[26] But before sending universities a cease-and-desist order, it's worth at least exploring how DEI statements might be framed and used in ways that respect these values—all of them—rather than sacrificing some for the sake of the others.

The four sections of this chapter grapple with these individual challenges to diversity statements one by one, in each case offering advice about how to meet the challenges. Along the way, what I hope to show is that thinking through these issues ultimately requires us to think seriously about what a university sees its mission to be.

On that last question, I'm a pluralist. My claim in what follows is *not* that every university needs to emphasize DEI values to the extent that mine has. I'm glad that the University of California, where I work, embraces the values it does, but that's not what I'm defending here. Here, I'm asking what should follow *if* a university believes that advancing diversity, equity, and inclusion is crucial to its mission. All too often, debates over diversity statements—like each of the debates to come in this book—distract us from the more fundamental question: What does a university want to be?

Loyalty Oaths

This chapter opened with Heather Mac Donald's policy argument that universities are overly focused on "the trivialities of identity." But the claims we hear most against universities' current use of DEI statements are specifically legal ones. Take, for example, the claim that mandating diversity statements is little different, and no more constitutional, than the anti-Communist loyalty oaths that professors were forced to swear during the Cold War. It's an argument that hits close to home at the university where I teach, given our history. Nearly half of the faculty who lost their jobs nationwide for failing to forswear communism were fired by the University of California.[27] By 1969, when our Regents unanimously ordered that "no political test shall ever be considered in the appointment or promotion of any faculty member or employee,"[28] a series of court cases had made it clear that states couldn't use vague or overbroad oaths to weed out party members who didn't themselves intend to engage in criminal activity.[29] The loyalty oath requirement ascribed guilt by association, which the Constitution doesn't allow.

In light of this history, allegations that diversity statements are just political litmus tests or modern-day loyalty oaths are serious indeed. If universities are using DEI statements to weed out faculty who don't swear fealty to those values, history would seem to be repeating itself. We should be worried if faculty members are being forced to pledge allegiance to some political cause.

And yet if pledges of allegiance are the worry, there's an obvious solution: Don't ask faculty to pledge allegiance to anything. Flippant as that might sound, it leads to a concrete and crucial recommendation. To avoid imposing orthodoxies, universities that request diversity statements need to make it clear that they only want to know about someone's actions and plans, not their beliefs. Their goal should be to find out what someone has *done* to increase diversity, equity, and inclusion at their institution or in their field—not to ferret out general beliefs or political views, much less to demand that someone recite empty catchphrases about diversity's value.[30]

We can formalize this as a principle, the first of four in this chapter. Each comes from listening to critics and finding what I hope will be seen as good-faith responses to their worries.

> Principle 1: DEI statements should focus not on general statements of belief, but on concrete actions and plans that advance diversity, equity, and inclusion.

When the governor of Utah pushed for a statewide ban on diversity statements in 2023, he said it was "just awful" that "professors or employees have to sign these DEI statements before they can even qualify for a job."[31] But diversity statements just don't work like that. A DEI statement isn't some pre-written pledge that faculty *sign*. This is one crucial way that they differ from the anti-Communist oaths of the last century. Diversity statements are individualized reports that faculty write themselves—just as they write their own scholarly agendas or teaching statements when they apply for a job or promotion. I have yet to see something called a "diversity statement" that faculty don't draft but simply sign. If such a thing exists somewhere, I would enthusiastically join the critics protesting it.

Most thoughtful critics realize that this isn't what diversity statements look like. Their real worry is that universities, even if not literally asking for pledges, are looking for *signs of commitment*. They want to recruit and reward true believers to the cause—the cause being DEI. Much here turns on what is meant by "commitment." In his essay "Every University Should Reject Political 'Diversity Statements,'" John Tomasi—the president of Heterodox Academy, a group dedicated to viewpoint diversity in higher education—slides between two different meanings. One of his formulations sounds like a declaration of values: "saying what you believe and believing what you say"—or faking it. But another weaker sense of commitment he describes as something that can be "evidenced by stories from the past and/or . . . pledges for the future."[32] These are two different things, and academics aren't the only workers who can show commitment in either sense. A factory worker who makes widgets might be committed to her work in the sense that she believes in the product—the power of widgets to change lives. Another worker might not care about widgets at all, but he never misses a day of work and so gets top marks from supervisors for his "commitment" to the job.

When it comes to DEI, commitment in the second sense means that someone can show a track record of concrete steps taken, say, to ensure that a diverse set of students thrive in class, to mentor people with backgrounds that are underrepresented in their field, or to do research that addresses the needs and interests of a diverse community. If "signs of commitment" just require that an applicant has done work that advances these parts of a school's mission—again, at schools that *do* see DEI as integral to their mission—it's hard for me to see the problem. "What have you done, and what are you well positioned to do, to advance our mission?" is a pretty unavoidable question in hiring and promotion decisions, not just at universities.

But looking for signs of commitment could also mean that a university is looking for candidates to recite platitudes like "DEI is at the center of everything I do as a scholar" or "I strongly support University X's commitment to diversity, equity, and inclusion." Signs of commitment here are almost like those yard signs you used to see in left-leaning neighborhoods: "In this house, we believe Black lives matter, women's rights are human rights, no human is illegal" et cetera. Those signs state beliefs untethered to any particular actions. That's why they can be mass-produced and shared across the neighborhood. There is no way to know from reading them whether the beliefs are sincere and the signs are true.

Universities shouldn't reward this kind of thing, much less require it. Statements of belief that are unconnected to action are a waste of time, given how easily they can be faked, coached, or ghostwritten. Descriptions of actions, by contrast, can't be faked; someone has either made particular contributions or they haven't. Whether they did so as a true believer or just because it was part of their job description really shouldn't matter. Works, not faith, is what schools should demand.

This suggests an even more important reason why universities shouldn't request or reward pledges of allegiance: to protect the possibility of faculty dissent. If you ask someone to file a report about their *beliefs*, they can't simultaneously express contrary beliefs elsewhere without contradicting themselves. Reports of actions operate differently. Unlike compelled statements of belief, statements focused on action leave space for dissent by people who think DEI statements, or even their school's commitment to DEI itself, are bad ideas. To be clear, these dissenting views are probably best expressed outside the DEI statement, not within it. (After all, I've just said the statements are not supposed to be about beliefs!) A job application isn't necessarily the most appropriate place to argue for a change in the job description. But faculty should be able to argue against the way their school understands and values diversity in any number of other places, from faculty meetings to op-eds in the *New York Times*. They can dissent without hypocrisy as long as they weren't forced to state contrary beliefs within their diversity statements. And academic freedom should fully protect their dissent.

Seen this way, diversity statements start to look a lot more analogous to other, more familiar elements of applications and advancement files. Think about teaching statements. It's hardly controversial to ask faculty and faculty applicants to list what classes they've taught, to report scores and comments from their student evaluations, and to discuss any changes they've made or are planning in their classes. In other words, it's not controversial to require faculty to submit teaching statements that describe their actions and plans in the classroom.

What universities generally don't ask faculty to do is to pledge their commitment to some particular pedagogical theory or to rattle off platitudes about the joys of teaching. As a result, professors can write effective teaching statements *even if* they happen to believe that teaching is just a distraction from research or—to give a belief I actually argue for in chapter 2—that making advancement dependent on student teaching evaluations is a threat to academic freedom. I can make the latter argument here in this book, just as others can argue for a lower teaching load in the faculty senate, without contradicting anything said in our teaching statements. And that's because our teaching statements never require us to agree with the university's views on teaching or to state any other belief. All we are asked is what we've done in the classroom. If mandatory teaching statements can be required without requiring faculty to pledge allegiance to anything, why can't the same be true of DEI statements?

One possible response is that teaching is a necessary part of faculty members' jobs while DEI is some sort of *extraneous* political agenda, a fad imposed by woke administrators. Whether that's true or not turns out to be the question at the heart of the criticism we turn to next: the claim that DEI statements lead to unconstitutional viewpoint discrimination.

Viewpoint Discrimination

Were I in charge of things, as I'm surely not, I might ask faculty applicants for something along these lines:

> In addition to a cover letter, CV, research statement, and statement of teaching experience, we require a statement* describing your past and planned contributions to diversity, equity, and inclusion. General statements of belief about the value of diversity, equity,

> and inclusion will not be helpful. Instead, please focus on identifying shortcomings related to diversity, equity, and inclusion in your specific discipline, research area, or classes, and describe what you have done or plan to do to address those problems.

(*The prompt could ask instead for a description of DEI contributions *within* the research and teaching statements. Having a *separate* statement is not necessarily what matters.)

Framing the prompt like this hopefully goes a long way to address worries about loyalty oaths. But it doesn't eliminate viewpoint discrimination from the evaluation process. If faculty are being asked to identify DEI needs and to suggest effective ways to meet them, their views on both the needs and the potential solutions are going to get judged by review committees. We can't avoid it: this is viewpoint discrimination.

Viewpoint discrimination by government officials is generally unconstitutional,[33] and critics of diversity statements sometimes say that viewpoint discrimination, or at least discrimination based on political views, is forbidden in the faculty hiring process.[34] But those claims aren't quite right. The truth is that viewpoint discrimination is often unavoidable and perfectly constitutional in the university context, even at public universities where the First Amendment applies.

As a state actor, I can't tell my students what views they can express on the quad, and my university can't stop student groups from inviting speakers whose views it finds hateful or stupid. But in the classroom, I certainly tell students when they are wrong. (These distinctions will be explored further in chapter 5.) We grade students' papers and tests, judging some answers as better than others. The peer review system at the center of faculty hiring and tenure is nothing but viewpoint discrimination all the way down. And in an increasingly politicized world, it hardly helps to say that viewpoints can be judged as long as they're not "political."

When people say they're worried about viewpoint discrimination in faculty hiring and advancement, what they really seem to care about is discrimination based on *irrelevant* political or other viewpoints. If someone's political party or choice for president should never affect their tenure review, that's because it is presumably never relevant to a faculty job at a college or university. At the same time, while an applicant's views on capitalism can probably be considered when filling a chair in entrepreneurship at a business school, they are almost surely irrelevant to hiring in physics.[35]

The First Amendment scholar and former dean of Yale Law School, Robert Post, has explained what's going on here. Imagine, he says,

> a case in which a chemistry department awards research grants only to students who oppose abortion rights. Although we might be tempted to say about this case that the department's criteria for awarding grants are outrageously viewpoint discriminatory, what we would actually mean is that the criteria are completely *irrelevant* to any legitimate educational objective of the department.[36]

Post's insight here pushes us to reframe the question we've been asking. Ask not whether our evaluations of DEI statements are viewpoint discriminatory, he is telling us, for of course they are! Instead we should be asking whether the DEI contributions we're evaluating are relevant to the job in question and to the "legitimate educational objectives" of the department where that job is located.

> Principle 2: Universities should evaluate DEI contributions against the needs and objectives of a particular position or field.

Unfortunately, when it comes to the question we should be asking—whether DEI contributions are relevant to a job and field—critics more often assume the answer than argue for it. Take the report on DEI statements by the American Enterprise Institute, titled *Other Than Merit*. Its opening paragraph claims that "increasingly, universities are not hiring faculty based purely on the quality and promise of their scholarship. Rather, more and more candidates for professorships are also being screened on their commitment to 'diversity, equity, and inclusion.'"[37] Putting aside the issue of commitment covered in the previous section, it's the "purely" and "also" that beg the relevant question here. The AEI report simply assumes that DEI contributions are something extraneous to the "quality and promise" of a faculty member's scholarship.

Similarly question begging is columnist George Will, writing in the *Washington Post* that when UC Berkeley tried looking at applicants' diversity statements before the rest of their files, it was weeding people out "before considering the applicants' academic qualifications." Only those who "scored well in the diversity enthusiasm sweepstakes," he wrote, were "then evaluated as scholars."[38] Similarly, a lawyer who wanted to sue Berkeley for its use of DEI statements once claimed that it had rejected candidates "without even considering their teaching skills, their publication history, their potential for academic excellence or their ability to contribute to their field."[39] These are astonishing claims. Why should we assume that techniques that help engage a more diverse set of students does *not* count among a professor's "teaching skills"? (These techniques could include rethinking what readings to assign or what examples to focus on in class, finding better ways to learn how to pronounce uncommon names, or taking steps to ensure that class materials are accessible to people with various disabilities.) How is it not part of someone's merit as a scholar if their research focuses on topics of concern to groups whose needs have long been ignored? (Examples here are endless, but think of the nursing professor whose research about how bruises appear on dark skin has broadened the forensic evidence available in domestic violence cases.[40]) On what basis should we simply accept that mentorship that helps retain underrepresented minority professors is not part of the mentor's "ability to contribute to their field"?

None of this is to say that every DEI contribution will be relevant across different academic fields or jobs. In fact, one of the biggest lessons that comes from asking about relevance rather than viewpoint discrimination is that no single evaluation metric is ever going to work across the entire university. There can never be a one-size-fits-all "best" answer to a diversity statement prompt. The strongest answers will always vary by the needs of a particular field and the demands of a particular job. That shouldn't come as a surprise if we take seriously, here again, the analogy between DEI statements and the more familiar teaching or research statements that universities generally require. Who would ever think that the "best answer" for a required teaching statement would be the same in the theater department as in physics, law, or clinical medicine? Part of the concern about loyalty oaths no doubt springs from the misconception that there is one best or expected answer to a diversity prompt—one single oath to sign. There is not. Or if there is somewhere out there, there shouldn't be.

Focusing on relevance also shows us how to answer the question FIRE has long posed about whether DEI proponents would be similarly tolerant of mandatory patriotism statements. The force of the thought experiment comes from the unspoken assumption that contributing to diversity, equity, and inclusion is as irrelevant to most academic jobs as fostering patriotism would be.

But let's look at specifics. It's hard for me to believe that engaging in anything that could be described as a "contribution to patriotism" would have made me a better philosopher when I started out in that field as a junior academic. (My law career came later.) By contrast, contributions to diversity, equity, and inclusion within my subdiscipline, the philosophy of art, have transformed the field in the years since I joined. When I started graduate school in the late 1990s, a shocking amount of the profession's time was spent on two examples: Marcel Duchamp's *Fountain* (the urinal he entered into an art exhibition in 1917) and Beethoven's Fifth Symphony. Now when you look at leading work in the field, examples of aesthetic value come from street art, board games, Black expressive culture, eighteenth- and nineteenth-century shop signs, jokes, human bodies, or cultural appropriation.[41] Meanwhile the leading professional organization in the field has commissioned philosophers to design model syllabi to help teachers who might want to venture into new areas in aesthetics, or who just want to assign a more diverse set of authors and perspectives on the classic questions, like the definition of art or the nature of portraiture.[42] We now pay for philosophers of art to attend pipeline programs targeting undergraduate philosophy majors from backgrounds that are underrepresented in the field.[43] And we subsidize travel for scholars who are new to the field and don't yet have institutional funding. Each of these contributions to diversity, equity, and inclusion has made the philosophy of art a more vibrant field, far more visible in the top generalist journals in philosophy than when I began teaching. It has made this area of philosophy *philosophically* better.

Is there a comparable story someone could tell about how "contributions to patriotism" might have deepened the questions being asked in my field, increased enrollment, or otherwise improved its professional standing? And even if so, do we have reason to believe that similar stories can be told in departments across the university? To ask this isn't to imply that contributions to patriotism never have value, or that certain institutions (military academies,[44] for example) might not incorporate love of country into their mission. But what I have just described are concrete ways that teaching and research have improved in one of my fields due to an increased emphasis on diversity, equity, and inclusion, and I suspect that this would also be true in other departments, even if the specific needs and means of meeting them might be quite different. It's no accident that I just chose to focus on a discipline where I have expertise. I don't have the same level of knowledge about how fields like biology or math are lacking when it comes to diversity, equity, and inclusion. So I don't know what actions would count as DEI contributions in those fields. I do know something about what our needs are in philosophy and especially in law. That's what makes me qualified to judge diversity statements written by my colleagues *in those fields*.

If we're not just going to beg questions about what constitutes academic merit in particular fields, someone has to decide what qualifies and what doesn't. And that someone shouldn't be George Will opining in the *Washington Post* or the American Enterprise Institute dismissing diversity contributions as something "other than merit." Instead, we have to give experts in the various academic disciplines the primary authority to decide what work has merit. This is the fundamental point of academic freedom, as the next section will explain.

But first, it's worth pausing to underscore the stakes of the argument to this point. Claims about viewpoint discrimination end up turning on questions about what counts as academic merit: what it means to do your job well as a faculty member in a particular field. And insofar as doing your job involves advancing, in some way, the mission of the university where you work (or want to work), claims about viewpoint discrimination ultimately become questions about the mission of a university. No wonder the fight over diversity statements has inspired such passion.

Two decades ago, my university decided that diversity is "integral to [its] achievement of excellence."[45] This wasn't a neutral decision, but neither was the position it replaced. Because my university now sees DEI values as part of its mission, work that advances that aspect of the mission should be recognized and rewarded. Otherwise, what does it mean to say that we value those things? Judging who deserves those rewards can never be a neutral endeavor. That, in itself, is not a problem. What matters is who does the judging. And that brings us to the principles of academic freedom—the basis for the next critique.

Academic Freedom

Since the American Association of University Professors released its *1915 Declaration of Principles on Academic Freedom and Academic Tenure*, academic freedom in United States has been described as having "three elements: freedom of inquiry and research; freedom of teaching within the university or college; and freedom of extramural utterance and action."[46] In none of these areas does academic freedom give professors the freedom to say whatever they want. This is the kind of liberty the First Amendment generally gives speakers out in the world at large. By contrast, academic freedom involves responsibilities alongside its liberties. To quote the 1915 Declaration again, "The liberty of the scholar within the university to set forth his conclusions . . . is conditioned by their being conclusions gained by a scholar's method and held in a scholar's spirit."

The overarching responsibility is that faculty submit their work to the judgment of their peers. Their scholarship and teaching have to meet the professional standards of their discipline. This duty comes, though, with a corresponding liberty—in fact, a crucial one, perhaps the most basic point of academic freedom: the assurance that judgments of academic merit will be made free from the dictates of non-expert outsiders, whether those be university administrators, trustees, donors, legislators, or the general public.

To clarify where these principles are coming from: at state schools, academic freedom is protected under the Constitution. The Supreme Court has even called it "a special concern of the First Amendment."[47] But that was in a loyalty oath case where a state was trying to interfere with the makeup of a university's faculty. Constitutional case law has focused mostly on external threats. It's had far less to say about the academic freedom of faculty members claiming overreach by their universities, as compared to faculty, or their universities, claiming overreach by the state.[48]

As a result, the academic freedom issues raised by diversity statements are governed less clearly by constitutional doctrine than by policies like the AAUP's *1940 Statement of Principles on Academic Freedom and Tenure*, which over 250 schools have adopted, often incorporating the 1940 Statement's principles directly into their faculty handbooks or other contractual provisions. Some schools, including mine, have their own policies that spell out the freedoms and responsibilities of faculty; the University of California also now recognizes that non-faculty academic personnel like librarians share the same rights and responsibilities in their teaching and research work.[49]

Any differences in the details of these policies matter less for our purposes than what they have in common: a widespread commitment in American higher education to the idea that teaching and research at universities should be carried out free of institutional or governmental reprisal, subject only to the scholarly and pedagogical standards of a scholar's discipline, as judged primarily by other experts within the field. So what do these shared principles have to say about what the Academic Freedom Alliance called the "obvious threats to academic freedom" posed by DEI statements? The answer varies depending on what those threats are said to be.

To start with what is largely a nonstarter: Critics sometimes say that *requiring* diversity statements is the problem. They claim that making DEI statements optional rather than mandatory would better protect the academic freedom of faculty who think DEI contributions are bunk, who fear reprisals for their views, or who just want to keep their opinions to themselves. If the claim here is that forcing faculty to file a report violates academic freedom because it compels faculty to speak, those making the claim need to explain why teaching and research statements and the endless other reports faculty are forced to file to get jobs, grants, tenure, or promotion don't also threaten academic freedom. Submitting information for a performance evaluation does not automatically count as unconstitutionally compelled speech.

The distinction between mandatory and optional DEI statements doesn't end up doing much work, at least at schools that have decided that contributions to diversity, equity, and inclusion are something they value and reward. If DEI contributions are a plus factor in tenure or advancement, what's the difference between filing a mandatory statement that says "no DEI contributions during the review period"—as faculty who have taken a sabbatical might say in their mandatory teaching statements—as opposed to not filing an optional DEI statement? Either way, the person under review isn't going to get any "credit" in that area. Someone with no DEI contributions will be like someone whose teaching or service was weak: they'll still advance if other parts of the file (for example, their research) make up for it. In hiring, were everything else in their applications truly equal, a candidate who has DEI contributions will get the job over one who doesn't have them. That outcome wouldn't hinge on whether the statements were required or optional.

The real issue for those opposed to DEI likely isn't the mandatory nature of statements, but the university's choice to reward DEI contributions in the first place. This does raise a genuine academic freedom issue: insofar as diversity statement requirements flow from a university's recognition of DEI values as part of its mission, how a university's mission gets determined has big academic freedom implications. We'll wait to tackle that topic until the end of the book, but spoiler alert: Shared governance that involves faculty in the decision-making is at the heart of the answer. And, to be very clear, the argument here is not that schools *must* recognize DEI values within their mission. Whether to do so or not is the real question that fights over DEI statements may just be distracting us from asking.

At a school where DEI contributions *are* seen as components of merit, judging those contributions is unavoidable. And academic freedom requires that judgments of merit be made by experts within each discipline. In this regard, DEI contributions should be treated like all other aspects of academic merit. The standards of what counts as valuable can't be set by administrators or imposed from above. In the last section, I argued that no one-size-fits-all, single best answer to a diversity statement prompt can ever be possible. The additional requirement here is that we leave it to experts within those fields to determine their field or department's specific diversity needs and to set the criteria they'll use to evaluate the diversity statements they receive.

This doesn't mean there can't be top-down administrative advice about, say, what the law or university policy allows hiring and tenure committees to consider. It doesn't mean there can't be training about best practices being used elsewhere in the university or about techniques that have been shown to work to diversify the pipeline of graduate students and faculty applicants, or to improve retention.[50] It also doesn't mean that administrators can't offer incentives to departments that might otherwise remain uninterested in thinking about diversity. Sometimes the departments with the biggest DEI challenges are the ones least eager to confront them.

Even university-wide evaluation rubrics are possible, as long as they're general enough. Giving these rubrics meat—filling them in with substantive specifics—that's the part that has to happen bottom-up, starting with the faculty committees charged with hiring or tenure. Here, once again, evaluating diversity contributions proves no different from the evaluation of every other component in an application or advancement file.

> Principle 3: To preserve academic freedom, DEI statements should be evaluated bottom-up, by disciplinary experts in each field.

This principle helps answer another academic freedom worry sometimes raised about diversity statements: that terms like *diversity, equity,* and *inclusion* are "very squishy," "often vague," and "rarely defined with specificity."[51] The same can be said, after all, for nearly every marker of academic excellence. It's not like faculty applicants are normally told with any specificity what a department will view as great scholarship or teaching. I have absolutely no idea why the many schools that declined to hire me made the choices they did. The nature of academic evaluation—particularly when done through peer review, as academic freedom demands—is such that explicit criteria for what counts as good are highly and rightly contested, seldom made transparent, and unlikely to cut across different fields. There is just no algorithm for what will get you a job as a professor at any particular school.

Strangely, the same critics who see diversity statements as squishy and hopelessly vague have also referred to them as political litmus tests. So are the requirements too specific or too ambiguous? I read the critics as saying that they're both at once. On their view, evaluative criteria for DEI statements are left vague in order to mask the very specific commitments that "everyone knows" evaluators actually want to hear.[52] But if we take academic freedom seriously—if we leave the evaluation of diversity statements to the responsible discretion of experts within each field, as we do with every other aspect of hiring and tenure review—then we shouldn't expect explicit rules.

Before moving on, though, we need to take seriously the claim that "everyone knows" what universities are *really* talking about when they talk about diversity. As John Cochrane, a senior fellow at Stanford's Hoover Institution, once blogged:

> My friends (anonymous!) in the [University of California] system report that the criteria are clear and the word is out: Don't try to be clever. . . . Don't write vibrant essays on the importance of ideological, political or religious diversity. . . . Are you thinking of writing about your hil[l]billy elegy background, your time in the military, your support for gun rights and Trump, and how this background and viewpoint would enrich a faculty and staff that likely has absolutely zero people like you? Don't bother. We all know what "diversity" means.[53]

What "everyone" is said to know is that only some types of diversity get included in universities' attempts at diversification. This simmering suspicion has boiled over since the campus protests over Israel and Gaza began. Do DEI officials care about stopping antisemitism, and does inclusion extend to Jewish students and faculty? That's what Republicans at the House hearings wanted to know. And what about intellectual diversity? Does increasing the number of conservatives on university faculties not count as a DEI issue? If universities really cared about academic freedom, shouldn't they be trying to create a more politically diverse faculty?[54]

The charges of antisemitism raise genuine inclusion issues and, in doing so, offer a reminder that "DEI" combines three separate concepts, all too often run together (including in this book). Many schools' diversity needs don't include increasing the number of Jewish students or faculty, but that in no way means that Jewish students and faculty never face discrimination—which is to say, threats to their full inclusion. Addressing the latter is made even more complicated by the conflation of anti-Zionism and antisemitism. Since the first targets an idea and the second an identity, recent hostilities force the question of whether ideas and identities should be treated differently within universities' DEI efforts. And that is the same question raised by claims about ideological diversity on the faculty.

As a professor at a state university, where the mission includes a commitment to serving the people of our state, I feel I have a professional duty to ensure that students of all races, gender identities, sexual orientations, and religions flourish in my classes. If one group is doing less well, it's my responsibility to, at the very least, give my teaching and my school environment a hard look to see if we could be doing something to eliminate that disparity. That's what I understand "equity" in DEI to mean: that any identity-based differences in student or faculty success demand, at minimum, some soul-searching about whether and how we could be doing things better. Not to ask that question is to assume that some races, genders, sexual orientations, or religious identities are just inherently better than others. That's an idea DEI proponents reject, just as, of course, we'd reject any official attempt to get a student or colleague to change their sexual orientation or gender or religion to one we perceive as "better."

I can't say the same thing when it comes to ideological diversity. The point of education, and of rational argument more generally, is to change what people think. To put the point a different way: I'd be upset if all the racial groups represented in California weren't able to thrive at our state's public universities. But I certainly don't think the same is true of all of the ideas the people of California hold. Deciding which ideas merit discussion in university classrooms and in academic research is the whole point of academic freedom, where disciplinary expertise is used to sort ideas into better and worse. This is what distinguishes university classrooms and labs from the unregulated marketplace of ideas that the First Amendment protects out in the public sphere, where it's said that "there is no such thing as a false idea."[55] We'll return to this distinction in chapter 5.

To say that viewpoint diversity is different in kind from the identity-based grounds of diversity that DEI efforts generally target is *not* to deny that both matter, or to ignore that people with certain beliefs have been subjected to stereotyping or other forms of unjust discrimination, just as people with certain identities too often experience. Nor is it to deny the important correlations between political beliefs and particular backgrounds and identities. As Musa al-Gharbi has argued, "policies and practices that alienate socially conservative or religious perspectives will disproportionately affect" people who are Black or Hispanic, and from working-class and/or rural backgrounds.[56]

The underrepresentation of conservatives in universities today is well known. And it certainly is a problem insofar as it leads to echo chambers within the university or to a greater disconnect, even distrust, between universities and certain segments of society. As the political scientist Steven Teles has argued, conservatives' absence may be due to the kind of structural or systemic injustice that liberals often emphasize, and that conservatives often downplay, when it comes to racism and sexism.[57] Perceptions of discrimination against conservatives within academia can narrow the pipeline of conservative job candidates even if the perceptions don't match reality. According to Teles, university culture, as it currently exists in many places, may be a smoother fit for liberals than conservatives, imposing a sort of "tax" on conservatives—even a need for the kind of concealment or "covering" that LGBTQ people know so well.[58] And because "incumbents choose their successors," as Teles puts it, there is a tendency toward inertia in academia that could discourage those interested in currently underexplored topics from pursuing those interests. (Then again, this inertia is one of the main reasons DEI efforts in hiring have been necessary in the first place.)

These structural barriers, and their politically lopsided effects, give rise to two final lines of criticism against DEI statements. The first is the worry that faculty just can't be trusted to administer them fairly. A generous opponent of mine once said that he'd "be okay with diversity statements if Brian Soucek were the one reading them all." But I'm not, he said, so as a prophylactic measure against ideologues who just want to entrench orthodoxy on campus, it's better to do away with diversity statements entirely than to try improving their use in the ways I've been suggesting. This type of skepticism goes too far, as least as a defense of academic freedom, which it purports to be. If faculty can't be trusted to engage in good-faith evaluation of their peers, academic freedom is a hopeless enterprise. As we've seen, academic freedom at its core is the idea that academic merit should be judged by experts in the various disciplines. Without the possibility of good-faith peer review, there is nothing left. This isn't to deny that a system of peer review isn't always susceptible to outside interference, to factions that form within departments or entire fields, or to self-interest, laziness, or bias. Sometimes groups of disciplinary experts turn into reactionary cartels, enforcing orthodoxies and resisting new ideas. Peer review, conducted as it is by human beings, necessarily shares humans' many flaws.

But to say all of this is to express a concern about academic freedom itself, not just about DEI statements. It's curious that some critics raise these worries, call for reform, and even allow for legislative interference, only when it comes to evaluations of DEI contributions, but not to any of the many other evaluations that get made by the exact same people in the course of faculty hiring and advancement. The following chapter pushes this point further by comparing the attention paid to diversity statements to that which student teaching evaluations have typically received.

Still one more related academic freedom worry remains, though. Insofar as conservatives inside and outside the academy *view* DEI statements as a liberal litmus test, it doesn't really matter whether they actually are used in that way. As Professor Teles noted, the perception of bias—even if false—can be enough to discourage people from entering the profession. And it's enough to cause the public to lose faith in the expertise that universities exist to develop and deploy. This, to me, is the hardest of all the challenges to diversity statements. Perceptions, even misperceptions, about diversity statements can all too easily become reality. Hiring committees don't have to be misusing DEI statements for those who aren't in the room to believe that their contributions won't be valued, and to decide that it's not worth applying or even training for those positions in the first place. This itself could distort the pool of experts on which academic freedom relies. It could end up having the same effect as a litmus test.

So is banning DEI statements the only answer? To my mind, it's much too early for that. If misperceptions really are the danger, correcting perceptions is surely worth trying. Most of the loudest criticisms of DEI statements come from people who have never actually used them. They've never read a stack of diversity statements as part of a hiring or advancement process.[59] As such, they've never gotten the chance to see just how diverse the contributions described in those statements can be.[60]

Universities that embrace DEI values as part of their mission need to do a better job explaining why they're asking for diversity statements.

They need to signal more clearly their openness to the wide variety of ways that we can better meet the needs of a diverse student body and a diverse public. What actions are likely to meet those needs can't be predetermined. The university may have set the goals, but it's up to those within the university to determine how those goals are best met. It's not likely to happen in the same way across departments. And, importantly, although universities' DEI goals—fostering teaching and research that addresses a broadly diverse public—are often focused on identity traits like race or gender, it in no way follows that the *means* of achieving those goals must be race- or gender-conscious as well. My own DEI statements, for example, always include the fact that I have developed free course readers to save students from having to shoulder the expense of commercial textbooks. Efforts aimed at first-generation students, who may come to school knowing less than their peers about how to succeed, are similarly race-neutral in their means, if not their ends. Faculty who aspire to "color-blindness" thus should be able to find plenty of ways to promote their university's DEI goals, unless they think that the goals themselves are the problem.

Finally, given the baggage currently weighing down terms like "DEI," universities might need to consider redescribing their requirements to more accurately reflect the breadth of contributions they want to hear about—and to avoid triggering applicants who have come to see these particular words as dog whistles for the Left. Instead of asking for a "diversity statement," a university could point to a relevant policy or strategic goal—at my university, this would be Regents Policy 4400, discussed in the next section—and ask what faculty have done or plan to do to advance it. Catchwords or jargon might be making some DEI policies appear more ideologically narrow than they currently are or need to be.

All of these suggestions, however, assume that critics of DEI statements are arguing in good faith. I'm speaking here to those who are. And yet it's remarkable how often people insist on abandoning diversity statements entirely before even considering suggestions about how they can be improved. Critics rushing to put a stop to DEI statements need to explain what schools should be doing instead to advance their DEI commitments. Thoughts and prayers aren't enough here. And ideally, those same critics should also explain why they're so quick to give up on this one type of faculty evaluation while ignoring others that are even more demonstrably problematic. (See, again, the chapter to come.) If critics of DEI statements aren't willing to do any of this, perhaps their problem isn't with the statements, but with the idea of universities valuing diversity, equity, and inclusion in the first place. We can have that conversation instead.

The distrust that has built up around DEI statements—at least in some circles, including those that have been losing their long-standing demographic stranglehold on academia—is partly a failure to recognize that, done the right way, diversity statements are meant to reward DEI contributions from *all* faculty, not just those of particular, previously underrepresented backgrounds. That said, in addition to rewarding contributions *to* diverse populations both inside and outside the university, it's also true that DEI statements have additionally been used to *create* a more diverse population within our universities. And their use in diversifying university faculties has given rise to another kind of critique: that DEI statements are just a thinly veiled attempt at race discrimination in hiring.

Race Discrimination

The US Supreme Court has now spent several decades pushing American antidiscrimination law ever closer to the notion that, to quote an iconic (dissenting) opinion from 1896, "Our Constitution is color-blind, and neither knows nor tolerates classes among citizens."[61] The fight over affirmative action has been the primary site of the shift. In 2023 the court moved a step closer to color-blind constitutionalism when it struck down race-conscious admissions policies at Harvard and the University of North Carolina, holding that a student's race cannot itself be a factor that helps students get admitted.

Some states were there already. California, most notably, passed a statewide referendum in 1996, reaffirmed with even more support in 2020, amending its constitution to ban "preferential treatment . . . on the basis of race, sex, color, ethnicity, or national origin" in public schools and employment.[62] As a matter of state law, universities in California (as in eight other states) cannot give candidates a boost in faculty hiring or in student admissions based on their race or gender.

What's a school in those states to do, then, if it wants to diversify its student body or, more relevantly here, its faculty, but can't directly consider race or gender in admissions or hiring? Requiring job applicants to submit diversity statements may seem like an answer. Critics allege that they allow universities "to continue to take race and gender into account in ways that will be 'invisible to outsiders.'"[63] Some say that diversity statements give applicants space to reveal information that schools cannot ask about directly. This is why at least one critic has singled out the University of California's use of diversity statements as a race discrimination lawsuit waiting to happen.[64]

The critics aren't wrong that diversity statements are being used as a tool to diversify the faculty. At the University of California, for example, some of the most active experimentation and criticism surrounding diversity statements stemmed from a $2 million grant the state legislature awarded in 2016 to promote "best practices in equal employment opportunity." UC spent that money on initiatives to "increas[e] the presence of underrepresented minorities (African-American, Chicano(a)/Latino(a)/Hispanic, and Native American) and women" on faculty in ways consistent with California's affirmative action ban.[65] One of the suggested "best practices" that emerged that year: expanding the use of DEI statements in evaluating faculty applicants.

When the legislature renewed funding in the following years, some of its grant money went to campuses that were looking to experiment with the way job applications get read. For example, in 2018–19, the committees hiring for five jobs in the life sciences at UC Berkeley, and for eight positions spread across different colleges and schools at UC Davis, all started their review by looking only at applicants' anonymized diversity statements. Those that met a cutoff score set by the committees then made it to the next round, where the applicants' names and the rest of their application materials were unveiled. This had widely publicized and criticized effects. Berkeley's committee, for example, winnowed 894 applicants down to 214 after they reviewed the DEI statements. The initial pool was 42% female, 3% African American, and 13% Hispanic, while those numbers rose to 60%, 6%, and 23%, respectively, in the following round.[66] Reaction in some quarters was furious, though it often conflated UC's use of diversity statements in these few experimental searches with our general hiring practices. In fact, one lesson from these experiments was that looking at diversity statements by themselves was too limited; it makes little sense to spend too much time on the DEI contributions of someone who works in an area where you're not looking to hire. In subsequent searches, hiring committees have paired DEI statements with research statements on first-pass review, or just included them as one of the many application documents reviewed all at once. What UC's experiments did make clear was that both the use of diversity statements and the order in which applications are read can significantly affect the demographic makeup of the pool that ultimately gets considered. Of course, this means that the old way of doing things had its own demographic effects. Neither choice is neutral.

All of this is to say that diversity statements *have* been used in faculty recruitment as a means of diversifying the faculty, especially in places where race- and gender-conscious hiring is prohibited. So we need to ask whether schools like the University of California have been requiring diversity statements "as a way to launder diversity hiring and get around antidiscrimination laws," as critics have alleged.[67] Are diversity statements just a way of crediting race and gender through winks and nods rather than checkboxes or quotas?[68]

The answer is no. Of course, bad intent can enter the hiring process through diversity statements no less than it traditionally has through every other part of job applications. Everything from an applicant's name and schools attended, to the old boys' network of recommenders, to research topics seen as gendered or racialized can be used improperly to discriminate. But when they're used the right way, diversity statements don't evade the law—or, worse, violate it behind closed doors. They actually do exactly what color-blind courts have consistently *instructed* schools to do instead of using race explicitly in admissions or hiring.

A little detour into equal protection law is needed here. For the past few decades, when the Supreme Court has struck down affirmative action policies as unconstitutional, it has applied what's called strict scrutiny. Because affirmative action policies classify people based on race, the court holds them to the same exacting constitutional test as Jim Crow and anti-miscegenation laws: they survive only if they're "narrowly tailored" to advance a "compelling governmental interest."[69]

The narrow tailoring prong of the test basically asks whether explicit racial classifications are necessary. And time and again, the court has found that race-conscious means are *unnecessary* because methods that don't classify people based on race could be used instead. So, for example, Louisville and Seattle were barred from taking students' race into account when assigning them to public schools because the court said they could instead promote integration through targeted recruitment efforts, funding for magnet schools, strategic site selection for new schools, and redrawn attendance zones. These alternatives would all be chosen with an eye to their demographic impacts, but they wouldn't require the government to classify individual students based on their race.[70] Similarly, the court has said that if a public university could achieve its diversity goals by accepting, say, the top 10% of students at each public high school in the state,[71] explicit consideration of student's race in admissions would become unnecessary—and therefore unconstitutional under the current test.

Mandated diversity statements are like Top 10% plans: even if they are put in place because we hope they'll increase the number of underrepresented minorities at a given institution, they apply to everyone across the board, regardless of race. And they don't require any individual to disclose their race or other identity traits. Again, they are used with the intention that they'll have racially disparate impacts—otherwise they wouldn't be effective in diversifying the faculty. But initiatives like these not only continue to be constitutional,[72] they actually provide courts a basis for striking down other selection methods that would look to race more explicitly (like using racial checkboxes on an application).

The Supreme Court reaffirmed this point even in its most recent affirmative action decision. "Nothing in this opinion," the majority wrote in the Harvard/UNC cases, "should be construed as prohibiting universities from considering an applicant's discussion of how race affected his or her life, be it through discrimination, inspiration, or otherwise."[73] In other words, universities do not discriminate based on race if they consider how someone's racial background or race-based experiences gave that particular person a "unique ability to contribute to the university."[74]

To bring this back to diversity statements, what this means is that candidates may choose to draw upon their identity and background when describing their past and planned contributions to diversity, equity, and inclusion. Or they can choose not to mention anything about their identity. But hiring committees, to put it crassly, shouldn't award or subtract points *because of* the person's racial identity. That is what the law prohibits. What universities *can* reward, even in states that ban affirmative action, are descriptions of how a candidate's background or identity has helped prepare them to identify and carry out concrete actions that improve diversity, equity, and inclusion at their institution, in their research, or within their academic field. So a faculty candidate who grew up in a Spanish-speaking household where no one had previously attended college would not get a preference for that alone. Their diversity statement should be rated highly only insofar as it describes how, for example, their language skills have made their particular research possible, or how their first-generation background has made them a more effective mentor to certain students. This is the "unique ability to contribute to the university" that the Supreme Court recognized in the analogous context of university admissions.

According to current legal doctrine, there are right ways and wrong ways for universities to achieve greater diversity. The goal itself is constitutional, even if some means of achieving it aren't. Using race-neutral means such as diversity statements is one of the right ways. It's a way of *complying* with the law—even in states that ban affirmative action preferences—not skirting or subverting it.

This brings us then to the last of this chapter's principles:

> Principle 4: Universities that require diversity statements should not ask about, or reward, a person's identity in itself, but they can consider how a person's identity or background may impact their unique ability to engage in work that contributes to diversity, equity, and inclusion.

: : :

Diversity statements have been used to diversify university faculties. But it's important to reiterate that this is *not* the only reason why universities ask for diversity statements. Consider the University of California once again. Critics often act like diversity statements are a recent innovation, imposed on faculty by DEI bureaucrats and other administrators who want a faculty that is less white, male, and straight. The history says otherwise.[75]

Twenty years ago, the University of California's president convened a task force on diversity, and the Academic Senate crafted a statement that became Regents Policy 4400, still in effect today. The policy talks of diversity as "integral to the University's achievement of excellence."[76] The ten years that followed saw intense debate within the faculty, and between faculty and administrators, on whether to add language to the university's *Academic Personnel Manual* about contributions to diversity, equity, and inclusion. These years of wordsmithing, which might seem like a wonky sideshow, are actually what genuine shared governance looks like. The university's faculty and administration were jointly deciding whether and how DEI contributions would be rewarded in hiring, tenure, and promotion. They were deciding whether DEI contributions would be seen as an element of faculty merit.

UC policy now highlights DEI contributions as something that should be "credited in the same way as other faculty achievements" in teaching, research, and service.[77] This was done in part to address the fact that contributions to this part of the university's mission—especially mentorship of students coming from underrepresented backgrounds—have not always been evenly shouldered among the faculty. If the university says that diversity is integral to its mission, it only makes sense that it should reward work that contributes to that aspect of the mission. And to reward those contributions in hiring and advancement, the university needs a way for faculty to report what contributions they've made. Hence the need for diversity statements.

Diversity statements, then, aren't useful only to help diversify the faculty. They have another purpose too, which cuts across race and gender lines. Requiring them helps universities endorse and reward contributions to DEI as something they value. It expresses the university's view that DEI is intrinsic to its mission. And the requirement pushes faculty of *all* races and genders to consider how they and their departments may be succeeding or failing in advancing this part of their university's mission.

In March 2025, the University of California abruptly announced an end to its use of diversity statements in faculty hiring, as opposed to advancement. No consultation with the faculty was involved: the Regents, without any public discussion or vote, issued an order to the president, who delegated the announcement to the provost.[78] Nothing had changed at the University of California aside from anxiety levels about potential attacks from Washington. To those looking for ways to appease the Trump administration, the use of DEI statements in hiring must have seemed like something expendable and too often misunderstood. But even then, the fact that the University of California retained its use of diversity statements in advancement files shows that their purpose is not just to diversify the faculty; it is also, and even more importantly, meant to nudge faculty already employed to think about what they are doing to advance values that UC continues to see as "integral to [its] achievement of excellence."[79]

Not every university needs to value diversity, equity, and inclusion as an essential part of its mission. It's a choice. I'll say it again: I'm a pluralist when it comes to universities' missions. Not every school needs to make the choice that my own university has. But those that do shouldn't hide the ball. They should make it clear that they'll reward work that contributes to this aspect of their mission, and they should ask faculty and faculty applicants to report what contributions they've made. If schools don't do so, we might have good reason to doubt the extent to which they actually do see DEI as intrinsic to their mission in the first place.

The debate over DEI statements has reached its current intensity because at some level, people realize that what's at stake goes far beyond the paperwork in an HR file. What's at stake is the role that diversity, equity, and inclusion will play—or not—within a university's mission. Choices about that are unavoidable, and unavoidably value-laden. There is not a neutral option. No matter what they decide, universities end up expressing a view. They speak through what they choose to reward.

2 *Distraction and Hypocrisy*

Ignoring the Real Threats to Academic Freedom

Diversity statements and the topic soon to come, institutional speech, have each spawned endless op-eds and faculty resolutions, university policies and state legislation. The attention they've gotten is striking, especially when you compare it to the silence surrounding much greater threats to academic freedom in the United States. Two of the worst threats are discussed so little that you might laugh when I mention them. I'm talking here about student teaching evaluations and *U.S. News* rankings.

Neither is a joke. If you want to see faculty hiring and promotion getting distorted along race and gender lines, or find professors censoring themselves and changing how they do their jobs, focusing on diversity statements is a distraction. Student teaching evaluations are doing the real work. And if academic freedom is your university's brand (or more charitably, its most cherished value), then you probably shouldn't let a struggling news magazine drive decisions about what kinds of students get admitted, which faculty get hired, and where money gets spent at your university. To put it mildly, schools undercut their devotion to academic freedom when they commit to institutional neutrality while outsourcing their institutional identity.

So why do diversity statements and institutional speech get so much more attention than student evaluations and college rankings? Does distraction here serve some purpose? And if so, who benefits from it?

In asking these questions, this chapter bridges those on either side of it. The distractions of the surrounding chapters mask the hypocrisy identified in this one: that those who are so loudly worried about universities going beyond their proper mission—whether by advancing diversity or forsaking "neutrality"—are looking away as that mission gets redefined by those least qualified to do so.

Student Teaching Evaluations

In the last chapter, we heard critics arguing that by requiring DEI statements, universities pressure faculty to act in ways that "everyone knows" are favored; they skew the demographics of who gets hired and promoted; and they violate academic freedom—the idea that academic merit should be defined and judged by disciplinary experts, not outsourced to administrators or outside amateurs.

Chapter 1 offered responses to each of these worries. But whether or not you were convinced by them, consider: diversity statements can't possibly approach student teaching evaluations in the extent to which they distort how faculty act and speak; in their racially and sexually disparate impact on faculty hiring and advancement; and in the power they outsource to non-disciplinary experts to make academic judgments. After all, when it comes to student teaching evaluations, the judges—students—are non-experts by definition.

Every fall, I teach first-semester law students, most of whom arrive with no previous knowledge about the topic of my class, civil procedure. At semester's end, the students go online to rate how I did. They fill out teaching evaluations, a mix of 1-to-5 ratings and open-ended answers to questions my university asks about me. Some of the questions make good sense and elicit feedback that only students could offer. Did students feel I treated them with respect? Did I make myself available to answer their questions? Were the course objectives clearly explained? Who better than students to ask about those things, since they're in the classroom day in and day out. Student evaluations might also be one of the best indicators of whether professors are reaching people from a diverse variety of backgrounds. Nothing in what follows is meant to suggest that students shouldn't be empowered to provide feedback about their experience in the classroom.

But each year, students in my class are also asked to rate things like my "demonstrated mastery of the subject." Never mind that everything most of them know about the subject came from me. If I'd been wrong, or at least convincingly wrong, about every single thing I taught them, most would have no way of knowing. Students also rate the "overall educational value of the course" and the "overall teaching effectiveness of the instructor." Here again, in their first semester of law school, they make these judgments with few comparisons of other law school classes, without yet understanding how the material they learned relates to their future jobs, and without necessarily having any pedagogical experience of their own. Judgment about my merit as a teacher gets handed off to people who are not, or not yet, expert on most of the things on which I'm judged.

And yet their judgments have incredible power. When I applied for my current job, the only thing UC Davis knew about my teaching was what classes I'd previously offered and what scores the students in those classes had given me. Were I to apply for another job now, my application probably wouldn't provide much more information about my teaching skills. Some schools ask for a personal statement about a candidate's approach to teaching. And when I went up for tenure, my file included reports from three of my colleagues who had visited my classes. But teaching evaluations are the one thing nearly every school requires. Whether or not they're sufficient to show a faculty member's skill at teaching, they are almost always necessary. A 2010 survey found that student teaching evaluations were used at 94% of schools and, according to deans, "were usually their main source of information about the quality of classroom teaching."[1] Additional, external ratings like those on the website Rate My Professors may not be put to any official use, but they can still exert reputational pressure since they're freely available online, often near the top of an academic's Google results.

By reducing weeks of classroom time, office hours, email exchanges, and exams to a number between one and five, the scores my colleagues and I receive have an instant communicability. They turn different teachers, teaching styles, and types of classes in wildly varied fields into suddenly comparable digits, doing what sociologists call commensuration, "turning qualities into quantities on a shared metric."[2] Notably, this is a power that student evaluations share with the rankings systems we'll turn to next. One reason why student evaluations and university rankings both fly under the radar compared to other threats to academic freedom is surely because of the perceived objectivity of numbers they employ. Unlike the messy realities they are meant to represent, numbers appear neutral, unquestionable. But none of the judgments in this book are neutral—that's the whole point.

And one of the worst ways that student evaluations are not neutral is in the race, gender, and other types of bias often concealed within their numbers. In 2018 a Canadian arbitrator hearing a claim against Ryerson University found that the "largely uncontested evidence" showed student evaluations to be skewed according to "race, gender, accent, age and 'attractiveness,'" making them "imperfect at best and downright biased and unreliable at worst."[3] Faculty in the Ryerson case argued that racial and gender bias in student teaching scores made their use in hiring and advancement not just ill-advised but illegal.[4] Similar questions have been raised in the United States, where federal law prohibits employment tests that have a sufficiently large disparate effect based on a protected identity category like race, sex, or national origin, unless they test for something sufficiently related to the job and "consistent with business necessity."[5] In short, the legality of using teaching evaluations for employment depends on how differently they affect different racial groups or genders, and also on how effective they are at measuring something universities obviously have a right to care about: the quality of their faculty's teaching. Unfortunately, for decades now, studies have made clear that student teaching evaluations struggle in both regards.

On the question of whether student evaluations measure job-related achievement, the title of a 2016 meta-analysis of decades of empirical studies summed up its conclusion: "Student evaluation of teaching ratings and student learning are not related." The analysis reviewed ninety-seven studies in which students were randomly assigned to a class with multiple sections, taught by different instructors, but given the same exam. If student teaching evaluations truly measured good teaching, we would expect that students with the most highly rated instructors would do best on the exam. But psychologist Bob Uttl and colleagues found that wasn't so. "Despite more than 75 years of sustained effort, there is presently no evidence supporting the widespread belief that students learn more from professors who receive higher [student] ratings. If anything, the latest large sample studies show that students who were taught by highly rated professors in prerequisites perform more poorly in follow up courses."[6] Uttl concludes that student evaluations reflect student satisfaction, not student learning. So for student evaluations to be related to some business necessity, as the law requires, universities would need to be in the business of satisfying students rather than educating them.

Things get even more problematic when universities use student teaching evaluations to compare the quality of professors across fields. In a 2017 study at NYU, the average student rating in English classes was 4.29, while classes in math averaged 3.68.[7] Other studies have found significant differences between English, history, languages, sociology, and political science, on the one hand, and math, computer science, engineering, and chemistry, on the other.[8] Direct comparisons across the university would systematically disadvantage faculty going up for tenure or promotion in some fields rather than others.

On the question of whether faculty get different results based on their race or gender, the studies are grim. Studying racial differences in student evaluations has long been complicated by the fact that there just aren't enough faculty of certain racial groups to compare. One early study by Usha Chowdhary found that students gave her a lower rating in the section where she wore traditional Indian clothes than in one where she only wore Western clothing.[9] In 2010 Landon Reid, a psychologist, turned to Rate My Professors to gather thousands of ratings from the top twenty-five liberal arts colleges.[10] (Because that website gives students a chance to rate their professors' "hotness," it has also been a central source of data for studies showing that good looks lead to higher teaching scores.[11]) Reid's study found that grouping non-white faculty together obscures differences *among* underrepresented racial groups in the bias they face. It specifically understates how scores given to white professors differ from those given to Asian and, especially, Black faculty in student evaluations of instructors' overall quality, helpfulness, and clarity. Reid's study did not find similar differences between white and Latino faculty.

Bringing together national origin and gender, a more recent study of over half a million student surveys at an Australian university found that female instructors from non-English-speaking countries—comprising 38% of the faculty—were far less likely than men from English-speaking countries to get high evaluation scores from local students, whether male or female.[12] In the worst case, foreign female instructors in the sciences were only 42% as likely as local male instructors to get high scores from local male students. Lesser but still significant national origin and gender differences were observed in the business, medical, engineering, and arts and sciences faculties too.

Focusing solely on gender, economist Friederike Mengel and colleagues looked at nearly twenty thousand student evaluations at a university in the Netherlands, where students are randomly assigned to instructors but graded through centralized exams. They found in 2018 that "female faculty receive systematically lower teaching evaluations than their male colleagues despite the fact that neither students' current or future grades nor their study hours are affected by the gender of the instructor."[13] Mengel's study found that students even rated *textbooks* worse when they were assigned by a female professor. In a study of online classes, where researchers could switch the name and picture that students see, students gave professors an average 4.35 out of 5 for promptness when they thought their professor was male; those thought to be female got a 3.55, despite the fact that they graded and returned students' assignments in the same amount of time.[14] That study also found that professors received better ratings in fairness, enthusiasm, respectfulness, praise, and professionalism when students thought they were male. As the study's authors put it, "Male instructors are often afforded an automatic credibility in terms of their professionalism, expertise, and effectiveness as instructors." And the time it takes female faculty to overcome this differential obviously impacts the amount of time they have for research and service activities, the other things that determine whether someone gets a job, tenure, or promotion.

Even the rating scale used in student evaluations has been shown to affect the gender differentials in the results. A 2019 study by sociologists Lauren Rivera and András Tilcsik found that simply switching from a ten-point to a six-point scale reduced the gap between ratings of male and female professors. The reason: students were far more willing to give men a ten (22% versus 13% for female instructors), whereas they gave sixes almost equally regardless of gender. Rivera and Tilcsik's finding reinforced previous studies that have found ascriptions of "genius" or "brilliance" to be deeply gendered. "Because a 6/6 rating did not signify exceptional or brilliant performance as strongly as a 10/10 rating, women—who were less likely than men to be seen as brilliant teachers—benefitted from being assessed on a 6-point rather than 10-point scale."[15]

Together, studies like these raise tough questions about whether student teaching evaluations are even legal when used to determine a candidate's teaching skill or to award raises or promotions to current faculty. The uselessness of student evaluations as a marker of teaching prowess makes even unintended disparate impacts based on race and gender legally problematic. Why, after all, should an employer not be legally liable for relying on a test that is a barrier to women and certain minority candidates *and* has little or no relation to the job in question?

But put that aside. For my purposes here, the point is not to predict the outcome of a lawsuit, but to see what effect student evaluations have on what professors say and do in the classroom. That, after all, is the main threat to academic freedom.

A tenured law professor, not at my school, once told me that she stopped giving midterms in a course we both teach, even though she believes the studies showing that formative assessment and mid-semester feedback improve student learning. Students who are angry about their grades give lower teaching evaluation scores, she told me. It's just not worth it. Better to wait and grade students only after evaluations are in. I was a little scandalized to hear this. My friend was making what she knew to be a bad teaching choice in order to—what exactly? Get a better raise? Improve her chances of a job offer at a better school? From up on my academic-freedom high horse, it sounded like she was pandering to the students she should have been teaching. (I was probably also a little jealous of the time she wasn't spending grading in the middle of the semester.)

Soon after our talk, an economist at Georgia Tech, Whitney Buser, published a study that looked at almost twelve hundred introductory economics students at different types of colleges and universities in the United States.[16] Buser and her colleagues asked students to rate their professors at two points during the semester: on the second day of class and the day after students received their first midterm grade. The researchers found little evidence of bias in the first scores but found significant gender differences after grades came back. In other words, they were able to show that students take out their frustrations over grades in demonstrably gendered ways. What my friend had been describing was much more than just risk aversion or laziness on her part. My friend was actively avoiding sex discrimination. Joining me on my high horse would have cost her something it didn't cost me.

My uncharitable accusation of pandering isn't off the mark more generally though. Study after study has shown that students give better course evaluations when they expect to get higher grades in the class.[17] When Wellesley College instituted a grade ceiling in 2004, capping the class average at 3.33, the number of students "strongly recommending" their classes went down by 5%.[18] Fifteen years later, Wellesley gave up on the policy.

Students also give higher teaching evaluations in classes where "it [is] possible to get an A without much work," as Rate My Professors puts it, and they are more likely to enroll in classes where they expect good grades. Professors know this and clearly feel pressure to respond.[19] In one study at a California State University campus, 72% of the faculty surveyed thought that student evaluations cause teachers to water down their course content.[20] Untenured faculty are likely to feel even more pressure, with some studies showing higher average grades in their classes than in those of tenured faculty.[21]

As the social psychologist Wolfgang Stroebe notes, "In the 1980s, the time when [student teaching evaluations] became major information sources in faculty evaluations, grades began to rise . . . at a rate of 0.10 to 0.15 GPA points per decade."[22] In fifty years, from 1963 to 2013, the percentage of A's given in the United States rose from around 15% to 45%.[23] If Stroebe is right in connecting the "customer is always right" mentality of contemporary student teaching evaluations with the ever-increasing clustering of student grades at the top end of the scale, it is hard to imagine many other ways that academic judgment in American universities has been so thoroughly affected.

Student evaluations exert pressure on what professors say, in addition to what they do. In a large-scale survey in 1999, 34% of the professors surveyed said that they censored themselves out of concern for students' reactions, and 10% of those professors answered an open-ended question by identifying negative student evaluations as the thing they feared. Half of the surveyed faculty who self-censor said they didn't express certain viewpoints to avoid hurt feelings or confusion on the students' part, and as those running the survey noted, this answer, too, could have been driven in part by a concern about evaluations.[24] More recent studies have found that students "who perceive their professors to be political allies rate courses more favorably than do students who perceive their professors to be political foes."[25] So professors are punished on their evaluations if they depart too far from the political leanings of their students, no matter which direction.

This, in turn, may cause some professors to avoid discussing certain topics altogether. In a 2021 report about large-scale surveys of academics in the UK, Canada, and the United States, Eric Kaufmann shared comments by faculty who steered away from discussions of abortion, transgender issues, sexuality, and Israel/Palestine because of fears that students would penalize them on their evaluations.[26] In a 2017 essay, Harvard law professor Jeannie Suk Gersen wrote, "About a dozen new teachers of criminal law at multiple institutions have told me that they are not including rape law in their courses, arguing that it's not worth the risk of complaints of discomfort by students."[27] On the other hand, another law professor, Khiara Bridges at UC Berkeley, has argued more recently that student evaluations may cause professors to *add* new material. "A professor of criminal law who neglects to explore how the blackletter law that she analyzes in the class interacts with inequality along the lines of class and race is more likely than ever to hear about it . . . in the end-of-semester student evaluations."[28] Either way, student comments end up shaping what gets taught.

: : :

When I said at the outset of this discussion that student teaching evaluations have flown under the radar in comparison to diversity statements, I certainly didn't mean to suggest that they haven't come under withering criticism. Part of my point, in fact, is to emphasize how extensively and creatively they have been empirically studied—in contrast to the still largely anecdotal conversations surrounding DEI statements.

But criticisms of student teaching evaluations seldom focus specifically on their threat to *academic freedom*.[29] The problem here isn't that instructors may not feel they can say whatever they want in class. The threat to academic freedom is the systematic outsourcing of judgments about academic merit to people with limited expertise in the subject. When it comes to evaluating teaching, this outsourcing happens throughout higher education, in public schools and private schools, rich schools and underfunded schools, red states and blue states alike. It's everywhere. Yet the decades of studies showing the racism, sexism, and uselessness of student teaching evaluations haven't produced anything like the kind of popular outcry or legislative action that diversity statements have recently received.

These divergent reactions are especially notable if you remember what got people so worked up about diversity statements in the first place. Recall (from the last chapter) critics' fears that diversity statements will have a disparate impact on the racial and gender makeup of university faculties; that mandated DEI statements shift power from faculty to administration (and the diversity professionals who increasingly fill its ranks); that no matter how diversity statements get framed, "everyone knows" what universities really want faculty to say in order to pass their ideological litmus test; and ultimately, that DEI is a distraction from what universities should really care about: academic merit.

If those are the reasons why critics fret about diversity statements, we might expect to find those critics positively beside themselves at the thought of student teaching evaluations. Consider first the racially and gendered disparate impact of student teaching evaluations, which has been demonstrated for decades. Faculty who are not white or male either suffer the consequences of lower scores or have to put in more effort than their colleagues to raise them, taking time away from their research and other academic work. Why does the *potential* disparate impact of DEI statements garner so much more outrage than the *demonstrated* disparate impact of student teaching evaluations, which are far more widely used? Could the answer have anything to do with the difference in who bears the brunt of the impact?

Second, even if diversity statements were imposed by administrators—something not true at my university, by the way—the use of student teaching evaluations generally are, too. Even worse, whereas diversity statements (at least when done right) are judged by faculty within the field doing the hiring or advancement, student teaching evaluations are, by definition, evaluations by students. Academic judgment is outsourced by design.

Third, for all the work that "everyone knows" arguments do when it comes to diversity statements, we don't have to rely on that kind of conjecture when it comes to student evaluations. We have actual empirical data from countless studies showing that students punish faculty for their perceived ideology, their rigor, and any ways they depart from students' stereotypes of professors in that field. Unlike diversity statements, student teaching evaluations have long been part of nearly every faculty member's professional life. We've all used them. So unlike diversity statements, which are still new in most places, faculty around the world have spent years experiencing firsthand the pressure to shape their teaching, censor their views, and alter their self-presentation around the preferences expressed in evaluations that get incorporated into their review files. Sometimes student evaluations even get posted publicly, increasing their coercive effect even more.

Finally, the charge that diversity statements involve something "other than merit" is especially rich, given that student teaching evaluations have been shown to have no relation to merit whatsoever. Student teaching evaluations are simply no good at scoring teachers' ability to teach. What they do tell us is how much students like someone. And the quest for likability is correlated with a lack of rigor that has led to rampant grade inflation—an *actual* corrosion of merit judgments within the university, and one that can be graphed out for all to see.

The lack of outrage about all of this—really, any of this—is telling. In chapter 1, I kept urging us to compare DEI statements to the other standard elements of faculty job and tenure applications. We should use those as a model for how best to frame and evaluate DEI statements, I argued. Here the comparison reveals something darker. It shows that the worries we keep hearing about diversity statements—worries that have led already to legislative interventions across the country—those worries are far worse, and far better supported empirically, when it comes to student teaching evaluations, used at nearly every university in the United States.

The campus speech and academic freedom advocacy organizations that have so much to say about diversity statements have, to my knowledge, never launched a campaign against the biased, speech-distorting, or grade-diluting effects of student teaching evaluations. Similarly, in the twelve years I have taught at my current university, only one issue has provoked a faculty-wide resolution—two of them, in fact, in one year: diversity statements. After garnering 265 online comments in 2020, a resolution saying diversity statements should not be mandatory lost 441–426, while another calling them "a useful part of a holistic review" ended up winning 486–317. By contrast, the issue of student teaching evaluations prompted only one committee (on which I served), whose report seems to have generated little comment at all.

And while almost half of state legislatures have considered or passed bills to prohibit DEI statements, and the Trump administration has targeted them at the federal level, some of the most recent legislative action surrounding teaching evaluations actually goes the opposite direction. A bill that passed the Ohio Senate would require annual performance reviews for faculty in which, for the teaching component, student evaluations would make up at least half the score.[30] Ironically, given the variety of biases proven to infect student evaluations, the Ohio bill would make schools ask students whether their faculty "create a classroom atmosphere free of political, racial, gender, and religious bias."

Critics and legislators have bypassed any attempt to reform or improve DEI statements, preferring just to ban them outright. But those same critics and legislators have simply ignored the demonstrated problems with student teaching evaluations—or, as in Ohio, they've tried to double down on their use. To say all of this is not just to shout, "Look over there!" in hopes that critics of diversity statements might get distracted and start talking about something else. The critics are distracted already. They're looking away, inexplicably, from the fact that the very things they claim to fear about diversity statements have long been proven true of student teaching evaluations. At this point, at every panel I'm asked to join about diversity statements, and to every reporter who calls while writing yet another article about them, I want to say: "I hear your worries, I really do, but have you heard about this thing universities are using called 'student teaching evaluations'?"

The Rankings Racket

The threat that student teaching evaluations pose to academic freedom comes from giving non-experts the power to judge academic merit. Scored by students who prioritize different things than disciplinary experts would, faculty face a choice: stick to their own (and their peers') expert judgment of how best to do their jobs, or bow to outside pressure and do what it takes to get a good score.

If pandering was the predictable result of making student evaluation scores central to faculty members' professional success, it shouldn't come as a surprise that universities would also pander if they started getting scored. And pander they have. University rankings have the power to determine not just schools' prestige and bragging rights, but the quality of students, faculty, and funding they are able to attract. Once a ranker as influential as *U.S. News & World Report* chooses its evaluation formula, universities face a choice of their own. They can stick to their best judgment about academic matters like admissions, curriculum, faculty hiring, and the allocation of their resources, or they can cater to whatever criteria *U.S. News* has decided to privilege.

A 1957 US Supreme Court opinion, quoting South African scholars, emphasized "four essential freedoms" of a university: "to determine for itself on academic grounds who may teach, what may be taught, how it shall be taught, and who may be admitted to study."[31] Since *U.S. News* began ranking American colleges and universities in 1983, schools have increasingly outsourced to their ranker each of these four essential determinations, which give a university its character. Just to be clear, my concern here is not primarily with the specific directions in which outside rankings may have distorted which students get admitted, what kinds of faculty get hired, and where money gets spent at American universities. What I want to emphasize is how shocking it is—and how egregious a violation of academic freedom—that a private company like *U.S. News & World Report* should play any role in these decisions at all.

To see what types of academic decisions a ranking scheme can affect, just look at what *U.S. News* has weighed in recent years in its annual "Best Colleges" list. The factors that currently go into its ranking include graduation rates (26%, measured in two different ways) and first-year retention (5%); 20% for "peer" assessments, which really means surveys sent to college presidents, provosts, and admissions deans; a university's spending per student and faculty salaries (8% and 6%); students' standardized test scores, federal loan debt at graduation, and earnings compared to non-college graduates (5% each); and the student/faculty ratio (3%) along with the proportion of teaching faculty who are full-time

(2%). As part of a new emphasis on social mobility, two measures of success for students receiving Pell Grants are now used (totaling 11%). And in one of its newest changes, *U.S. News* has started including faculty citations in its ranking of national universities, with four different metrics that combined make up 4% of schools' total scores.[32]

From an academic freedom standpoint, some of the changes *U.S. News* has recently made to its rankings criteria are unambiguously good. For years, it gave significant weight to two factors—average salary of full-time professors (7% in the 2023 rankings) and average class size (8% that year)—that, together, presented universities with an especially perverse incentive: keep salaries high for a small number of full-time faculty while using low-paid adjunct instructors to offer as many class sections as possible. Universities' increasing reliance on instructors who lack long-term contracts, much less tenure, is nothing short of an academic freedom catastrophe. In fall 2022, 68% of faculty in the United States had contingent appointments—not tenured or tenure-track—and almost half of the instructors in American higher education had positions that were not full-time.[33] Contingent faculty are less likely than permanent faculty to participate in shared governance at their university, not least because that work often goes uncompensated. A recent survey found that only 46% of non-tenure-track faculty believe their administration guarantees their academic freedom in the classroom.[34] And contingent faculty are far more vulnerable to the coercive power of student teaching evaluations and other outside pressures, since their at-will employment often hinges on good reviews and is threatened by public controversy. The causes and potential solutions to this crisis are complex—and largely beyond my expertise.[35] But a ranking system that *rewarded* the casualization of academic labor certainly made things worse. To its credit, *U.S. News* has now taken away this incentive. In its recent rankings, it considers the salaries of *all* full-time instructors, not just professors; it looks at the ratio of full-time to part-time instructors; and it has ditched class size as a factor entirely.

I'm glad that *U.S. News* is no longer rewarding adjunctification, just as I am personally happy to see its rankings doing more to reward social mobility than, say, alumni giving rates, as it used to do. But the real academic freedom scandal comes less from what *U.S. News* chooses to reward in any given year than from the fact that universities let these rewards guide their decision-making. Questions about what kinds of instructional staff to hire and how strongly to prioritize social mobility within a university's mission—or whether to include it at all—are judgments that go to the very core of a university's academic identity. Shared governance exists precisely to make judgments like these. Decisions should be the product of joint effort among a university's faculty, administration, and trustees—not that of a private company trying to juice interest in its most lucrative product.

Just as I said in the previous section, critics who worry, in the context of DEI statements, that social justice concerns are being imposed on faculty, or that faculty hiring is being skewed by mandates from administrators, should presumably be livid at the thought that some unaccountable entity *outside* academia might be putting a thumb on the scale of who gets hired—and admitted—at our universities. But I've yet to see an angry letter or policy statement about this from FIRE, the Academic Freedom Alliance, or any of the other usual suspects.

Now some might respond that *U.S. News* isn't asking anyone to pledge allegiance to anything; it's not telling anyone what to teach or study. *U.S. News* just compiles statistics. It isn't out there getting faculty members fired or chilling their speech. On this view, *U.S. News* rankings might be bad for higher education—that's a view widely shared and often said in print—but it is not specifically a menace to *academic freedom*. That's wrong.

Unlike, say, legislative "gag orders" that prevent faculty from teaching certain subjects or force certain departments to close, the academic freedom threat of rankings does not come from directly silencing or firing faculty. It is more insidious. When a particular ranking scheme dominates the market like the *U.S. News* rankings have, it is bound to affect what faculty are hired to teach and what students are there to be taught. A dominant ranking scheme places a nearly irresistible pressure on a university to warp its identity around the metric of the day, shifting its priorities in admissions, hiring, and spending. As Wendy Nelson Espeland and Michael Sauder concluded in their indispensable study of law school rankings: "Rankings created new conceptualizations of how schools compared to one another, what it meant to be successful, and how identity is constructed and maintained."[36] Over time, whom you hire and admit, and what you fund, end up determining who you are as a university.

To see just how corrosive rankings can be to academic freedom, we don't need to look any further than the hero (or foil) of the chapter that follows, the university that, more than any other, has made academic freedom its defining brand: the University of Chicago. The next chapter will describe the campaigns being waged across the country to get other universities to adopt Chicago's free speech and institutional neutrality policies. But even as it evangelizes about what a school must do to be a genuine university, the University of Chicago has shown itself surprisingly willing to outsource some of its most fundamental academic decisions to *U.S. News*.[37]

Consider its fabled core curriculum. According to the University of Chicago's Admissions Office, "The Core is known for its small, Socratic-style classes capped at a maximum of 19 students where learning takes place through discussion based [around] primary texts."[38] (My first job out of graduate school was teaching one of these classes.) Why the cap at nineteen students, you might wonder? Did Chicago's long experience with the core curriculum or advice from education experts lead to the conclusion that nineteen students is the magic number? The school's student newspaper, *The Chicago Maroon*, tells a different story. After dropping to fifteenth in the 2006 *U.S. News* rankings, Chicago's dean of college enrollment scheduled a meeting in Washington, DC, between top administrators and the *U.S. News* staff. "That trip proved fruitful," the *Maroon* says. Among the changes Chicago made to get its rankings back on track was "the effort to cap core class size at 19 students, the level at which U.S. News and World Report defines a small class."[39]

Rankings also lurk behind the dramatic changes to the University of Chicago's undergraduate admissions practices in the two decades since I taught there. When I arrived in 2005, assembling the college's distinctively quirky, idea-loving student body was seen as so central to the university's character that all faculty were asked to read undergraduate admissions files. Chicago prided itself on refusing to join the Common App, the application form used by most universities in the United States. Instead, it had the "Uncommon Application," which asked famously idiosyncratic questions meant to draw out the uniqueness of the students applying—and to communicate the school's own uniqueness. As the dean of admissions from that time, Ted O'Neill, described the old system: "Those of us who worked in the admissions office at Chicago were happy with what we were getting—relatively fewer applications, but better, more informed, more targeted applications."[40] He went on: "But that isn't enough these days. Presidents and boards of trustees want more, better targeted or not, and eventually word came that we must abandon the Uncommon."[41] In 2008, its first year using the Common App, Chicago had a 9% increase in applications.[42] Three years before the change, its acceptance rate was about 40%; three years after the change, it was 16%, eventually falling to 5%, even as the number of undergraduates almost doubled. Not coincidentally, Chicago's *U.S. News* ranking during that period rose from a steady eighth or ninth in the country (and a low of fifteenth) up to third, where it stayed from 2017 to 2019.[43]

What does the University of Chicago's application system have to do with academic freedom, you might wonder? Chicago, after all, was still able to add some—though not all—of its "uncommon" essay prompts as supplemental essays on the Common App. (It did have to drop questions about what applicants were reading.) As Dean O'Neill explained, by using the Common App, Chicago was forced to ask questions that they didn't want students to answer. "Take, for instance, asking about an applicant's major. We know that most students frequently change majors, and are even encouraged to do so by our core curriculum, so why ask them to label themselves so early, and so meaninglessly?"[44] The way you select your students, in other words, can not only change the kind of students you get, but, less obviously, it can help establish the academic norms that those students bring with them when they come.

In 2024, the University of Chicago dropped from number six to twelve on *U.S. News*, falling out of the Top 10 for the first time since 2006. Chicago's academic quality almost certainly hadn't changed. *U.S. News* had just overhauled its criteria, and the new ones, which I described earlier, no longer consider average class size or the educational attainment of faculty, two of Chicago's previous strengths. The rankings now give more emphasis to outcomes measures, including social mobility, where, according to *U.S. News*, Chicago comes in 190th in the nation.

The arbitrariness of year-to-year changes in rankings is not itself an academic freedom problem. *U.S. News* has the right to rank schools on any metric it wants. The academic freedom problem only arises when universities decide to alter their own identity to match whatever *U.S. News* decides it values at any given moment.

To put it more concretely, social mobility is an admirable goal for a university, and many students are justifiably interested in it when they consider where to apply. But social mobility is not a key part of every university's mission. There is no reason all universities need to make that their aim. Whether they do emphasize social mobility as part of their mission or not is something each university needs to decide for itself—ideally for reasons better than "because *U.S. News* said so."

: : :

Rankings are homogenizers.[45] They can't reward uniqueness, because things that are unique can't be ordered along a single line. It would be a great shame, I think, if a school as historically idiosyncratic as the University of Chicago turned itself into Princeton, the perennial winner of the *U.S. News* sweepstakes. But it would be an even greater shame if it did so in order to win the favor of a private digital media company. To mangle one of Chicago's beloved Great Books: What shall it profit a university if it gains the top spot but loses its soul?[46]

Homogeneity is a threat to higher education. And it's a villain that reappears throughout this book. At every turn, there is someone claiming some necessary sameness, some single way things must be done or understood. Academic merit can only be defined one way; universities need to keep their mouths shut or they won't be real universities anymore; when it comes to free speech and academic freedom, everyone should be more like the University of Chicago.

I've said a bit about Chicago and rankings not, or not primarily, to call it out as a hypocrite for outsourcing key choices about its academic identity even as it preaches academic freedom. The real lesson here is that a university with its own distinctive identity—something the University of Chicago has long had—is a wonderful, fragile thing. It's the *distinctiveness* that other schools should emulate, not the identity itself. The whole point of having opinionated universities, after all, depends on their not all sharing the same opinions.

3 *Institutional Speech*
Silence Is Not Always Silent

No matter what a university chooses to do to promote diversity or to regulate expression—the big topic already covered and the one still to come—it has to choose *something*. And its choices say something about what values it sees as part of its mission, and how those values should be understood and balanced. None of the options count as neutral.

Universities of course can also choose to say things through words. And those choices, too, end up expressing a view about their mission. It might not always seem that way, though. Universities sometimes decide to take some topics off the table entirely. When that happens, a university's silence might not appear to express anything at all. Take electoral politics, for example. Universities can't make endorsements without endangering their tax-exempt status—or in my university's case, violating state law. So no one reasonably thinks that my university is tipping its hand by refusing to endorse a presidential candidate. Here, silence is just silence, and neutrality seems possible.

That possibility has proven alluring. Calls for "institutional neutrality" have grown significantly louder in the wake of the October 2023 attacks in Israel and their aftermath. Some say that if universities hadn't spent years weighing in on political topics, from George Floyd and Black Lives Matter to Russia's invasion of Ukraine, few would have found their failures to speak about Israel or Gaza significant. The deep alienation and polarization caused by some university statements—and silences—surrounding October 7 might have been avoided if universities had institutionalized a policy of principled silence beforehand. The University of Chicago, whose neutrality policy dates back at least to the Kalven

Committee Report of 1967, is repeatedly held up as the model other universities should have followed.[1]

But Chicago's silence isn't total. It doesn't extend to all of what the Kalven Report referred to as "the political and social issues of the day." The University of Chicago doesn't even remain categorically silent on narrower categories like foreign affairs. (Compare the claim cited in the introduction, that "the University of Wisconsin does not have a foreign policy."[2]) In recent years, the University of Chicago has spoken out on both the DACA program and President Trump's "Muslim ban."

The University of Chicago's neutrality mandate is meant to cover all political and social issues of the day, *except for those* that "threaten the very mission of the university and its values of free inquiry." The Kalven Report says the university actually has an "obligation . . . to defend its interests and its values." Chicago's neutrality thus begins where its mission leaves off. The upshot is that Chicago-style commitments to institutional neutrality turn out to be no different from debates over diversity statements or, as we'll soon see, freedom of expression policies. They all reduce to questions about the scope of a university's mission. And since those questions have no neutral answers, calls for institutional neutrality don't ultimately deliver what they promise.

This chapter advances this argument both in regard to institutional speech and to speech by units within an institution—the schools, departments, and centers whose expression takes an even more complicated variety of forms, with their own distinctive possibilities and dangers. Most of what follows is about whether and how universities or their units *can* speak. But "can" does not imply "should." Even after the pretense of neutrality is discarded in favor of more forthright debate about a university's mission, a different and difficult challenge remains: deciding whether any given statement will effectively advance that mission. This chapter and the next both take that challenge seriously.

Kalvenist Missionaries

Institutional neutrality is an export business at the University of Chicago, and recently business has been booming. Even before interest in Chicago's Kalven Report began taking off in 2023, a well-funded effort to promote another of Chicago's speech policies had been underway for years. More than a hundred universities have adopted the so-called Chicago Principles, based on a 2015 report by the University of Chicago's Committee on Freedom of Expression, headed by First Amendment scholar Geoffrey Stone. Its ascendancy didn't come about by accident. The year the committee's report was released, FIRE launched a national campaign to convince universities to endorse it; around the same time, the American Council of Trustees and Alumni (ACTA) wrote to over nineteen thousand university trustees across the country promoting the Chicago Principles.[3] Fast-forward ten years and a bill that narrowly passed the House of Representatives in 2024 expressed the sense of Congress that *all* universities, or at least all nonsectarian ones, should do two things: ban diversity statements and adopt the Chicago Principles.[4]

The Chicago Principles are mainly concerned with free speech on campus—the topic of chapter 5. But they incorporate, uncited and sometimes unnoticed, the Kalven Report's insistence that the university must remain silent if its members are to speak freely:

> Debate or deliberation may not be suppressed because the ideas put forth are thought by some or even by most members of the University community to be offensive, unwise, immoral, or wrong-headed. It is for the individual members of the University community, *not for the University as an institution*, to make those judgments for themselves, and to act on those judgments not by seeking to suppress speech, but by openly and vigorously contesting the ideas that they oppose.[5]

Having been so successful in evangelizing for the Chicago Principles, it's unsurprising that FIRE, ACTA, and others have more recently turned to promoting the Kalven Report as well. In February 2024, FIRE teamed up with two other advocacy organizations, Heterodox Academy and the Academic Freedom Alliance, to call on university trustees to adopt an institutional neutrality policy by the start of the following academic year. Citing what it referred to as "the University of Chicago's famous *Kalven Report* of 1967," the three groups wrote that "it is time to restore truth-seeking as the primary mission of higher education by adopting a policy of institutional neutrality on social and political issues that do not concern core academic matters or institutional operations."[6]

The following week, an article in the *Chronicle of Higher Education* asked: "Is Institutional Neutrality Catching On?"[7] The answer seemed, and seems, to be yes.[8] But the conversions to neutrality have taken various forms, not all consensual.[9] Some are little more than suggestions, like that of Columbia's relatively powerless University Senate, which advised in February 2024 that "the University and its leaders should refrain from taking political positions in their institutional capacity . . . except in the rare case when the University has a compelling institutional interest, such as a legal obligation, that requires it to do so."[10] (This is a stricter test even than Kalven's.) Others consist of commitments—which is to say, *statements*—by university presidents pledging to limit their use of statements going forward. The president of Holy Cross recognized the irony by calling his new policy "Our Statement on Statements."[11]

More binding commitments to institutional neutrality have come from college and university boards of trustees—some, like those at Ohio State and Claremont McKenna, explicitly referencing or incorporating the Kalven Report.[12] And then there are neutrality mandates that are imposed from outside. In 2023, a new state law in North Carolina dictated that every public university there "shall remain neutral, as an institution, on the political controversies of the day." Indiana passed a law the following year requiring university boards to adopt policies banning institutional and departmental statements on "political, moral, or ideological issues" unless they affect "the core mission of the institution and its values of free inquiry, free expression, and intellectual diversity."[13]

So what is this Kalven Report, which so many schools are now wanting to emulate, if not borrow outright?

In May 1966, "one of the first major sit-ins of a university administration building" occurred at the University of Chicago, prompted by its president's decision to provide class ranks to draft boards on students' request.[14] The following January, two hundred University of Chicago students picketed a bank downtown, then rallied on campus, demanding that their university cut off ties with the bank unless it divested from apartheid South Africa.[15] In June 1967, students again took over the Administration Building, returning to the issue of class rankings. This time, fifty-eight of those students received suspensions from a faculty disciplinary committee chaired by law professor and First Amendment scholar Harry Kalven.[16]

In the months between the divestment and second draft protests—from February to May 1967—Professor Kalven had been appointed by

Chicago's president to chair another important committee as well. This was a group of seven faculty tasked with examining "The Role of the University in Political and Social Action"—also the title of its resulting report.[17] The Kalven Report, as it's more commonly known, describes its aim modestly, as simply "providing a point of departure for discussion in the University community" about what its political and social role should be.[18] This "point of departure" is a reaffirmation of "a few old truths and a cherished tradition," a reference to a path-marking statement adopted in 1899, under the University of Chicago's first president, William Rainey Harper, declaring "that the University, as such, does not appear as a disputant on either side upon any public question."[19]

To justify this tradition, the Kalven Report starts by defining the mission and purpose of the university. And here, both context and a switch from "University" to "university" indicate that the Kalven Report means to refer to universities generally, not just the University of Chicago. "The mission of the university," it says, "is the discovery, improvement, and dissemination of knowledge. . . . A university faithful to its mission will provide enduring challenges to social values, policies, practices, and institutions."

But who is to do the challenging? According to the report, "The instrument of dissent and criticism is the individual faculty member or the individual student. The university is the home and sponsor of critics; it is not itself the critic." The explanation for why this is so gets a bit murkier, so I'll just quote. A university, the report says,

> is a community which cannot take collective action on the issues of the day without endangering the conditions for its existence and effectiveness. There is no mechanism by which it can reach a collective position without inhibiting that full freedom of dissent on which it thrives. It cannot insist that all of its members favor a given view of social policy; if it takes collective action, therefore, it does so at the price of censuring any minority who do not agree with the view adopted.

The argument seems to be that an institution's *positions* or *views* or *collective actions*—it's notable that the Kalven Report treats these interchangeably—necessarily endanger its members' *academic freedom*, without which the university cannot "perform its mission": fostering teaching and research that will "challenge existing social arrangements." Carrying out the university's "proper role in political and social action" thus turns out to depend on maintaining its "neutrality as an institution."

Much can be said of the central argument here—and has been.[20] Why, for example, can't a university take collective action without *insisting* that all of its members share its view? Why should we think that anyone who disagrees is thereby *censured*? Some of Kalven's supporters talk as if voicing an opinion for an institution necessarily means speaking for all of the institution's members, or sending the message that there can be only one correct view.[21] Neither is true. The idea that a group can't express a collective position without inhibiting the "full freedom of dissent" is especially curious in a committee report that itself includes a dissent from one of its members. (Professor George Stigler attached a "special comment" disagreeing with the report's view on the university's actions as employer and property owner.)[22]

As Robert Post has argued, the notion that institutional statements are inherently incompatible with academic freedom is undermined by the Kalven Report's later, less categorical push for "a heavy *presumption* against the university taking collective action or expressing opinions."[23] Post argues that the Kalven Report is best understood as an empirical claim that faculty are likely to feel pressured to conform to official positions taken by their employer.[24] That claim seems intuitive in some circumstances, but not all. As Post asks, does anyone really think Chicago's faculty would have felt pressure to change what they taught or wrote simply because their employer had decided to divest from South Africa—as more than 150 other universities in fact went on to do?[25]

If the chilling effect of institutional statements can be this variable, it seems a little overwrought to claim—as Geoffrey Stone, author of the Chicago Principles has done—that "once a university takes sides, it is no longer a university."[26] I'll call this the strong claim for institutional neutrality, or hard-line Kalvenism: the claim that neutrality is a necessary condition for a university even to be a university. The University of Chicago is not the only place where that strong claim has been made.

In fact, for all its newfound popularity, the Kalven Report has never been the only game in town. Like most faculty committee reports, the Kalven Report didn't have much influence outside the University of

Chicago for much of its existence.[27] When, in November 1969, the American Association of University Professors took up the subject of institutional neutrality, it did so without any reference to Kalven at all.[28] Instead of taking its own position, the AAUP's Council briefly stated the arguments on each side of the debate and called for further discussion from its membership, which it went on to publish.

The AAUP's summary of the pro-neutrality position made the strong claim: that open dialogue and academic freedom are "possible only if the institution within which this dialogue is to take place is itself, *as an institution*, neutral on the issues being debated."[29] Respondents to the AAUP's call for further discussion also made the strong claim, again without mentioning the Kalven Report. As historian Winton Solberg put it, the "principle of institutional neutrality"—the idea that the university as a corporate body is obligated "to refrain from official pronouncements on disputed political, moral, philosophical, and scientific issues"—is "essential to the proper functioning of a genuine university."[30]

When in 2017 the Goldwater Institute began popularizing the Kalven Report, turning Kalven's principles into model legislation, it claimed that "when a university, as an institution, takes a strong stand on a major public debate, this inherently pressures faculty and students to toe the official university line, thereby inhibiting their freedom to speak and decide for themselves."[31] Universities that take stands *inherently* inhibit academic freedom, which is *possible only if* institutions stay neutral. When they don't, they are *no longer a university*, or at least no longer a *genuine* university. These are the central tenets of Kalvenism, according to its most hard-line version.

Is Neutrality Possible?

Where hard-line Kalvenism sees institutional neutrality as a necessary condition for academic freedom, Robert Post's argument is that the two are only contingently connected. Whether a university that expresses an opinion thereby chills the speech of its members is an empirical question, and one that admits of widely different answers depending, presumably, on what the opinion is about, how the university goes about expressing it, and what academic freedom protections lurk in the background, both in policy and practice.

Post strikes me as clearly correct in recognizing that non-neutrality—which is to say, institutional opinionatedness—can have varied effects on academic freedom, from severely chilling to nearly unnoticed. And it's a good thing that neutrality isn't a necessary condition for academic freedom.[32] Because in many cases, neutrality isn't even an option. As the philosopher Robert Paul Wolff wrote in his still-essential 1969 book, *The Ideal of the University*, "The doctrine of value neutrality suffers from the worst disability which can afflict a norm: what it prescribes is not wrong; it is impossible."[33] I see two different routes leading to this conclusion. One, which was also Wolff's, avoids a blind spot within the Kalven Report: some of the controversies it addresses *require* that the university take sides. These issues leave no space for neutrality because they involve expressive actions, not just words, in contexts where choosing one action or another is unavoidable. The present book is structured to make this point. The overarching claim here is that many of a university's actions are just as expressive as its statements, so treating the two as something categorically separate makes little sense—or at least requires more argument than institutional neutrality proponents normally give us.[34]

The other path begins with something the Kalven Report explicitly says, as opposed to something it ignores. This is the Kalven Report's carve-out: the exception it makes for institutional statements addressing threats to a university's mission. A university that says we'll be neutral unless our mission requires us not to be is not really neutral at all, since it always has to take a stand on what its mission requires. Insofar as there's no neutral choice about what a university's mission should be, the vision of neutrality promised by the Kalven Report is bound to be illusory.

To start, then, down the first of these two paths, we just need to return to the controversies that prompted the Kalven Report in the first place: providing rankings to the Draft Board and divesting from South Africa. Both share something in common. Compared, say, to the emails and press releases sent out after October 7, 2023, a statement about whether the University of Chicago will provide class ranks or alter its investment strategy is more than just a statement; it's an announcement of something the university plans to *do*. And while it might seem like a university can stay neutral by refusing to issue a statement about foreign wars, it doesn't have a similar option when it comes to class ranks or divestment. The school either chooses to share the rankings or not, to continue investing in South Africa or to stop doing so.

Addressing a new divestment controversy nearly forty years after the Kalven Report, Chicago's Geoffrey Stone wrote, "Those who demand divestment want the University to make a *statement* about what is morally, politically, and socially 'right.' And that is precisely what the University should not do."[35] Stone doesn't acknowledge that a decision to continue investing in something makes a statement of its own. Preserving the status quo is not the same thing as neutrality. More broadly, Stone fails to recognize just how routinely universities, through their actions, make statements about what is morally, politically, and socially right. His argument against doing so would prove far too much.

Just look at the names universities give their schools, buildings, classrooms, and the scholarships and chairs they award. Universities *express* something with these choices.[36] I am lucky to work at King Hall, named after Martin Luther King Jr.; his words are on my school's walls and a statue of him stands in our lobby. Some other law schools near mine haven't been so fortunate. UC Berkeley no longer refers to its law school as Boalt Hall, having discovered how grossly anti-Chinese its namesake was.[37] And the first law school in California, once known as UC Hastings, is now UC Law SF—a much less catchy name, but one that's at least not as strongly associated with the massacre of Native Americans.[38] Renaming efforts like these strike some as hopelessly woke.[39] But keeping a name is no less value-laden. Inertia isn't neutral; it's just a choice to put tradition, or branding, over other considerations that are at stake when making what turn out to be unavoidably political and expressive decisions.

In 2017, Yale University renamed one of its residential colleges, previously named for one of the nineteenth century's leading advocates for slavery and theorists of southern secession, John C. Calhoun.[40] In doing so, Yale rightly recognized that "the University speaks through its building names," and that "when the University speaks, it chooses its message in light of its mission." According to the committee charged with setting standards for renaming, "One of the values the University rightly communicates is the importance of genuine inclusiveness for all those who will make it a leading center for research and teaching in the years to come."[41] To better communicate that message, Yale decided to honor the mathematician, computer scientist, and rear admiral Grace

Murray Hopper in place of Calhoun. But by renaming the school for this reason, Yale was doing "precisely what the University should not do," according to Stone. It was "mak[ing] a *statement* about what is morally, politically, and socially 'right'"—and, of course, which is morally, politically, and socially wrong.[42]

Professor Stone's own university is no different from Yale in this regard. Just recently, the University of Chicago renamed what was formerly its Oriental Institute. After first giving it the Kentucky Fried Chicken treatment, referring to it in marketing materials only by its initials, OI, Chicago now calls it the Institute for the Study of Ancient Cultures. It justified the name change as a more accurate description of the institute's work, but also as an attempt to avoid the "pejorative connotations of the word ['oriental.']" This wasn't the institute's first naming incident either: in 1968, the shah of Iran pledged $3 million for what would have become the "Mohammad Reza Pahlavi building," which never came to pass.[43] The University of Chicago, it seems, sometimes just lets a controversial name quietly fade away. The same year it renamed the OI, Chicago got rid of its Robert A. Millikan Distinguished Service chair, giving its holder a new title, named after the economist D. Gale Johnson. This happened, without fanfare, after Caltech had removed Millikan's name from one of its buildings because of his involvement with eugenics, and the University of Chicago had been publicly urged to follow suit.[44]

Another naming controversy gave rise to allegations that the University of Chicago was actually violating the Kalven Report. When the Milton Friedman Institute was proposed in 2008, a hundred faculty members wrote a letter protesting its $200 million endowment and prominent location on campus. Chicago's faculty senate met for the first time in a decade to discuss the matter. "When the University of Chicago invests so heavily in culturally and politically conservative thought," the faculty letter said, "we wonder about its commitment to strong intellectual diversity in the tradition of the Kalven Report." As a small compromise, the center was ultimately named the Milton Friedman Institute for Research in Economics—an attempt to focus more on Friedman's economic rather than ideological legacy. (After a merger in 2011, it became the Becker Friedman Institute for Research in Economics.)[45]

Ubiquitous and expressive as names are on nearly every campus, statements are also made, and heard, when universities decide what paintings or photographs to hang on their walls or what statues to erect or tear down on their lawns. Choices here include everything from the alumni portraits in so many hallways to Confederate monuments like Silent Sam, formerly at the entrance of the University of North Carolina. When I was in law school, there were seventy-six portraits in our building, but only six were of women.[46] My school was sending a message, intentionally or not. Its attempt to commission a more diverse set of portraits in the years since has been similarly expressive.

Is there a possibility of neutrality in decisions like these? Whether it is Calhoun or Hopper, a residential college needs a name, and these are bound to express a message, unless the colleges of Yale are just going to be labeled with letters or numbers. Similarly, the paintings on a university's walls need subjects, unless the school is going to forgo art entirely or move toward non-representational art. (Our federal courts have increasingly done this in recent years in an effort to avoid any appearance of partiality. It turns out that Lady Justice was no longer so effective at signaling neutrality once women were finally recognized as legal persons.)[47] Each of these choices comes at a cost, and probably not one that universities are willing to bear. Getting rid of names would eliminate major fundraising opportunities, and it could impact community-building on campus. The affection I had in college for my fellow Gonzagans—my dorm having been named after a Jesuit saint—might not have been fostered if I'd been assigned to something called Dorm E or Building 62. Likewise, a campus devoid of paintings or sculptures would be a more impoverished place, both aesthetically and in the connections it creates between present community members and those who came before. Universities regularly choose these other values over neutrality, presumably because they think the other values are more important in advancing the university's mission.

But what if universities tried to set neutral principles to govern who gets a portrait or a building named after them? This, in fact, is what the law school I attended was originally doing: alums and faculty who became a US president, a Supreme Court justice, or chief judge of a federal court of appeals were automatically approved for a portrait, as were the school's former deans.[48] This policy at least got the law school out of the business of picking and choosing which Supreme Court justices to honor. It sidestepped fights over whether students and faculty wanted the face of Justice Sotomayor but not Justice Alito, or vice versa, looking at them from a classroom wall. The policy reduced conflict by taking certain issues off the table—one of the arguments made on behalf of institutional neutrality generally.[49]

But making certain decisions automatic is not the same as making them neutral. "Neutral" principles really just change the level of generality at which a substantive debate takes place. My law school may not have been judging Sotomayor against Alito when it put up both their portraits, but it was still speaking loudly about what constitutes success for its graduates. Why honor federal appellate judges but not state supreme court judges? And why judges rather than advocates for civil rights or the poor—or, for that matter, successful prosecutors or corporate lawyers? A school ends up taking a stand about what it prizes even when making rules that are meant to ensure neutrality. And the stand it takes says something about how the school sees its mission. A law school that aims to produce the future leaders of America is quite different from one that aims to nurture competent and ethical members of the local bar, or one that seeks to increase access to justice. Each of those schools will have different pictures on their walls and different names on their buildings. There isn't a "neutral" choice among them.

Let's retrace this first path. The institutional neutrality debate encompasses institutional actions no less than the statements that institutions make. I say this as a descriptive matter, insofar as it reflects the actual controversies that led to the Kalven Report, written to guide the University of Chicago's *actions* concerning the draft and apartheid. But I also mean it as a normative claim: there is no reason to treat institutional statements as something categorically different from institutional actions, when both involve universities staking out positions on contested, politicized questions.

The actions demanded of universities—to divest, for example, or to choose who gets honored with a statue, building name, or graduation award—these don't allow space for neutrality. The choice to divest is no less *neutral* than continuing to support business activities in apartheid South Africa, Darfur, or Israel. And neither are decisions made at a higher level of generality: the decision, say, to maximize returns on the university endowment rather than using it to promote other social goods. Deciding what values a university might find important enough to overcome its profit motive ultimately brings us back to the question of the university's mission. And here we've once again reached the argument at the heart of this book. Institutional neutrality debates, just like the debate over DEI statements or the debate to come about campus speech, *all* turn out to be fights about a university's mission, where no position counts as neutral.

Remarkably, the Kalven Report itself recognizes the relevance of the university's mission not just to actions, but even to its verbal statements—the press releases and schoolwide emails that institutional neutrality commitments are normally understood to be about. This gets us to the second path, promised earlier, to the conclusion that the institutional neutrality sought by the Kalvenists turns out to be a mirage. Soon after it claims that the university "cannot take collective action on the issues of the day without endangering the conditions for its existence," the Kalven Report goes on to describe when a university not only can, but *must* take a stand.

> From time to time instances will arise in which the society, or segments of it, threaten the very mission of the university and its values of free inquiry. In such a crisis, it becomes the obligation of the university as an institution to oppose such measures and actively to defend its interests and its values.[50]

Perhaps the underlying argument here is that certain societal actions do more to endanger the conditions for a university's existence than institutional statements do. When societal threats outweigh the threat of collective speech, institutional statements are warranted—or even required. Making this call, though, requires a university to judge not just the extent of the threats involved, but more crucially, the scope of its mission. By its own lights, the Kalven Report makes choices about institutional speech dependent on a university's understanding of its mission.

To be clear, the Kalven Report is not alone in this. Nearly every recent neutrality mandate features a similar carve-out. Utah's 2023 guidance bars universities "from taking public positions on political, social, or unsettled issues that do not directly relate to the institution's mission, role, or pedagogical objectives."[51] The Goldwater Institute's model legislation allows for administrators to take positions on "the public policy controversies of the day" if it is "essential to the day-to-day functioning of the university."[52]

The University of Chicago's own experience in deciding when the Kalven Report allows (or compels) it to speak is instructive. After all, Chicago *has* weighed in on public policy controversies from time to time in the decades since the Kalven Report was written. Its critics sometimes allege hypocrisy here, suggesting that institutional neutrality is just a smoke screen that administrators deploy opportunistically whenever they don't want to take a particular stand.[53] My approach is different. I want to take the Kalven carve-out seriously, to presume that Chicago has tried to apply it in good faith, and to ask what this tells us about how the University of Chicago understands its mission—and how other schools might understand theirs differently.

Chicago has released statements and even filed court briefs on a number of high-profile political controversies in the last decade, including the Trump travel ban, the attempt to end the DACA program for Dreamers, and attacks on affirmative action in university admissions.[54] The recent affirmative action cases against Harvard and the University of North Carolina offer the easiest fit with the Kalven Report's exception for mission-related threats. As the last chapter noted, a university's choices about which students to admit is one of the core elements of its institutional academic freedom. So a lawsuit that takes away Chicago's ability to use race-conscious admissions to diversify its student body can easily be characterized as a "threat to the very mission of the university." This would compel it, in Kalven's words, to "oppose such measures and actively to defend its interests and its values."

It's worth pausing here, though, just to note what a major hole the Kalven carve-out bores through the logic of its argument for neutrality. Surely the university's work to defend affirmative action does more to promote an official, potentially chilling orthodoxy than would a decision to divest from South Africa or Sudan. And the university's choice to engage in race-conscious admissions surely has a far more concrete effect on faculty members' work than divestment decisions. It literally changes who will be sitting in their classrooms and labs. The first half of the Kalven Report suggests that taking a stand on political controversies as fraught as affirmative action will endanger the conditions for the university's "existence and effectiveness"; in the case of affirmative action, though, the second half of the report seems to accept the risk.

The University of Chicago's engagement with Trump-era immigration law offers a harder case. Two days after President Trump, during his first term, released an executive order barring immigrants and visitors from seven Muslim-majority countries (Iran, Iraq, Libya, Somalia, Sudan, Syria, and Yemen), Chicago's president and provost issued a statement decrying "unnecessary restrictions on the flow of talented scholars and students into the United States," which they said "damage the University's capacity to fulfill its highest aspirations in research, education, and impact." (The letter separately "reaffirm[ed], in the strongest terms, the commitment of the University of Chicago to . . . those members of our community with undocumented immigration status or who qualify for relief under the Deferred Action for Childhood Arrivals (DACA) program.")[55] Two weeks later, Chicago joined with sixteen other universities to file a brief asking a federal court to block Trump's Muslim ban. According to the brief, each of the universities "has a global mission" that depends on the schools' "ability to welcome international students, faculty, and scholars into their communities."[56]

The threat Trump's immigration restrictions posed to the University of Chicago's "global mission" wasn't fanciful. At the time it spoke out, Chicago had twenty-three students from Iran and one from Syria, and its Oriental Institute (still bearing that name) was running excavation projects in Iran and Iraq. And yet, if the claim was that Chicago's global mission depends on its ability to bring people from anywhere in the world to its Hyde Park campus, and to send its researchers throughout the entire world as well, any international disruption or policy that prevents that movement would presumably fall within the Kalven carve-out. When Chicago announced full-tuition scholarships for students affected by Russia's invasion of Ukraine in 2022, it noted its long history of welcoming scholars "during times of conflict and crisis," from World War II Europe to Afghanistan, Iraq, and post-hurricane Puerto Rico.[57] Is there any reason, given these precedents, that Chicago couldn't make a statement about the destruction of universities in Gaza in 2024?

Whatever the answer, the *structure* of the argument is what really matters here. Chicago found it appropriate to speak out against the travel ban only because Trump's policy posed a threat to the university's mission. That's a substantive judgment about the University of Chicago's particular mission. Not every university has a "global mission" like Chicago and its fellow brief-signers. A university focused on its local community, or on educating the people of its state, would see its role differently. For the state school, speaking out about Trump's travel ban might be no more appropriate than making a statement about water disputes in Honduras or tariff fights with China. In the Kalven Report's terms, these just aren't true threats to the missions of many, perhaps most, universities.

The Kalven Report puts a university in the business of debating the scope of its mission every time it considers whether to speak. Consider, then, how differently these debates might play out at different schools when they decide how to respond to something like the *Dobbs* decision, which ended the federal constitutional right to an abortion.[58] Deciding to speak about *Dobbs* is probably easiest at a secular university that has a medical school and other health sciences programs. A court decision that affects the ability of medical professionals to teach and practice evidence-based standards of care clearly implicates the mission of a university like that, especially if it's located in a state that banned abortions after *Dobbs*.

This is presumably the reason why Chicago's provost, the dean of its medical school, and the head of its health system jointly issued a statement on the day *Dobbs* was decided. The statement reaffirmed their university's commitment to "providing high-quality, evidence-based reproductive healthcare," including abortion.[59] Meanwhile the president of my own university—himself a physician—said something similar, if in somewhat stronger terms:

> The Court's decision is antithetical to the University of California's mission and values. We strongly support allowing individuals to access evidence-based health care services and to make decisions about their own care in consultation with their medical team. Despite this decision by the Court, we will continue to provide the full range of health care options possible in California, including reproductive health services.[60]

Elsewhere in his statement, the University of California's president went significantly further than that of the University of Chicago by expressing his concern that *Dobbs* "could pave the way for other fundamental rights to be removed." He pledged to "stand with California leaders and health care advocates who are taking critical steps to protect Californians' human rights." Where Chicago and UC both saw the provision of evidence-based health care as part of their missions, the University of California also emphasized its commitment to a particular, substantive vision of fundamental rights. (We might wonder what other fundamental rights UC would speak out about, and how it might balance them. Let's say the state or federal government were to narrow its conscience clauses, which allow medical providers to avoid performing procedures that they object to on religious grounds. Would the University of California speak out against that as an erosion of the fundamental right to freedom of religion? What if it affected the ability of trans patients to get care?[61])

On the other side of the abortion debate, religious schools with pro-life commitments also spoke up when *Dobbs* was decided, in their case because they saw *Dobbs* as *removing* a threat to their institutional missions. The president of Catholic University wrote of the "unholy idea that there is a constitutional right to kill unborn children," then announced an institutional commitment to more lovingly support mothers, fathers, and "the babies who are born into our community rather than aborted."[62]

The question of whether a university should speak about an issue as politically divisive as abortion becomes harder at schools that aren't religious or don't have a hospital or medical school. Some of those might still choose to speak out because, like the University of California, they see within their mission a commitment to advancing human rights, including a right to reproductive autonomy. Other universities, though, might feel justified in speaking out about *Dobbs* for an entirely different reason. They might speak simply because they have many students, staff, and faculty who have the potential to become pregnant. Why is that fact relevant to a university's *mission*? (After all, the university also has many students, staff, and faculty who owe federal income taxes, but that doesn't mean adjustments to individual tax brackets necessarily constitute a threat to any university's mission.) I think the best answer borrows a page from the University of Chicago's argument in the travel ban case. Just as Chicago worried that the Trump travel ban limited some students' ability to attend, other universities might feel that *Dobbs* does the same. If some students and faculty can't make the reproductive choices necessary to continue their schooling, teaching, or research, is that not a threat to the university's ability to carry out its mission? Where some schools self-identify as having a "global mission," others might see diversity or equity at the core of what they do. Schools in the latter camp would be more justified in speaking out about a decision like *Dobbs*, given its inequitable effects on pregnant people's ability to participate in the university's work.

The larger point here is this: when the University of Chicago applies the principles of the Kalven Report, including its carve-out for mission threats, it does so based on its self-understanding of its own mission. (In fact, these choices over time are part of what *constitutes* the university's mission.) But there is no reason why other schools need to define their missions the same way Chicago does. The University of Chicago, in other words, is not making a determination about what counts as genuine neutrality—much less a genuine university. If it decides to speak out about the travel ban but not, say, trans rights, Chicago is making a decidedly non-neutral judgment about its *own* institutional identity.

This is the why Kalvenism can't ultimately deliver the neutrality it promises. Let me be clear: the claim is not that neutrality is never possible because silence always conveys a message.[63] When a university has committed to remain silent on a category of issues that can be defined in a non-discretionary way—elections for public office and state referenda, for example—then its ensuing silence on those topics should not be seen as meaningful at all. But that's not what the Kalven Report does. It counsels silence on political and social controversies *that do not threaten the university's mission*. Embedded in this is the unavoidably value-laden question of what a given university's mission is understood to be. Kalven's loophole is what ensures that universities like Chicago will always be saying something—about their mission, if nothing else—even when they maintain the institutional silence the Kalven Report is famous for recommending.

Areas of Agreement

Hard-core Kalvenism, as we have seen, is the belief that universities that fail to stay neutral on political and social issues endanger the academic freedom that is necessary for a genuine university to exist.

My argument, which lacks a correspondingly catchy name, starts with the recognition that universities' actions are often as politically freighted as any statements they might make. Uproars over diversity statement requirements and campus speech regulations make this clear, but so, too, do the more everyday, but still political, decisions that universities make about admissions, curricula, honors, or even the names and images that their buildings bear. Choosing one course of action over another in each of these areas is often unavoidable, and none of the choices can be characterized as neutral. The Kalven Report and its progeny recognize this to a certain extent, and for that reason allow universities to express themselves when they are doing or saying things to defend or advance their mission. This is all well and good, except for the fact that it requires a university to define the scope of its mission. And here again, there are no neutral options. Talk of neutrality just doesn't get us very far.

There is less distance between these two positions than might first appear, however. If the Chicago stance can be caricatured (unfairly) as "universities should always stay silent," it would be equally unfair to cast me as arguing that universities, lacking a resort to neutrality, can do nothing but speak. The Kalven Report, as we've just seen, has allowed Chicago to speak out on any number of divisive political and social issues. And for my part, I want to emphasize that "can speak" in no way implies "should speak." Institutional statements are often unwise, even if they're not incompatible with the essence of a university. Between never speak and always speak is the messy middle ground of when to sometimes speak.

In recent years, there have been a number of attempts to go beyond Kalven and explore this middle ground. Some of these attempts have even come from within the University of Chicago. Tom Ginsburg, the founding faculty director of Chicago's Forum for Free Inquiry and Expression, has proven to be both a leading defender and modifier of his school's approach. Rather than making neutrality definitional to any genuine university, Ginsburg describes it as "a core norm, constitutive of at least one great research university."[64] He backs away from the notion that institutional neutrality is a necessary condition for academic freedom, and instead defends it as an aspiration—a standard, rather than a rule—that directs a university's energies to activities more productive than statement-making. A commitment to neutrality, Ginsburg argues, keeps universities focused on their "core work" rather than on "normal political contestation." And Ginsburg's untethering of institutional neutrality from academic freedom turns out to open a new export market for the Kalven Report: Ginsburg has recently argued that it provides a model not just for universities, but for corporations as well.[65]

Outside of the University of Chicago, Heterodox Academy has developed its own "model of statement neutrality" that attempts to clarify "unwieldy features" of the Kalven Report and say more about when universities *do* need to speak.[66] Heterodox begins with the Kalvenist premise that a university that speaks on things that don't "directly, significantly, and specifically affect[] the academic mission of the institution" will chill dissenters, replace "scholarly discourse with simplistic position statements," waste institutional energy, and undermine its prestige and trust with the public. But Heterodox goes importantly beyond Kalven by acknowledging—as I have been arguing here—that "academic missions vary," so decisions about when to speak should vary across institutions as well. Not every university has to be Chicago. As Heterodox puts it: "While all colleges and universities share the University of Chicago's foundational commitment to the acquisition and transmission of knowledge, context matters too." Some schools have chosen to "pursue knowledge within a particular intellectual, political/social, racial, gendered, or religious tradition." Some "aspire to social goals that are quite broad, such as 'social justice' or 'democracy' or the 'general welfare' of a particular state." Each, then, needs to "apply the principle of neutrality in light of their institution's unique history and mission."[67] I couldn't agree more.

Other important new institutional speech policies impose silence without invoking neutrality at all. Harvard's Institutional Voice report, from May 2024, goes so far as to say that "the university as an institution can never be neutral" because it "has a responsibility to speak out and protect its core function": cultivating an environment that fosters "free inquiry, intellectual expertise, and productive argument among divergent points of view."[68] The analogous committee at Yale noted, in its October 2024 report, that "leaders may choose not to speak on a given matter without professing neutrality."[69] These policies, like a similar one at UCLA, root their limits on institutional speech primarily on the limited nature of university leaders' *expertise*.[70]

Professor Ginsburg's prudential reasoning for choosing institutional silence, Heterodox Academy's pluralism about university missions, and Harvard's and Yale's rejection of neutrality all count as welcome departures from hard-line Kalvenism. But what about any moves to the middle on my side? If my arguments against neutrality have left the impression that I think institutional speech should be unfettered, it's time to correct that.

One guide here comes from Princeton, which touts its tradition of "institutional restraint" as distinct from Chicago's "institutional neutrality." Princeton shares with Chicago a "strong presumption" against making statements or investment decisions that are meant to affect external political or social debates. But this presumption can give way when there is a "direct and serious contradiction between an investment and a central value of the University"—a "value-laden institution," in the words of William G. Bowen, Princeton's former president. Standing up for its institutional values led Princeton to divest from South Africa, postpone final exams during the Vietnam War, and condemn as "inconsistent with the University's commitment to 'the fair and equal treatment of all persons'" the invitation for a segregationist governor to speak on campus in 1963.[71] (Princeton's president offered this condemnation even while defending the governor's right to speak.) More recently, Yale's new policy on "institutional voice" rejects "precise formulas" in favor of "discernment and active responsiveness to a variety of relevant considerations, in light of the mission of the university."[72]

I am, of course, fully on board with the idea that a university should be thinking about its mission and values when it decides whether to issue statements or not. In fact, I'm tempted to say that the growing pile of committee reports and recommendations about institutional statements could all be replaced with something like this: "The university and its departments should make official statements only when doing so advances their mission." That said, my conception of universities' missions—both in their potential variation and the scope of what they might include—is probably broader than that of many advocates for restraint. Take the policy recently adopted at UCLA, which recommends that "university leaders should not make statements on societal, political and public matters unless those matters directly affect the university's ability to support a research and educational environment where free expression thrives."[73] Why is free expression singled out as the only part of a university's mission that statements can be used to advance? And what work do we think the adverbs in all these statements are supposed to do? Do issues need to relate "directly," "directly and seriously," or "directly, significantly, and specifically" to the university's mission before the institution can speak? Do these differences in wording ever make a difference in outcomes?

Instead of hard-line cans and can'ts, I see a sliding scale that recognizes the importance both of a university's mission and its need for restraint. The more central an issue is to the core functioning or mission of a particular university, the less that university should be swayed by prudential considerations that might otherwise counsel silence. Concerns about coercive or chilling effects on dissenters within the institution, backlash from donors or legislators, anger or reduced trust from the public, or wasted resources—these should hold less sway when one of the university's most deeply held values is at stake. Better to stand up for its identity and face the consequences. Some values are so central to a university's identity that it might be better for those who reject those values—those who feel alienated by the university's defense of them—to consider attending, working at, or donating to another school instead. On other issues closer to the periphery of a school's mission, consequentialist concerns are more likely to justify restraint and, perhaps, silence. On those issues, the support an institutional statement might provide to one part of the community might be outweighed by the alienating or chilling effects it has on another group, or by the anger or retaliation the statement prompts from outsiders.

Importantly, though, we shouldn't treat the costs of institutional statements as set in stone. These costs can vary at least as much based on what a university does as what it might say. This is especially true when it comes to what a university does to protect academic freedom. A university's *actual* commitments to academic freedom, embodied in policy and consistent practice, can hugely reduce the costs of institutional speech. At a school where protections are well established, dissenters will be more confident that they can disagree with institutional positions without fear of retribution. It's just not true, or needn't be, that taking a collective position inevitably comes "at the price of censuring any minority who do not agree," as the Kalven Report would have it.

Kalvenists argue that institutional expression categorically endangers academic freedom. I'd argue that a robust commitment to academic freedom is what makes it *permissible* for universities to express their positions. That said, it bears repeating that the permissibility of issuing a statement still doesn't equate to the wisdom of making it—a truth that holds for statements at every level of the institution, as we'll soon see.

Department Statements

Does everything just said about institutional statements also apply to statements by units *within* an institution? In other words, if an institution commits to something like the Kalven principles, would their departments necessarily need to stay neutral as well? And at universities that reject the Kalven Report, does it follow that the university's departments, schools, and centers should be equally free to speak their mind?

Not necessarily. There are a few good reasons why someone might favor statements from universities but not their subunits. And there are at least two reasons why someone might want to allow statements by departments even if they think institutional statements are inadvisable.

Departmental speech might be seen as more problematic than institutional speech because it can cause confusion about who the department speaks for. If the Department of Comparative Literature at Cornell University makes a statement about Gaza,[74] will students or donors or the general public think it speaks for Cornell? Academic freedom has long been premised on the notion that a university's faculty members don't speak for the university.[75] But people still get confused about this. And if that's true of a university's faculty, confusion is even more likely when a university's *units* have something to say. The Cornell University Department of Comparative Literature, after all, has "Cornell University" in its very name. When it speaks as a department, it might be seen as leveraging the university's name, possibly in service of a cause the university itself doesn't support.[76] Speakers shouldn't benefit from listeners' confusion about who is speaking. To take a page from trademark law, universities have a right to avoid consumer confusion about their brand.

Importantly, trademark law also protects against tarnishment of a brand.[77] And universities are surely worried about this too. They might fear that their reputation will take a hit if intemperate or unpopular speech by one of their departments sparks bad press and popular outrage.[78] Department speech isn't unique in this; unpopular statements by faculty or student groups can tarnish a university's brand too. Just look at the controversy started by the thirty-some student groups at Harvard who called Israel "entirely responsible" for the Hamas attack on October 7, 2023.[79] Universities can't do much about this, however, when it comes to faculty and students, due to academic freedom and First Amendment protections. Whether that's true also of departmental speech is a much harder question, in part because the academic freedom of departments, as departments, is an unsettled topic. Universities might not be able to distance themselves from the speech of their units in the same way it can from the speech of their faculty, and as a result, they might have more leeway in controlling it.

The final and most significant way that departmental speech is potentially more dangerous than institutional speech is in its potential to chill dissenting views. Faculty will surely feel more pressure to fall in line with colleagues who vote for their promotion, or with the chair or dean who sets their salary, committee assignments, and teaching schedules, compared to a university president who probably doesn't know their name.[80] Graduate students, who are even less likely to come in contact with a university president, may think twice before refusing to sign a statement made by the people who will judge their dissertation and write their recommendations. The potential chilling effects here are serious—and almost certainly worse at the department level than in the university as a whole.[81]

At the same time, there are reasons to think that departmental statements might have certain advantages over statements issued by the institution as a whole. Kalvenists often argue that university presidents should speak less because they're unlikely to have special expertise on the topics they're called to speak about. As Brian Leiter asked during the pro-Palestinian protests on his campus: Why would anyone want to hear whether the chemist who heads the University of Chicago thinks the violence in Gaza legally qualifies as genocide?[82] Certain centers and departments on campus, however, *do* specialize in questions like that. And their disciplinary expertise might be the very thing that makes statements from a department more valuable than statements from a university itself.

This point, if true, comes with a built-in limit: departments are only specially situated in this way to make statements on issues that fall within their zone of competence. This limit is not unlike the Kalven Report's carve-out—the claim that universities are allowed to speak on issues relevant to their mission.[83] Departments, on this view, would be able to speak about their own operations and about issues that fall within their disciplinary wheelhouse, however controversial or "political" those issues might be. Society might benefit from hearing a professional consensus, say, from a medical school about COVID or from law school deans about the threat to the rule of law on January 6, 2021.[84]

A second advantage of departmental speech stems from its potential role in university governance. Just as it is important for administrators and trustees to engage in what the AAUP calls "joint planning and effort" with the faculty as a body,[85] so, too, might institutional decision-making benefit from the views of individual departments, centers, or schools. To silence them is potentially to ignore the ways university policies and conduct affect different parts of the university in different ways. And it undercuts powerful collective organizing within the university. A statement that the Faculty of Arts and Sciences or the School of Law has lost confidence in the university president is a very different thing than a petition signed by individual faculty. Leveraging the power of a group's collective identity is, of course, the reason why many are suspicious of institutional and departmental statements in the first place. Sometimes using the institutional name gives too much heft to a statement that actually has only divided support. But when a department or school really does believe something, its influence is unduly diminished when it can't speak in its own name.

The problem here is deciding when it's accurate to say that a department "really does believe something." And that problem can be added to those already on the list: the possible coercion and chilling of department members who don't share the opinions of their colleagues and supervisors; and the confusion, or reputational harm, that can occur when listeners confuse speech *within* the university with speech *by* the university. If these are the problems, what are the solutions? And is departmental speech even worth the trouble of finding and implementing them?

The last question is a little misleading if it suggests that statements are something departments might want to try out sometime down the line, if they could just find a safe way of doing so. In reality, department statements are ubiquitous. On my campus, it was hard to find a departmental website that did not have a statement about racial justice after George Floyd's murder in 2020.[86] The longtime dean of my law school posted statements on critical race theory, the military's refusal to hire transgender troops during the Trump administration, the January 6 attacks, the significance of Martin Luther King Jr. Day, and the rise in violence against Asian Americans. Hardly any of these statements caused controversy. Some were hardly noticed, which is an issue of its own.

What *did* provoke controversy, media attention, and new policies from the University of California's Academic Senate and Board of Regents were the statements of "solidarity with the people of Palestine" that gender studies departments throughout the country signed in May 2021, in the midst of that year's fighting in Gaza.[87] On my campus, in addition to gender studies, nine other departments and programs, along with over fifty individual faculty members, crafted their own solidarity statement, describing how our students had been affected by the conflict and calling for changes in US funding for Israel.[88]

Other members of our faculty responded at the time by protesting to campus counsel that the solidarity statements were "blatant political advocacy, and a misuse of state-funded . . . resources."[89] The critics pointed to a California law that prohibits the use of the University of California's name in support of any "political, religious, sociological, or economic movement, activity, or program."[90] They worried that faculty and students who disagreed with the department's positions would be afraid to express their views. They asked how the Israeli-Palestinian conflict fell within the expertise of the departments that signed the statement. And they called on the university to develop policies to regulate departmental statements and endorsements going forward. In other words, they raised each of the problems I identified a moment ago.

First, confusion about *who is speaking*. This, to me, is the easiest of the bunch. There is precedent here. A basic bargain of academic freedom is that if universities refuse ever to censor faculty speech, they also can't be seen as endorsing it; the university isn't responsible for what its faculty say. Faculty, in return, have a duty to avoid causing confusion on that point. That's why the amicus briefs that professors file in court tend to clarify that our school and job titles are provided "for identification purposes only," and that we are speaking "in our individual capacities, not on behalf of our institutions." Whether by choice or by university policy, departments could make similar disclaimers when they are expressing positions. Simply stating that a particular view is the department's and not necessarily that of its university should go a long way toward avoiding confusion.[91]

The second problem involves a different kind of confusion about who is speaking. Once it's established that the department doesn't speak for the university, who does it speak for? Put a different way: How does a department come to take a position on any particular issue?

When my dean released a statement after the Trump administration stopped hiring trans soldiers in 2017, his signature was at the bottom of the statement, but the statement itself made clear he wasn't speaking just for himself. As the letter said, "UC Davis School of Law strongly condemns the U.S. government's decision to limit the ability of transgender individuals to serve. . . . King Hall believes that this opportunity should be available to all."[92] The dean was speaking for the school—or, more poetically, the school was speaking through the dean.

Sometimes departmental statements come from the dean or chair, sometimes they are attributed to the school or department itself, and at other times messages come from "the faculty" or even "the faculty, students, and staff" of a department.[93] There is another option too: issuing a statement with individual signatures at the end. But it's not clear whether this makes something a *departmental statement*, even if it happens to be signed individually by every member of the department.

After my dean issued his statement on the trans military ban, one of our students, a veteran, wrote to say that he was part of King Hall and he didn't condemn the trans ban. He thought the letter was wrong, not just on policy but as a factual matter, since it suggested a consensus at King Hall that didn't exist. I responded at the time that just as a corporation isn't the same as any or all of its shareholders, the people who make up King Hall aren't the same as King Hall itself. But this answer really just restates the problem: What opinions are those of "King Hall itself," and how does King Hall, or we who work or go to school there, arrive at those opinions?

The University of California's Academic Senate took up this problem after the 2021 Israel-Gaza uproar and made what I thought to be a wise recommendation: that all departments develop, and make public, "standards governing the practice of issuing statements on controversial topics."[94] (Note the meta-issue here: after going through the proper channels and votes, the recommendations themselves came from "the Academic Senate," not from any particular faculty member, much less from all of us.) Departments should decide in advance whether their statements require a majority vote or something more, and who within the department (faculty, staff, and/or students) have the ability to vote. To avoid implicating dissenters, statements should specify what they represent: a majority view of department faculty, for example. In the alternative, departments could issue statements through their chair or with names of supporters individually listed.

At public universities like mine, these differences trigger significantly different legal obligations. A statement by a chair or dean, acting in their official capacity, or a statement made in the name of the department or school itself, almost surely counts as "government speech." The First Amendment doesn't require viewpoint neutrality in that case. When civil rights icon John Lewis came to speak at my school's commencement, and our dean lavished him with deserved praised, we didn't have to invite and praise a white supremacist the following year just to provide balance. (A dean's choice to give welcoming remarks at some conferences but not others probably deserves similar constitutional leeway.)

If, however, a school or department posts a statement signed by individual faculty members on its website or social media accounts, the First Amendment *would* require it to give similar space to dissenting views. Unless the unit (or its leader) endorses the original statement as its own through the procedures just mentioned, the department itself wouldn't have spoken; instead, it would have opened up what lawyers call a "limited public forum" for speech. Viewpoint discrimination is constitutionally prohibited there. More on this in chapter 5.

These different forms that departmental statements can take also affect the third problem—that of coerced agreement and chilled dissent. The threat is real, but it's one that's not unique to departmental *statements*. Decisions about any number of departmental actions—from graduation awards to curricular decisions to hiring priorities—can lead to similar fears of pressure and retaliation. Majoritarian decisions seldom reflect the will of everyone. But when it comes to statements, the chilling effect can vary based on the specific form that department statements take.

What at first might seem like the most defensible type of statements—ones that are individually signed by people who support them—could actually end up being the most threatening to academic freedom. Enemies of department statements, and institutional statements generally, all acknowledge that individual faculty have a right to make or sign statements. This is the basic premise of the Kalven Report: a university's "neutrality as an institution has its complement in the fullest freedom for its faculty and students as individuals to participate in political action and social protest." Statements made in the name of individuals rather than departments are also less likely to cause confusion about who is speaking. The signatures are right there, after all. But individually signed statements are likely the most coercive.

Consider an example from 2020, when the dean of Penn State Law wrote to the community to urge students, faculty, staff, and alumni to join her in signing a statement in order "to be on record . . . condemning racist violence, police brutality, and systematic racism against Black men and women." Calling the dean's request "a serious violation of academic freedom," University of Chicago Law School professor Brian Leiter argued that "the Dean of a law school should not be proclaiming the correct interpretation of public events, . . . let alone using her position to solicit support for her interpretation."[95] Whatever the merits of the first half of Leiter's claim, which I'll come right back to, it's surely true that the pressure to comply gets ratcheted up when your dean doesn't just sign a public statement herself, but publicly urges you to do so as well. Asking colleagues to "be on record" opposing racism—or anything else—raises the cost of dissent, not just for racists (or those who don't agree with the notion of "systematic racism"), but even for those who don't want to sign because they see statements as uselessly symbolic. Taking a roll call of individual faculty members' positions on divisive social issues is probably the most debate-chilling approach of all.

By contrast, speech by the unit's leader, whether on their own or speaking for the unit, does not necessarily strike me as a "serious threat to academic freedom." Quite a bit turns both on the academic freedom climate within the unit and the topic being addressed. A vengeful dean who brooks no dissent will surely chill faculty discussion not just on public statements, but on ordinary internal policy decisions too. One who makes clear that they welcome disagreement can afford to be more opinionated. In general, allowing unit heads to speak for their unit has a benefit and a drawback, both of which stem from the fact that deans and chairs are accountable to administrators above them.

Deans and chairs do not generally enjoy academic freedom in their capacity as deans or chairs, as opposed to their faculty roles. My university's academic freedom policy explicitly carves out the administrative activities of deans and chairs as unprotected, and no AAUP policies guarantee academic freedom for unit leadership when acting as administrators rather than faculty.[96] (Things are different in Canada.[97]) This means that when chairs or deans speak for their unit in a way that is at odds with the university's values, they can be replaced. This has the benefit of ensuring that department speech coming from department leaders will not stray too far from the position of the institution as a whole. But it can also be a downside. The at-will employment status of deans and chairs limits their independence: their capacity to speak out against university actions in ways that could be most useful for shared governance. A dean or chair who issued a statement criticizing the university's president for hoarding power and wielding it to shut down student protest could be replaced. A faculty that collectively issued the same critique on their behalf of their department could not be. This is what makes departmental statements such a potentially valuable form of intramural speech.

This leaves the final problem: What topics should departments be allowed to speak about? Is "allowed" even the right word here? Outside of legal limits, like the ban on electioneering, universities may not want to be in the business of policing what its schools and departments say. As I mentioned before, the academic freedom protection of departments is an underdeveloped issue. But erring on the side of freedom is almost certainly the right choice. Establishing a system to monitor or pre-approve or punish departmental statements might be a bigger threat to academic freedom than the statements themselves could ever be. But even if so, departments should still be asking themselves whether making or signing any particular statement is a good idea.

Departments should begin by asking whether a statement they are considering is predominantly focused internally or on the world beyond.

Departmental statements made in the wake of George Floyd's murder, for example, were obviously focused in significant part on issues of race and policing in Minnesota and across the country. But many also focused on how members of their own community were hurting or fearful. Some addressed policing issues on their campus, while others noted the effects of systemic racism within their field.[98] On my campus, the classics department wrote not just to express solidarity with the Black Lives Matter movement but also to acknowledge its own discipline's "historic and continued complicity with racist narratives."[99] One rule of thumb is that departments should always be able to issue statements about plans of their own. If a department is able to *act* in a particular way, it surely can *talk about* how it plans to act. So, the more internally focused a statement is, the more secure departments should feel in making it.

In 2020, the University of Chicago's English department made a statement announcing both its support for Black Lives Matter and its decision to prioritize "applicants who work in and with Black studies" for PhD admissions the following year. Some critics were outraged at what they saw as a political test for admissions. But Chicago's then-president Robert Zimmer responded with a more nuanced view. Zimmer clarified that Chicago's stance on institutional neutrality applies to departments no less than it does to the university itself. But as he saw it, the English department's statement could be understood not as a political test, but as the usual "prerogatives of an academic department to make decisions about the choice of scholarly directions it wants to emphasize." The latter, Zimmer added, would be "an important manifestation of academic freedom"—not a threat to it.[100]

Zimmer was right. As I've said repeatedly now, academic freedom means that disciplinary experts in a given field must have the primary authority to decide what and whom to teach. That authority obviously has its limits, political litmus tests and antidiscrimination law among them. If Chicago's English department planned to admit only Green Party members or Hispanic students, it would be acting beyond its proper powers. But if it chooses to emphasize a previously underemphasized set of interests within its field, it is doing exactly what a community of experts should be doing. It's notable that the following year, Chicago's English department announced it would only admit (not just prioritize!) students working on pre-1900 anglophone writing.

Strangely enough, unlike the emphasis on Black studies in 2020, the 2021 exclusion didn't make national news.

Statements focused primarily on the world outside the department raise the hardest questions. One is whether the topic falls within a department's disciplinary expertise. This is something different from the expertise some *within* the department might have. A statement that doesn't leverage a department's collective expertise lacks one of the main advantages that department speech can have over speech by university presidents. And Keith Whittington has suggested another reason why speech beyond a department's purview could be troublesome: a department whose faculty plans to continue speaking on external matters might want to judge potential new colleagues based on their views on those matters.[101] This could lead to the kind of viewpoint discrimination—or more precisely, *irrelevant* viewpoint discrimination—discussed as unconstitutional in chapter 1.

When considering what topics are fair game for statements, the level of generality matters. Any number of departments study power or systems of oppression. Because oppression often targets intersectional identities, it's not always possible to cabin the study of oppression into discrete categories: gender over here, race or national origin over there. Injustice anywhere may truly be a threat to justice everywhere. But does this give certain departments free rein to weigh in on any and all of the world's injustices? Were that the consequence, I think we would have defined the departments' distinctive competencies, their reasons for existence, at too high a level of generality. Ultimately, to believe in academic freedom is to give disciplinary experts within each field the primary authority for defining the bounds of their expertise. But a department that found it could speak on nearly anything would be one that thereby undermined the basis for its having the academic freedom to speak in the first place.

: : :

What I've just been offering are *prudential* guidelines, not necessarily rules to be enforced from above. As recent institutional speech policies like Yale's have recognized, good judgment about when to speak and what to speak about is more important—both at the departmental level *and* at the institutional level—than any analytic claims about neutrality.

I've defended the possibility of departmental speech and even emphasized its distinctive potential in contexts like shared governance. But to do this is hardly to argue that departments should be speaking more than they currently do. As with speech by the university as a whole, the costs of speaking are real, and the effects any statement will have on academic freedom and other values always have to be considered. As Robert Post has observed, there is hardly any context in the world in which *maximizing* speech is a good idea. Sharing every idea that comes into your head about a friend or partner is hardly the secret to a healthy relationship, and giving the longest talk or comment at a conference doesn't win any awards.[102] When our focus shifts from universities' or departments' *ability* to speak, to asking about the *desirability* of the many varied things institutions and their units get called upon to say, the gap between me and the neutrality hawks narrows considerably.

At this point, some might actually be looking for daylight between the Kalvenists, who counsel silence but admit exceptions, and those like me who would allow for speech but urge discretion. If our areas of agreement have turned out to be broader than at first expected, it may be worth asking for examples where we disagree about whether universities or their departments should speak.

The following chapter offers an entire category of such examples. And more importantly, by describing what I'll call "institutional counterspeech," the next chapter also helps remind us why all of this matters in the first place: why allowing universities to express their opinions can sometimes be worth the all-too-familiar costs.

4 *Institutional Counterspeech*

"The Remedy for Speech That Is False Is Speech That Is True"

The last chapter spoke briefly of restrictions on trans soldiers during the first Trump administration and the response it drew from the dean of my law school at the time. I mentioned the story to point out that the response, though signed by my dean, spoke explicitly and emphatically for the UC Davis School of Law, which condemned Trump's policy and urged its repeal. Left unexplained, though, was why my dean and school felt the need to make this statement in the first place.

Having been immersed in the Kalven Report and its progeny, we're all now primed to ask whether my school's mission was threatened by the military's discriminatory hiring policy. We are not a military academy, after all, so the policy did not affect who we admit, hire, or graduate. For us, the threat was less direct. The US military comes to my university each year to interview our students for employment. The military's trans ban violated our nondiscrimination policy. In theory, we could have just enforced our rules and refused to allow military recruiters access to our facilities. But a federal law—the Solomon Amendment—allows the government to cut off nearly all of a university's federal funding if any of its schools refuse to give military recruiters the same level of access they give other employers.[1] The UC Davis School of Law was forced, in other words, to choose between one of our core values and one of our university's core funding sources. We chose the funding.

Is that threat direct enough to convince the Kalvenists? Federal funding, especially at a large research university, is certainly sizable enough to affect its ability to carry out its mission. But the Solomon Amendment isn't a funding cut—it's a funding condition. Universities can keep their funding at the cost of hosting one employer who is unwilling to hire a subset of their students. The question under the Kalven Report, then, really should be whether a university's mission is threatened enough for it to speak out whenever its commitment to equality is hindered to this limited extent.

If that seems like a tough call, perhaps the problem is the Kalvenist framing of question. I think there is a better way to look at it. The harm Trump's trans ban caused our students didn't just come from beyond the university. It was, in significant part, a harm our university itself caused. To put it bluntly: the university, under pressure, had put a price on trans rights. The government may have forced our hand, but we were the ones who played it. The university caused harm by putting trans students in a situation where they had to endure discrimination at their own institution. It harmed our trans students by forcing them to see the price their institution was unwilling to pay for their equality. Even if those harms were outweighed by the enormous good that federal funding makes possible, the university still incurred a duty to mitigate the harm it caused, to whatever extent it could. Speaking out in support of trans students, and in opposition to laws that would harm them, was one important way the university could do that.

This is a chapter about institutional counterspeech. It's a chapter in which stories loom large. They are stories of universities causing harm, sometimes unavoidably, and trying to make up for it. This chapter describes a category of cases where I think a university should overcome any presumption it might have against making statements—the subject explored so fully in the last chapter. It should do so when it's making statements meant to counteract some harm that the university itself has caused. As we'll see, this category centrally includes cases where the source of the harm is the university's commitment to free speech—the topic of the next chapter.

Universities can be more permissive in how they regulate offensive speech by students, faculty, and outside speakers if those universities are also freer with their own speech. This is a point that often gets lost in debates over so-called institutional neutrality, where statements by universities are often dismissed as ineffectual. If, as we're often told, the answer to harmful speech on campus "is more speech, not enforced silence," speech by the university itself can be a crucial part of that answer.

Countering Inequality

The Trump trans ban in the military was not the first time schools like mine had been forced to weigh their federal funding against a minority's rights. Nearly the same thing occurred a decade earlier, when openly gay service members were barred under the Clinton administration's "Don't Ask, Don't Tell" policy. A group of law schools sued, alleging that the threat to deny them funding for enforcing their nondiscrimination policies violated their rights under the First Amendment. When the case reached the Supreme Court, the decision against the schools was unanimous. The Solomon Amendment, the Supreme Court said, "affects what law schools must *do*—afford equal access to military recruiters—not what they may or may not *say*." As the court suggested, the law schools "could put signs on the bulletin board next to the door, they could engage in speech, they could help organize student protests"—they could do any of this as long as they opened their facilities to the military as the law required.[2]

Interestingly, this is basically the model I proposed back in chapter 1 when talking about diversity statements. My argument there was that universities can reward faculty for what they *do*—advance the university's mission with regard to diversity—as long as they protect faculty's right to *say* that the mission, so defined, is misguided. Similarly here, the court allowed the federal government to condition funding on certain required actions so long as it preserved universities' right to speak out against those actions—to argue that what the government was doing was unwise or unjust. Preserving this freedom to speak was seen as sufficient to avoid any misimpression that universities themselves were endorsing policies like "Don't Ask, Don't Tell." As Chief Justice Roberts quipped: "We have held that high school students can appreciate the difference between speech a school sponsors and speech the school permits because legally required to do so. . . . Surely students have not lost that ability by the time they get to law school."[3] The takeaway here is this: Universities are sometimes forced or pressured to take actions that harm members of their community. Institutional speech can be a way of mitigating that harm by making clear that those actions aren't expressive of the university's own beliefs.

"Mitigating harm" is about as lifeless a phrase as I know, so let me tell a story to animate it.

Everyone associated with a university is familiar with their recurring blood drives. My school holds them once per quarter, and each time, our chancellor puts out a statement encouraging us all to participate. Well-meaning student groups work hard to help ensure that we meet our community's blood needs. Donating blood is one of the community service opportunities my law school's students and faculty are usually offered as part of our annual MLK Day of Service. And once a year, our campus competes with another nearby school to see who can give the most. Prizes are sometimes offered for those who participate.

But most gay men can't participate.[4] In the United States, any man who had sex with another man after 1977, even once, faced a lifetime ban on donating blood until 2015, when the life sentence became a one-year "deferral," shortened to three months during COVID. Only in 2023 did the FDA finally institute a new behavior-based guideline that looks to the type and amount of sex a potential donor has recently had. Until 2023, gay men needed to be effectively celibate in order to participate in the blood drives we were so regularly pushed to join. Shockingly few people who aren't gay or bisexual men seem to know about these restrictions. After decades of advances in detecting and preventing HIV, "That's still a thing?" was the general reaction I got when I was writing about the deferral in 2018. It *was* still a thing, though, and every email I got encouraging (or slightly shaming people into) participation in the quarterly blood drives felt like a slap in the face for those of us who were barred. One quarter I snatched one of the cheery "I'M A BLOOD DONOR" stickers and photoshopped it to read "I'D BE A BLOOD DONOR (IF THE FDA DIDN'T DISCRIMINATE AGAINST GAYS!)."

My university was arguably violating its own nondiscrimination policy by hosting an event—with prizes—where participation hinged both on sexual orientation and gender. This was the reason San Jose State University decided to discontinue campus blood drives in 2008. Its decision alarmed the nearby Stanford Blood Center, which gets 20% of its supply from blood drives at high schools and colleges; it called SJSU's decision a "seriously misguided effort to influence national policy."[5] (Treating SJSU's move as a boycott aimed at an external policy ignored the fact that the school was worried about engaging in discrimination itself.)

As a gay man unable to donate, I wasn't calling for a boycott. I thought the need for blood was just too great, and I had donated religiously from the time I became eligible until the time when I no longer was. Still, for my own university to violate its nondiscrimination policy without even acknowledging it, to celebrate a regular campuswide community event without ever noting that it excluded a significant part of the community, and to put me in the position of having to explain why I wasn't joining the effort with my (again, very well-meaning) colleagues and students—this hurt. So in early 2019, I decided to write to my university's chancellor to complain. Soon after, his speechwriter was in my office discussing the issue. The public statement that followed that April, signed by our chancellor, Gary May, began by announcing our next blood drive and, as usual, encouraging "all who are able to come give the gift of life." Then came the part I'd never heard before:

> I also want to acknowledge those in our community who would participate, were they not barred by federal restrictions on blood donations by men who have had sex with men (MSM).
>
> At the start of the AIDS epidemic in the early 1980s, the U.S. Food and Drug Administration imposed a lifetime deferral of blood donations by MSM. Since then, scientists have made huge strides in our understanding and testing of HIV. As a result, in 2015, the FDA shortened the deferral period for MSM to one year. Unfortunately, this policy continues to work as a ban on donations from most sexually active gay and bisexual men.
>
> UC Davis strongly supports the development of evidence-based policies that would allow blood donations from all who are safely able to give. UC Davis—and I personally—stand strongly against all forms of discrimination on the basis of gender or sexual orientation. By using those traits as a proxy for risk, the FDA's policy unnecessarily prevents some of our fellow students, staff and faculty from joining in this important and generous community effort.
>
> None of us able to donate blood should take for granted what a privilege it is and what a difference we can make. I look forward to the day when all who want to give blood and can do so safely are allowed to give this generous gift.[6]

UC Davis went on to attach this statement to all of its future blood drive announcements. Until the FDA's policy changed, every subsequent email included a link back to it.

Chancellor May's statement didn't affect my ability to donate blood. I'm quite sure it had zero effect on FDA policy. (The ineffectiveness of campus statements is one of the arguments sometimes made by their opponents.) Where it *was* effective, though, was in almost completely removing—for me, at least—the sting of exclusion I'd felt every time a blood drive was promoted on campus. The original statement, and the links back to it each quarter, probably educated at least some people about the FDA's outdated rules. But most of all, it made people like me feel that we weren't outsiders to our community.

If institutional statements can have this much power in making someone feel included, they can surely have just as much power to turn someone else *into* an outsider. This, I recognize, is the fundamental worry at the heart of the Kalven Report and other efforts to limit what universities say. But this is where the category of institutional speech that I'm describing in this chapter stands apart from other statements. The category of statements I'm describing are justified because they attempt to counteract something that *the university itself did* to harm or diminish one of the values it sees as integral to its mission. By choosing federal funding or public health needs over its nondiscrimination policy, the university—in both the trans military ban and the blood donation cases—participated in the exclusion of some of its members based on a protected identity characteristic. And sure, speaking out as my dean and chancellor did in those two cases has potentially exclusionary effects on those who think trans people shouldn't be in the military (or shouldn't exist), or those who think MSM donation restrictions are good public policy. (The 670 public comments submitted when the FDA was considering a policy change in 2016 included a large number of copy-pasted worries about "pressure from the radical Homosexual Lobby to ignore scientific evidence."[7]) But the danger of alienating people who hold these views isn't gratuitous in these cases; it's the by-product of a university trying to undo damage *it did* to some of its members and, importantly, to one of its institutional values.

I doubt this would be enough to justify a statement on a contested political issue under the Kalven Report or similar policies. The FDA's guidance itself doesn't "threaten the very mission of the university and its values of free inquiry," as Kalven would require. Harvard's policy, which speaks of "issues directly relevant to the university's operation," offers examples like admissions, curriculum, and research, none of which seem similar to the issue here. The recognition and support I felt from my chancellor's message could mean that statements like this are analogous to what some have called institutional empathy statements. The Harvard policy explicitly prohibits these, urging funding for counseling and other "pastoral" activities instead of institutional statements of support for affected groups. Heterodox Academy's proposed policy, by contrast, states that "Empathy is allowed." It goes on to caution, however, that "universities should . . . feel free to express concern and empathy, and share available resources and practical updates, as long as this practice does not amount to political/social opinion-signaling by other means." According to Heterodox, it's inappropriate for schools to draw "politically contested policy conclusions" in these statements—as my chancellor, speaking for our university, surely did.[8]

To be clear, the category of statements that I am describing here—a set of statements I think are highly important for an institution to make—are not the *same* as empathy statements. When Donald Trump was elected and some students were crying in my class the next morning, the statements my institution made offering counseling and other support services for affected students surely counted as empathy statements, and they show how hard it is to avoid political opinion-signaling: it's hard to imagine similar emails going out after Joe Biden's election, much less Barack Obama's or Bill Clinton's. These are different from the category of statements I'm describing here, in which a university is speaking to counter some harm *it* helped bring about. UC Davis had done nothing to cause the fear and sadness that some of our students felt after the Trump elections.

The category of statements I'm describing are more necessary than empathy statements. They're needed in order to bolster a value like equality that the university cherishes, but has chosen to subordinate to some other value. The stories of discrimination in the military and in blood donations show how statements of support and solidarity can help restore a sense of equality after the university—perhaps for good reason—has allowed or helped inequalities to fester. And this category of institutional *counterspeech*, as opposed to mere expressions of empathy, is especially important as a response to hate speech, something the university might have to allow, but which it is never bound to ignore.

Countering Other Speech

Here is one last story, again about my chancellor, Gary May. (I promise I'm not his publicist. This is more just a case of "write what you know.")

Early in 2023, the student chapter of Turning Point USA at UC Davis announced it would be bringing the organization's founder, Charlie Kirk, for a talk on campus. As a registered student organization, they had a constitutional right to do this; since we allow student groups to host speakers, a public university like mine can't impose viewpoint restrictions on who can come. But concern on campus was high. The previous semester had seen violence that prevented a different Turning Point speaker from giving a talk arguing against the existence of systemic racism.[9] In the meantime, Kirk had expressed hostility to the presence of transgender athletes in college sports, saying that "someone should have just took care of it the way we used to take care of things in the 1950s or 60s."[10]

Scrambling to avoid a repeat of the fall, the chancellor's office hosted a Town Hall on freedom of expression, where I argued that the First Amendment requires our university to regulate student groups evenhandedly, without regard to viewpoint, but little more. What the First Amendment does *not* require is for the university itself to stay neutral in what it says about a student group's choice of speakers. Just because we, as an institution, value freedom of expression doesn't mean we're required to praise all speech as a valuable contribution to the marketplace of ideas. Some speech is just trash. People say things that are bigoted, uninformed, and harmful, both to the search for truth and to the inclusive learning community we want to build. Vague institutional praise for freedom of expression isn't always the right response to that kind of speech—and it's certainly not a necessary one under the First Amendment.

Having argued all of that, I was still caught off guard by what the chancellor chose to say on the day Charlie Kirk came to campus in March 2023. A few hours before Kirk's event, Chancellor May released a short video in which he described Kirk as "a well-documented proponent of misinformation and hate, . . . who has advocated for violence against transgender individuals." Referencing our university's values, May said that "UC Davis stands with our transgender and non-binary Aggies [our nickname] in opposition to this hateful and divisive messaging." He explained what the First Amendment requires of us as an institution, concluding that "while I abhor the inflammatory speech of this speaker, UC policy permits the student organization to invite [him]." Along the way, the chancellor referred to Kirk's speech as "loathsome and hurtful," "offensive and clearly intended to shock and provoke."[11]

Kirk responded with outrage—and fast. He posted Chancellor May's video on Twitter with his own running commentary, threatening to sue for "slander" and warning May to "be really careful" because "he's supposed to remain neutral."[12] At that night's event, the warm-up speaker asked the crowd if they'd seen Gary May's video, then went on to address the second half of his talk directly to "Gary." In his own talk, Kirk mentioned Chancellor May and the video before he even thanked the police who were holding back protesters outside. More than half of his remarks were about the chancellor's speech and an op-ed in the local paper, which Kirk identified as the source of May's "defamatory" claim that Kirk had called for violence against trans people. Kirk even played most of the chancellor's video, telling his audience: "Not only did he lie about me, but . . . he actually has a bias toward what he wants to have happen here tonight." This was all the worse, according to Kirk, because it was "not some sort of deranged professor; this is someone in a leadership position."[13]

Here was a case where a university's leader didn't just respond to a controversial event with an empathy statement afterward; he actually changed the course of the event itself. Instead of waiting until Kirk had come after our trans students, or students who are immigrants, or any of Kirk's other standard targets, the chancellor had made himself the target. Institutional counterspeech, in this case, got in front of the message it was countering. Charlie Kirk got his platform to speak at Davis, but he found himself having to use most of it addressing our institution's values. By stating those so emphatically in advance, the chancellor's video had reset the terms of the debate.

What my chancellor did would certainly be prohibited under neutrality policies like the University of Chicago's. The Chicago Principles flat-out dictate that judging ideas "to be offensive, unwise, immoral, or wrong-headed . . . is for the individual members of the University community, not for the University as an institution" to do. UC Davis, by contrast, stood with its trans students in opposition to ideas it branded as both hateful and misinformed. Here, I think Davis was right and the Chicago Principles get it wrong. Counterspeech cases like these are the kind of institutional statements most worth fighting for.[14] When institutions have sacrificed one of their closely held values, they need to make up for it, even if the sacrifice might not have been avoidable, or if avoiding it might not have been wise, all things considered. In the Charlie Kirk case, my university was forced to host a speaker whom it never would have invited itself. It was bound to do so by the First Amendment, which protects a value—freedom of expression—that is central to the university's mission. But in honoring this value and doing what the law requires, the university was endangering another of its values: the equal inclusion of community members regardless of their gender identity. The chancellor's speech reduced a harm that the university would otherwise have helped bring about.

Speaking out in this way isn't the *only* action the university could have chosen. UC Davis could have invited speakers and funded other events to advance trans rights. It could devote more resources, as Harvard's Institutional Voice report recommends, to counseling and support services for students affected by anti-trans animus. It could commit to admitting or hiring more trans and nonbinary students, staff, and faculty to reduce feelings of isolation. But why should proponents of *neutrality* see any of those actions as somehow preferable to a statement? They all make the university's non-neutral commitments clear. The only reason I can see why they might be preferrable to a statement is if they advance the university's mission more effectively. Sometimes statements are just talk, after all.

But here, the chancellor's statement was more than that. It *did* more. For one thing, it took the pressure of responding away from those who were most affected by Kirk's presence. This was especially valuable since counterspeech by trans or undocumented students might have required them to out themselves and become even more of a target. Institutional counterspeech put the university and its leaders in the crosshairs instead.

The statement that Kirk felt the need to respond to was, as he said, not just that of a "deranged professor" but of university leadership, speaking for the university itself. This matters. For as an institution of higher education, a university has a unique ability and need to use its speech to help establish norms that are conducive to advancing knowledge. A university can—and should—call out misinformation and dehumanization as inconsistent with those norms. As Professors Kristine Bowman and Katharine Gelber have argued, this kind of institutional speech helps to undermine the perceived authority of people who engage in hate speech. It can stop them from resetting campus expectations about what kind of expression the university exists to foster.[15] By distancing itself from those who engage in speech like Kirk's, the university distinguishes its aim—developing expertise and advancing knowledge—from the hurly-burly of speech in the world at large, where the First Amendment says that "there is no such thing as a false idea."[16]

This doesn't mean that the university needs to engage in counterspeech every time someone on campus says something the university disagrees with. It should be especially cautious when a faculty member's research proves offensive to some. If an economist were to argue for immigration restrictions, or an administrative law professor were to argue that the DACA program exceeded the president's powers, any number of people on campus might be genuinely hurt. Legal and policy questions like those are far more than theoretical to community members who are immigrants, who wait to be reunited with family members, or who could be deported if DACA were rescinded. But a university shouldn't speak out against research that conflicts with its own values and hurts some of its students simply because, as an employer, it is in some sense responsible for producing that research.

So what makes this different from the choice to speak out against Charlie Kirk in order to counter harms the university helped cause? As with all other choices about when to speak, everything turns on the potential costs. When the chancellor speaks out against what he sees as misinformation and hate speech on the part of an outside speaker, he is reinforcing the values of expertise and respectful dialogue that the university's work depends on. If that causes student groups to be more discerning in the invitations they extend in the future, that's a good thing. In fact, that's education. By contrast, were the chancellor to speak out publicly against a professor's research, he would be suggesting that people the university has hired for their expertise should not follow that expertise wherever it leads, however unpopular.[17] The chancellor would be signaling ambivalence about the value of academic freedom. The better option there is to leave opposition to other experts in the field. That's how academic progress occurs. Unlike those targeted by Kirk's speech, other experts are well positioned to respond in the case of the professor's research—far better positioned, in fact, than school administrators.

: : :

Beneath the frequent attacks on institutional statements, there's a running suspicion that they're just a waste of time. Combine that with the potential drawbacks of institutional speech, and campaigns to get universities to stay quiet may seem to make a lot of sense. This chapter's stories have aimed to show that institutional statements really can matter. And the common thread connecting the statements in these stories is this: All were made to counterbalance some harm that the university itself had helped or allowed to happen.

In situations like these, the university may need to speak—and not *just* about its own complicity in the harm. Counteracting the harm might require the university to go further and take a stand on the substantive issue at the root of the harm. The issue could be discrimination in the military, for example, or eligibility criteria for blood donations—not topics we'd normally expect (or perhaps, want) a university to speak about as an institution. My school made a statement about military hiring policies not because that's generally within our zone of expertise, but because those policies plus the Solomon Amendment had pushed us to participate in discrimination against our students. Reasserting the value that we'd let slip in this instance—our commitment to equality—was necessary, and that meant standing with our transgender students and speaking out clearly against the Trump administration's hiring policy, just as the Supreme Court had encouraged universities to do in the "Don't Ask, Don't Tell" era.

Sometimes *speech* is the root cause of the harm that needs counteracting through institutional counterspeech. Universities often permit speech that is inconsistent with some of the university's values in order to advance another of its values, freedom of expression. They allow equality or inclusion, or rationality or expertise, to take a hit for the sake of free speech, whether by choice or because it's required by law. This decision is often the right one, either because of the legal liabilities involved, or because of the dangers of giving any official the power to censor expression. The correctness of the choice, however, doesn't mean that its costs aren't real. Speaking out institutionally in favor of the value that was sacrificed can sometimes lessen those costs and reduce the harm. In some cases, this just means saying "We believe in rational argument," or "We stand by the academic freedom of our faculty even if we don't endorse the particular conclusions they reach." At other times, however, it might mean pointing out the harmfulness or falsehood of some idea the university was complicit in spreading.

Of course, counterspeech isn't the university's only option. Sometimes harmful speech can be regulated outright. That is the topic of the chapter to come. But before getting there, let's just note how deeply intertwined institutional counterspeech and the regulation of speech turn out to be.

I said in the last chapter that institutional speech has to be premised on unwavering protection for those who dissent. That remains true here in this discussion of institutional counterspeech. It's the protection the university guarantees Charlie Kirk and the student group that invited him—the steadfast refusal to shut down the event—that makes the chancellor's statement in opposition to Kirk an appropriate one. Otherwise, it would be nothing but a threat of censorship.

But this works both ways. What this chapter has shown is that *an institution's ability to speak out against those who reject its values makes its toleration of their speech less costly*. A university's ability to engage in counterspeech thus gives it less need to regulate speech that it finds harmful. And with that thought, this chapter's bridge from speech by universities to the regulation of speech *at* universities is now complete.

5 *Regulating Campus Speech*
When More Speech Isn't Necessarily Better

Having looked already at what universities subsidize and what they say, this chapter turns to what they censor. But it's important to remember that all three—subsidizing, speaking, *and* censoring—are just different ways that universities express the values that drive their mission. Deciding on these values is unavoidable, and unavoidably opinionated.

The tumult on university campuses in 2024, in the wake of the Israel-Hamas war, served as a reminder that no matter how "neutral" universities purport to be in their statements or investments, they still have to come down one way or another on what types of expression they are willing to permit on campus. There is always some point at which the right to protest gets trumped by some other value: limiting disruption, preventing violence or property damage, pacifying donors or legislators, or avoiding discrimination. On the quads and similarly public parts of campus where the protests generally occurred, a university's goal is—or should be—to allow as much room for expression as is compatible with its other needs. But one thing the protests made clear is that universities differ in how they balance those other needs against each other, and against freedom of expression.

Universities are more than just their quads. Other parts of campus require a different balancing of values—which is to say, different rules. Offices on campus need to run efficiently. Dorms are filled with students who deserve some measure of peace in their temporary homes. And in classrooms, studios, and labs, maximizing the sheer amount of speech often isn't the goal at all.[1] In fact, as we'll soon see, expanding free speech rights in the classroom can actually undermine the value that matters most there: academic freedom.

This chapter looks at the regulation of speech across these different parts of campus. But I don't mean to give anything like an exhaustive guide to the legal landscape. Others have done that, and done it well.[2] Instead, this chapter considers the choices universities face about how to regulate campus speech by focusing on two sets of court cases where universities' choices were challenged and overruled. In both sets of cases, freedom of expression runs headlong into other values, like inclusion, equality, and expertise. One line of cases, which has already made it briefly to the US Supreme Court, targets the anti-harassment rules and bias response teams that many universities have established to make their campuses more inclusive. The second case says that professors have a right to misgender their students in class—or so some have mistakenly claimed.

Both sets of cases come to the courts at a time when coordinated advocacy campaigns and selective reporting about the speech climate on our campuses have given rise to crisis narratives and deepening mistrust about the commitment to open discourse in American universities. Deciding cases against this background, increasingly conservative federal courts have begun substituting their own opinions for those of universities about how to balance free speech against the other values that are crucial to their mission, whether out on the quad or inside the classroom.

Quad Speech

When universities balance free expression against values like nondiscrimination or inclusion, they don't act with total freedom.[3] Public universities are bound on one side by the complex doctrine that has built up around the free speech clause of the First Amendment. As a reminder from chapter 1, the First Amendment doesn't automatically apply to private schools, but many schools voluntarily commit themselves to the Constitution's protections for speech. I'll say more shortly about what these protections involve and how they vary across different parts of campus.

But universities are constrained from the other side too. Title VI (of the 1964 Civil Rights Act) protects against race, color, and national origin discrimination, and Title IX (of the Education Amendments of 1972) protects against gender discrimination, not just at public schools, but at all schools that receive federal funding—which nearly every college and university does. Department of Education regulations interpret Title VI as extending to "shared ancestry or ethnic characteristics," which is how antisemitism and anti-Muslim animus get covered, even though religion itself is not a protected ground.[4] And Biden administration regulations, which were challenged in courts across the country (and which the second Trump administration has worked to undo), interpreted Title IX's language about sex discrimination to include discrimination based on sexual orientation and gender identity.[5] Administrative interpretations of federal laws are thus at the heart of some of the fiercest recent debates over equality on campus, from protests over Israel and Hamas to proper pronoun usage and trans athletes in college sports. As these examples suggest, speech is often at the heart of the race and gender discrimination that federal law prohibits.

To protect against the race- and sex-based harassment that Titles VI and IX prohibit, the Department of Education has the power to cut federal funding to a university that knowingly allows a racially or sexually hostile environment to arise on campus. More often, though, when the Department of Education gets complaints, it works with schools to reach an agreement about what needs to be done to fix and prevent the problem. (This, at least, was the practice before the second Trump administration began taking more unilateral action.) Students and others on campus can also sue universities directly, and in a 1999 case called *Davis v. Monroe County Board of Education*, the Supreme Court defined the point at which a school would be held liable: the sexual or racial hostility must be "so severe, pervasive, and objectively offensive that it can be said to deprive the victims of access to the educational opportunities or benefits provided by the school."[6] The *Davis* standard draws the line at which schools *must* act to stop a hostile environment, even if the hostility arises from speech—racist slurs, jokes, chants, or pictures, for example—instead of, or in addition to, racist or sexist conduct like assault or stalking. Once this line gets crossed, schools can be held liable in court, or could lose federal funding, if they don't adequately respond.

In recent years, however, campus speech advocates and, increasingly, federal courts have redescribed the *Davis* line. Originally drawn to mark the point where universities *must* act, the *Davis* line is now being treated by some as the point where universities first *may* act. At least when it comes to hostile speech, anything short of the *Davis* line is said to be protected under the First Amendment. "*Davis* properly drew the line between protected and unprotected speech in the context of harassment," according to FIRE, one of the leading advocacy organizations. In 2018, FIRE reviewed the harassment policies at 411 colleges and universities and concluded that 374 of them restrict constitutionally protected speech, which it defined as speech that doesn't rise to the "severe, pervasive, and objectively offensive" standard from *Davis*. The problem, though, is that *Davis* was defining antidiscrimination liability for schools, not protection for speech. FIRE assumes *Davis* defined both. The ceiling of what's protected as speech is, for FIRE, the floor of what's actionable as harassment. Were that the case, universities would be liable under the First Amendment for taking steps to stop hostile speech until the moment when they were liable under antidiscrimination law because they *failed* to stop a hostile environment from arising.

(A quick legal aside: There is a close constitutional parallel here in the context of state aid for religious schools, where the establishment clause prohibits government from promoting religion while the free exercise clause prohibits government from disfavoring it. The Supreme Court has long insisted that there is "constitutional room, or play in the joints, between what the Establishment Clause permits and the Free Exercise Clause compels."[7] The question for school speech codes is whether there shouldn't be similar play in the joints between what free speech law allows and equality law requires.)

The problem only gets worse when we acknowledge that racially or sexually hostile environments often don't result from just one speaker.[8] Think of the claims made by some Jewish students who have felt, in the wake of pro-Palestinian campus protests, that a climate of pervasive antisemitism was affecting their opportunity to get an education. A Title VI complaint filed at my own university alleged that the hostility came from many directions: students rallying with chants and signs perceived as anti-Jewish; anonymous graffiti; social media posts from students, student organizations, and a professor; comments made in lectures by outside speakers; letters published in the student newspaper; statements signed by faculty; a resource list published by the library; and, notably, a departmental statement by the Asian American studies department.[9]

Here's the problem: Imagine a simplified world in which "Level 10" hostility got us to the *Davis* line. At Level 10, the educational environment will have become illegally hostile. A moment ago, I was pointing to the problem where, according to FIRE, a school can't do anything to stop a person's hostile speech until it reaches Level 10. But an even harder problem arises when five speakers each engage in Level 2 hostility. Collectively, their speech will have created a hostile educational environment (5 × 2 = 10), but the university would be unable to stop the speech of any of the five independent speakers, none of whom has crossed the *Davis* threshold on their own. What is a university to do in this case?

In its investigations of antisemitism on college campuses during the 2023–24 school year, the Biden administration made it clear that doing nothing is not an option. Resolving complaints at the University of Michigan, for example, the Department of Education's Office of Civil Rights voiced concern that "the University appears not to have taken steps to assess whether incidents about which it had notice individually *or cumulatively* created a hostile environment for students, faculty, or staff."[10] Going forward, the University of Michigan agreed to educate its employees and members of student government about the school's obligation to respond to all individual incidents of hostile speech or conduct, "as well as [to] view incidents *cumulatively* to determine if a hostile environment may exist in the University's programs and activities." This includes incidents off-campus and on social media, if they create a hostile environment at the university "based upon the totality of the circumstances."[11]

FIRE called this "a field day for would-be censors," "a completely new standard that needlessly pits First Amendment rights against federal anti-discrimination law, dangling the threat of punishment over every discussion."[12] The problem, as FIRE saw it, was that worries about the cumulative effects of hostile but constitutionally protected speech would cause speakers on campus to "face formal investigations for expressing themselves." "To avoid federal anti-discrimination investigations and loss of funding, schools will have little choice but to begin systematically investigating protected speech at protests, in class, and even online."[13]

The challenge here is real. To see that, we don't have to accept FIRE's claim that speech has to reach Level 10 hostility before a school can address it. (In fact, the Department of Education itself uses a somewhat lower standard, asking if hostile speech is "severe *or* pervasive" rather than FIRE's and *Davis*'s "severe and pervasive" test.) There is surely some speech—call it Level 2, as before—that is undeniably protected on its own. A letter to the student newspaper claiming that Israel has committed genocide would be one example of this. This is not the kind of expression that a university can legally ban. But it's certainly conceivable that anti-Israel sentiment could cumulatively become pervasive enough on campus that some Jewish students no longer feel welcome. Again, what is a school to do? According to the Department of Education:

> Schools have a number of tools for responding to a hostile environment—including tools that do not restrict any rights protected by the First Amendment. To meet its obligation, a university can, among other steps, communicate its opposition to stereotypical, derogatory opinions; provide counseling and support for students affected by harassment; or take steps to establish a welcoming and respectful school campus, which could include making clear that the school values, and is determined to fully include in the campus community, students of all races, colors, and national origins.[14]

It's striking how prominently different forms of institutional counterspeech feature in this list. Were those to be restricted by an institutional neutrality policy, either chosen or imposed from outside, universities' options for dealing with potentially hostile educational environments would be dramatically narrowed.

This is not to say that institutional counterspeech is the only option for dealing with hostile speech in the places on campus where speech receives the most protection—spaces like the quad. People who harass others or who violate laws against threats, incitement, or other categories of unprotected speech can face school discipline or even criminal sanctions. If the hostility is targeted, a university can take steps to separate the source from the target. Roommates can be moved, class sections swapped, or, when a stronger response is needed, people can sometimes be ordered to keep their distance from those who have complained. But these are heavy-handed options.

Somewhat less concerning from a First Amendment perspective is mandatory training, whether for particular people, certain groups, or the campus as a whole. Perhaps counterintuitively, the more targeted interventions here are likely the most problematic from a First Amendment perspective. Ordering training for the entire campus is certainly more burdensome than requiring just a few people to attend, but the latter involves singling out particular people for things they have said, and that can look like retaliation or viewpoint discrimination. When it comes to free speech, broader burdens are sometimes more constitutional than narrower ones that fail to treat everyone the same.

Another option is to invite a particular speaker to discuss how their expression affects other people or the campus climate. These meetings can vary in how punitive they seem, so determining their constitutionality is sometimes hard. As the presidents of Harvard, MIT, and Penn infamously told Congress, it depends on the context. Being called to a mandatory meeting with a Title IX Coordinator or a Dean of Students is a far different thing than having a conversation with your residential advisor or one of your professors. It's hardly uncommon for a professor like me, who teaches at a professional school, to speak with a student during office hours about the way they're coming across to classmates or how they might present themselves more professionally in their emails. I can't imagine that this is a First Amendment problem, even though I'm of course trying to change their manner of expression. By contrast, mandatory counseling with university administrators who have disciplinary powers would present a much different constraint on speech.

The remaining and least intrusive options for addressing hostile speech include many of those that the Department of Education suggested above. Offering counseling and support services to affected community members—that is, to the listeners, not the speakers—is one such possibility. University counterspeech is another. As I argued in the last chapter, a university can respond to hostile speech, even if it is fully protected, by opposing or condemning that speech and by making the university's own values clear.

All of these options, from the most to least punitive, have one thing in common: a university can only employ them as a response to hostile speech if it knows about the hostility. In other words, universities need some system in place for receiving and investigating reports of bias. As the Department of Education has said, "Without a mechanism in place to monitor for future incidents and assess its school climate efforts, a school's response may not be reasonably calculated to prevent recurrence."[15] And yet the possibility that protected speech might spark such an investigation is exactly what has caused FIRE so much alarm.

These mechanisms for reporting and investigating hostile expression have also sparked litigation. In recent years, they have become the target of a shockingly effective legal campaign brought by a young speech advocacy organization, Speech First. Funded less by its $5 lifetime membership dues than by an undisclosed network of conservative donors,[16] Speech First filed its first lawsuit just months after it was founded in 2018. In a complaint that almost immediately got support from President Trump's Department of Justice, Speech First attacked the University of Michigan's definition of harassing speech as well as the university's Bias Response Team, a group responsible for collecting and responding to allegations of speech or conduct motivated "by the offender's bias against a race, color, ethnicity, national origin, sex, gender identity or expression, sexual orientation, disability, age or religion."[17]

The Michigan suit was just the first of many. In each, the story proved largely the same: after filing suit, Speech First would immediately ask for a preliminary injunction, an order that would put the challenged policies on hold. Trial courts would say no, which gave Speech First the chance to go directly to the federal courts of appeals. These are divided into twelve geographic regions, and Speech First got quick wins in the Fifth, Sixth, Tenth, and Eleventh Circuits, followed by favorable settlements with the University of Texas, the University of Michigan, Oklahoma State, and the University of Central Florida, the defendants in those four cases. Speech First lost in the Fourth and Seventh Circuits, but even there, the universities they sued—Virginia Tech and the University of Illinois—settled anyway. Iowa State settled before its case even reached the Eighth Circuit. And if Virginia Tech had not dismantled its Bias Response Team, the US Supreme Court was poised to reconsider Speech First's loss in the Fourth Circuit during its October 2024 term.[18] It's a staggering record for a legal organization's first six years. Only mid-Atlantic, northeastern, and West Coast schools have so far been spared Speech First's attack. Everywhere else, universities have been ordered or pressured to narrow their harassment policies and abandon their bias response teams, dramatically limiting their menu of options for balancing freedom of expression against equity and inclusion.

You might think that such dramatic changes to university policies must have been ordered because Speech First had exposed embarrassing cases of cancel culture or liberal intolerance on these campuses. You'd be wrong.

In fact, in *none* of its cases has Speech First described a single instance of a university student or employee being disciplined because of something they'd said. Instead, Speech First has brought its cases on behalf of anonymous students, listed in court complaints as "Student A," "Student B," et cetera, who say they *want to* "speak passionately and repeatedly" about conservative issues like "gun rights, illegal immigration, and abortion," but they are afraid to do so because of their universities' speech policies.[19] These lawsuits challenge the policies as written, not as they've ever been applied to any particular speaker. Ordinarily, this might cause problems with what lawyers call "standing": the constitutional requirement that cases in federal court involve concrete, not just hypothetical, injuries that the court can do something to fix. In the *Speech First* cases, courts are being asked to imagine the fears of unnamed students and decide whether those fears are reasonable, even at universities whose administrators have filed sworn statements promising that they would never punish the kinds of things these students wanted to say.[20] The courts' refusal to credit those promises show just how deep public distrust of universities has grown, at least in some quarters.

Since the *Speech First* opinions all came before discovery or trial, where evidence is gathered and presented, judges on the courts of appeals had to rely on their own intuitions about the objective likelihood of future punishment—the reasonableness of the students' fears—presumably based on things they had read elsewhere about the state of free speech on college campuses.[21] The Fifth Circuit, for example, quoted an open letter from *Harper's Magazine* on "our current national condition" in which it's said that "institutional leaders . . . are delivering hasty and disproportionate punishment" for controversial speech. One of the Eleventh Circuit judges quoted approvingly from the Chicago Principles before concluding wildly that "[a] university that turns itself into an asylum from controversy has ceased to be a university; it has just become an asylum."[22] And presented with the inconvenient fact that the University of Michigan had *never* disciplined a student for doing what Speech First's members said they wanted to do—have an "intellectual debate"—the Sixth Circuit simply replied that "the lack of discipline against students could just as well indicate that speech has already been chilled."[23] Heads Speech First wins, tails the university loses.

It's troubling that these courts were willing to assume that universities are itching to discipline their students, or at least their conservative students, for speaking out on political issues. But even worse were the courts' jaded views about some of universities' best options *other than discipline* for addressing speech that threatens to make campuses more racially or sexually hostile. For one thing, several of the *Speech First* opinions punish universities for trying to clarify what counts as harassment under their policies. (This, by the way, is often the first requirement the Department of Education imposes in its resolution agreements with universities facing complaints.) In some cases, courts found that university harassment policies were vague *because* they were too detailed. As the Fifth Circuit complained about the University of Texas, its "definition of verbal harassment consumes nearly a full page of small type. This alone might raise questions about vagueness." Notably, this comes just pages after the court complained that terms like "harassment," "incivility," and "bias" "beg for clarification." Even UT's attempt to stress its commitment to free speech was said to confuse things. Here's the language that perplexed the court: "To make an argument for or against the substance of any political, religious, philosophical, ideological, or academic idea is not verbal harassment, even if some listeners are offended by the argument or idea."[24]

In the Eleventh Circuit case, the court faulted the University of Central Florida for employing "a gestaltish 'totality of known circumstances' approach to" its definition of harassment. UCF, like many schools, offered a list of considerations that were meant to help determine whether speech doesn't just feel harassing, but is objectively so. According to these considerations, it would be less *reasonable* to see speech as harassment if it "implicates concerns related to academic freedom or protected speech." Amazingly, the Eleventh Circuit complained that UCF's use of the word "reasonabl[e]" was itself "pretty amorphous." This is an especially rich claim in an opinion that, in its own words, was deciding whether the district court had applied the law "in an *unreasonable* . . . manner" when it found that "Speech First's members could not *reasonably* believe that they would be punished." The court ultimately concluded that UCF's harassment policy would "cause a *reasonable* student to fear expressing potentially unpopular beliefs," apparently forgetting just how amorphous the word was at the center of its holding.[25]

In addition to punishing universities for saying too much about the meaning of harassment, the *Speech First* courts also chided them for creating bias response teams to respond to it. According to a study by Speech First in 2022, 456 schools had established something akin to a bias response team: a group charged with collecting, investigating, and responding to allegations of bias or discrimination.[26] Importantly, none of the teams Speech First sued to disband had any disciplinary authority of their own. So what made them so fearsome? According to Speech First, it's the fact that these teams could *refer* cases to student affairs officials or the police, who do have disciplinary power. And yet anyone can file a complaint with a university's Title IX office or the local police if they think there's been a violation of antidiscrimination or criminal law. It's unclear why offering another pathway for reporting and sorting such claims should be enough to create a constitutional injury.[27] Aside from referring claims for discipline, some bias response teams have the power to invite students accused of bias to a voluntary meeting or to facilitate conversations with those who reported them. Even here, some courts found an "objective chill" to student speech, simply refusing to believe that these meetings would be understood as voluntary or that they wouldn't affect students' professional prospects.[28]

Finally, and most troublingly of all, several of the *Speech First* opinions took issue with the language that universities use when dealing with speech complaints. The response team at UT Austin, the Fifth Circuit noted, "describes its work, judgmentally, in terms of 'targets' and 'initiators' of incidents."[29] The Eleventh Circuit wrote similarly that "no reasonable college student"—there's that amorphous word "reasonable" again!—"wants to run the risk of being accused of 'offensive,' 'hostile,' 'negative,' or 'harmful' conduct—let alone 'hate or bias.'"[30] But if language like this is enough to intimidate and chill "the average college-aged student . . . from exercising her free-speech rights," as the Eleventh Circuit held, then the potential for institutional counter-speech starts to look pretty bleak. If a university were to brand certain speakers as hateful or misinformed, would that also count as chilling? What would this mean for the First Amendment rights of universities themselves, if they are seen to be constitutionally injuring speakers on campus simply by calling them out as offensive or wrong? At times, the *Speech First* opinions seem to conflate universities that *discipline* certain types of speech on campus with those that merely *speak out* against it.

This can't be what the First Amendment requires. Return to my office chats, mentioned earlier, with students whose expression is overly informal or alienating. No one wants to be told that they sound unprofessional or come across like a jerk. And in telling them those things, my aim is clearly to change the way they speak. I *am* trying to chill certain types of expression, it turns out! But surely my attempt at persuasion, even when we acknowledge the power asymmetry in a conversation between me and my students, has to be treated differently than a disciplinary measure. Counseling students not to use "Hey!" as their salutation on an email is a much different thing than referring a student for discipline, even if both are attempts to change the way someone talks. Characterizing someone's speech in unflattering terms or trying to convince them that their speech leaves something to be desired—these cannot be what the First Amendment prohibits, at least not in an institution that's dedicated to education.

If the *Speech First* cases stand for the idea that universities can't even speak out against hostile speech, at least until it reaches the *Davis* threshold; that they can't invite students to discuss the effects of their speech or to meet with affected listeners; that they shouldn't make it too easy to report incidents of bias or to give administrators the ability to investigate whether speech is protected or potentially subject to discipline; and that schools shouldn't explain and publicize, at least in too much detail, what their harassment policies prohibit—what then *can* universities do if they want to prevent their campus from becoming a racially or sexually hostile place? How in particular can universities address the problem of cumulative hostilities, the protected but offensive speech acts that, when combined, have made certain university campuses feel so inhospitable to so many groups, especially recently?

It's just not enough to fall back, as so many speech advocates have, on the truism that hate speech is protected under the US Constitution. To do that is to disregard the people who are subjected to hate speech on a daily basis. Telling them to "toughen up" is not a sufficient answer—*especially* not from anyone who also happens to endorse the Kalven Report, which rests on the idea that faculty are too fragile to do their jobs if their university makes statements they oppose. It's pretty rich to ridicule protections and support for students while treating faculty like snowflakes.[31]

There is some room for hope, though, that the effects of hostile speech are starting to get noticed. *Speech First* won its impressive victories at least in part through procedural maneuvers that ensured courts would hear only from would-be speakers, not those who would be affected by their expression. By contrast, recent Title VI complaints from Jewish students have centered the concerns of people subjected to cumulative hostilities, many of which are speech-based. Republicans in Congress and officials in the Trump administration have suddenly taken an interest in the effects that hostile campus speech can have on its audience—at least on some audiences. Going forward, it will be interesting to see how this political realignment of the parties affected might also affect the balance that judges and others feel is proper when navigating collisions between speech and inclusion on campus.

: : :

What the *Speech First* cases and advocacy like FIRE's have done is to narrow or eliminate the "play in the joints" or breathing room between speech that is untouchable under the First Amendment and speech that is hostile enough to violate antidiscrimination law. And yet it's precisely in that breathing room that universities find space to decide how they want to balance freedom of expression with other values that drive their mission.[32]

A private, research-driven institution like the University of Chicago or MIT will likely want to strike this balance differently than a small liberal arts college, where most students know each other and live on campus together, or at a religious school or one where racial justice or gender equality or some other social value is at the center of the school's mission. A professional school like mine may feel the need to socialize its students into the norms of our profession, particularly if it cares about helping first-generation students successfully enter the field. And schools like mine certainly care about ensuring that students don't run afoul of state licensing requirements or the demands of future employers. This requires a balance that is a bit more speech restrictive than that which we might expect to find elsewhere within the university. Similarly, a medical school always has to worry about the quality of care its patients receive. "Doing no harm" in that context may require its own particular balance of order, efficiency, and calm against the disruption that freewheeling expression can cause. Free speech advocates sometimes run all of these contexts together, assuming that the same balance is appropriate everywhere.[33]

Each of the different types and parts of universities is likely to make a different decision—within certain bounds, of course—about how they respond to disruptive speech: what they regulate, what they try to dissuade, and what they speak out against. Institutional neutrality policies limit the third option. The *Speech First* cases tend to conflate the first and second. The net result is that universities become ever more confined in their ability to express their distinctive mission through their approach to campus speech.

Classroom Speech

From a free speech perspective, few places are as constitutionally complicated as a university. Different spaces and activities on campus are dedicated to very different purposes, and they should be subject to different constraints as a result. Aside from running together the *regulation* of speech from attempts to *influence* or *counter* it, the *Speech First* courts were also wrong to ignore the fact that not all speech on university campuses is subject to the same constitutional rules. That mistake isn't theirs alone.

Often lost in the discourse about campus speech is the fact that universities are far more than just their quads, where the First Amendment's strictest rules apply and speech generally has to be left as free, or nearly as free, as it is in "traditional public forums" like city parks and sidewalks.[34] Universities are also huge employers, with offices running everything from HR and parking to admissions and fundraising. They curate museum exhibitions and sponsor concerts, theatrical performances, and lecture series. Universities provide housing in their dorms; they operate sports teams with sometimes embarrassing budgets; and they fund student groups, which often use that money to sponsor speech of their own choosing. At public universities and other schools that have committed to First Amendment principles, each of these "spaces" comes with different rules. And that's before we even get to the classrooms and labs that are dedicated to teaching and research. This section is primarily focused on *those* spaces, and the academic freedom protections—and responsibilities—that govern there. In the classroom, expanding freedom of speech is not the same thing as protecting academic freedom. Oftentimes, one can actually undermine the other.

Before getting there, it might be useful quickly to differentiate speech in classrooms from some of the other main spaces on campus. To simplify things a bit, let's look at just two of these: what I'll call the quad and the bulletin board.

: : :

"The quad" stands for the real and metaphorical spaces where the rules that we most commonly associate with the First Amendment apply. This is the space that tends to swallow the rest of campus, at least in the minds of many reporters, campus speech advocates, and, unfortunately, judges. Part of the reason quad law, as we might call it, looms so large is because it's what applies to many of the most widely reported controversies on university campuses. The encampments set up to protest the violence in Israel and Gaza are only the latest examples. Quad law is what governs the most visible campus spaces—the ones generally open for public access.

In spaces like the quad, universities cannot force anyone to speak and, with very limited exceptions, they can't treat speakers differently based on what they're saying. Aside from exceptions like harassment, defamation, incitement, obscenity, and intellectual property violations, universities can only regulate the time, place, and manner of speech on the quad, not its content. It can cap how loudly protesters are amplified but not what they say, even if what they say is hateful or inaccurate. One way to think about this is to imagine a white noise machine or protesters with blank banners and placards. If university regulations would bar the noise machine because of how loud it is or what time of night it's playing, or if the blank signs would be prohibited because they're staked into the ground or left up too long, we can be fairly confident that the content of the expression is not what's being regulated. Time, place, and manner rules like these are allowed as long as they leave open other means of communication, and they aren't gratuitously broad. Does that test seem vague? That's part of the reason why even schools bound by the First Amendment still have significant wiggle room for deciding how to balance freedom of expression with other of their values.

Rules change when we move from the quad to campus "bulletin boards," by which I mean places or programs where the university sponsors the speech of others with a particular purpose in mind. Content discrimination is possible in these spaces as long as it's reasonably related to their purpose. So, for example, my law school could say that the bulletin board outside the dean's office can be used only for announcements about events in our building. Another bulletin board (or email distribution list, et cetera) might be made available for posting opinions on current events, but only by members of the law school. I've just described content and speaker discrimination, respectively. That's allowed in these spaces, unlike on the quad. What's not allowed is viewpoint discrimination. The university can't limit postings to conservative causes but not liberal ones, or the other way around.

The bulletin board is a metaphor for a much larger set of what lawyers call "limited public forums," which, at universities, importantly include school-funded student organizations. The last chapter's story about Charlie Kirk, who was invited by my university's student chapter of Turning Point USA, involved limited public forum doctrine. That's what constrained our options about how to respond. My university could theoretically decide that student activity funds can never be spent on outside speakers. But once it allows them, it's constitutionally prohibited from canceling speeches because it dislikes what the speaker might say.

That brings us finally to the classroom, lab, or studio—spaces dedicated to teaching and research. In these, viewpoint discrimination is pervasive and entirely proper, at least when the viewpoints and the criteria for judging them are relevant to the class or research project. As chapter

1 pointed out, viewpoint discrimination occurs every time a professor grades a student. And content discrimination, also allowed, occurs every time professors guide classroom discussion back to the topic at hand. Compelled speech, though constitutionally prohibited on the quad, occurs each time professors like me cold-call our students. And while there may be no such thing as a false idea on the quad, there certainly is in my class. In the classroom, professors can maintain a level of decorum, demand reasoned arguments rather than misinformation or personal attacks, and expect that professional standards will be maintained. None of this is true on the lawns beyond our classroom windows.

What matters in the classroom isn't that students—or for that matter, professors—have as much freedom to speak as possible. The freedom that matters in the classroom is *academic freedom*. And while we encountered some of what academic freedom allows and demands in chapter 1, there is no better way to see how it differs from ordinary free speech principles than through a recent and troubling blockbuster of a case, *Meriwether v. Hartop*.

:::

If you've heard of *Meriwether*, you probably know it as the case that gave public university professors a First Amendment right to misgender their students in class. It didn't actually do that—I'll explain why later—but that's how the case has been widely (mis)understood, and that perception itself has been enough to set back transgender rights, not just on college campuses.[35]

Nicholas Meriwether is a philosophy professor at Shawnee State University in Ohio, which since 2016 has required its professors to use transgender students' preferred pronouns, "regardless of the professor's convictions on the subject." Meriwether's own convictions on the subject are strong: he believes God immutably fixes a person's biological sex at the moment of conception. In spring 2018, a trans woman, known in court documents as Jane Doe, showed up for Meriwether's political philosophy class. On the first day, Meriwether called her "sir" because, as he'd later say, "Doe appeared male." Meriwether continued calling her Mr. Doe even after she corrected him and his university issued a reprimand. Eventually, Meriwether sued Shawnee State on free speech and religious freedom grounds, claiming that the university was infringing his academic freedom by forcing him to say things in class that he did not believe. The trial court didn't buy it; it dismissed the case at the outset. But the Sixth Circuit—the federal court of appeals for Ohio, Michigan, Kentucky, and Tennessee—overturned that decision, finding that Meriwether had stated First Amendment claims that were plausible enough to deserve evidence gathering and a possible trial.

Because Meriwether is a government employee, winning his speech claim meant surviving a three-step test. First, public employees generally have to show that the speech at issue didn't arise as part of their job duties. This requirement comes from a 2006 case called *Garcetti v. Ceballos*, and its rationale is straightforward, at least as it applies to most government jobs. When the parking office issues tickets, its employees don't have a free speech right to add a zero to the fine or to write little personal notes at the top. Government offices wouldn't run if bosses were unable to limit or direct what their employees say while doing their work.

University professors aren't necessarily like other government employees though. Professors aren't (or shouldn't be) told by some boss how to teach or what to research in the same way that workers in the parking office can be instructed how to do their jobs or interact with customers. As described in the AAUP's foundational 1915 Declaration, which we've encountered before, faculty "are the appointees, but not in any proper sense the employees" of a university.[36] Academic freedom requires this independence, and recognizing this, the Supreme Court in *Garcetti* left open the possibility that "expression related to academic scholarship or classroom instruction" should perhaps be treated differently than other government employee speech. In *Meriwether*, the Sixth Circuit joined the Fourth and Ninth Circuits in deciding that *Garcetti* doesn't apply to teaching and research, meaning that public university professors in those circuits have broader free speech protections than other government workers.

This is all to say that at step one of the government employee speech test, the Sixth Circuit said—I think correctly—that *Garcetti* doesn't apply to Meriwether. His claim advanced to step two, which asks whether the government employee was speaking on a matter of public concern. Courts have decided that they don't want to hear constitutional cases about workplace gripes and gossip. They want to step in only when the state might be preventing its workers from helping shape public opinion.

This second prong of the government employee speech test has proven tricky when it comes to speech by professors. (As is already becoming clear, the traditional test fits awkwardly with the peculiar nature of academic work.)[37] Many of the liveliest debates within particular academic disciplines aren't exactly "matters of public concern" to the world at large. Think of questions like how we should translate the first lines of *The Odyssey* or whether Kripke or Frege offered the better account of proper names. The general public may not care about either question, but classicists and philosophers of language certainly do, and academic freedom exists to protect both.

As a result, courts have generally and wisely taken a broad view of "matters of public concern" when it comes to university teaching and research.[38] That's what the *Meriwether* court saw itself as doing, and that's where its opinion starts to go off track. To the court, Meriwether's misgendering of Jane Doe was a way of "wading into" a national debate over pronoun usage. Each time he referred to her as a man, he was expressing a deeply contested view about gender identity. But that just can't be right. Discriminatory action is *always* expressive. If I were to say that the women in my classes need to sit behind the men, I'd surely be expressing a view on gender. I would also be violating Title IX, the equal protection clause of the US Constitution, and a slew of state laws. Meriwether, similarly, was *doing* something, not just discussing something, when he called on Ms. Doe as "Mr. Doe," over her objections. He was treating his trans students differently than his cisgender students.

But let's move on. Having said in step one that the *Garcetti* test doesn't apply to university teaching and, in step two, that Meriwether's misgendering of Doe counted as speech on a matter of public concern, the court of appeals made it to step three, which is a balancing test: Was the value of Meriwether's expression outweighed by the disruption it caused at his workplace, whether to his students or to the university itself? Here the Sixth Circuit loaded up the expressive-value side of the scales by suggesting that academic freedom itself was at stake. Pasting together a greatest hits list of Supreme Court dicta on academic freedom, shorn of their context, the court of appeals wrote that the classroom is "peculiarly the marketplace of ideas" (which is false);[39] that "Our Nation is deeply committed to safeguarding academic freedom" (also false, but it should be true);[40] that academic freedom "is of transcendent value . . . and not merely to the teachers concerned" (true);[41] and that "'To impose any strait jacket upon the intellectual leaders in our colleges and universities would imperil the future of our Nation.'"[42] This final claim could be true, but it's easily misread. Academic freedom isn't violated just because a professor is constrained; the problem arises when the "strait jacket" is *imposed* by the government or others who lack the relevant expertise to judge academic work.

This is the crux of the issue. Academic freedom is decidedly *not* an unconstrained right for professors (or students) to say anything they want in class. As one hundred other law professors and I wrote in a brief in the *Meriwether* case, "Academic freedom [in the classroom] protects professors' right to make *pedagogical* judgments, informed by their scholarly expertise, about how best to *discuss* issues that are *relevant* to the courses they have been hired to teach."[43] On this definition, *Meriwether* is not a case about academic freedom at all. Meriwether didn't have *pedagogical* reasons for misgendering Jane Doe or other trans students. He had religious views about gender identity. He was not *discussing* these views; as I said before, he was *calling on* Jane Doe, putting her in the position of having to respond to a name that isn't hers. And even if this weren't true—even if we *were* to see Meriwether's misgendering as an expression of his viewpoint—this would mean that Professor Meriwether was repeatedly expressing his views on gender identity in every single class session, no matter that day's topic. This would be like a professor ranting about Trump or the Yankees in every class. It would be a violation of a teacher's professional responsibilities, unprotected under any reasonable account of academic freedom.

The *Meriwether* judges' mistake was to untether academic freedom from the *disciplinary expertise* that justifies it. As the historian and academic freedom expert Joan Wallach Scott once wrote in a similar context, "By collapsing the distinction between free speech and academic freedom, they deny the authority of knowledge and of the teacher who purveys it."[44] Unlike the largely unfettered freedom at the heart of quad law, where there are no wrong ideas, hate speech is allowed, and the marketplace of ideas goes largely unregulated, academic freedom is a realm of rights that come with responsibilities. Professors have freedom from outside constraints only insofar as they hew to the standards internal to their field. They have the right to decide what and how to teach only as long as their choices are relevant to the class they've been assigned and can be defended on scholarly and pedagogical grounds.

By reducing academic freedom to free speech, the law of the classroom to quad law, the *Meriwether* court constitutionalized the possibility of in-class indoctrination, a world where professors can rant on topics that are outside of their expertise and irrelevant to the class they're teaching. Meriwether's personal religious and moral beliefs, after all, would have led him to misgender Jane Doe even if he were teaching soil biology rather than political philosophy. The irony here is that conservative judges on the Sixth Circuit were constitutionally protecting the very thing—indoctrination in the classroom—that red state legislatures have offered as their reason for meddling in university affairs, and that surveys have shown as a primary cause of the conservatives' reduced faith in universities.[45]

Reducing academic freedom to free speech, treating the classroom no differently than the quad, thus ends up contributing to a wider contemporary assault on education and expertise—in fact, an assault on expertise *in* education. And it's important to notice that, in *Meriwether*, this happens by *expanding* free speech rights in the classroom.

The idea that expanding free speech protections can count as an attack on academic freedom may come as a surprise, since we're more familiar with attacks that take the form of censorship, as when politicians or donors try to silence certain research or classroom topics.[46] Interestingly, when a group at Princeton recently issued a set of principles for "revitaliz[ing] free and vigorous inquiry" on campus, they were so suspicious of administrators' and faculty members' commitment to free speech and academic freedom that they were willing, in some cases, even to permit legislative meddling. Facing criticism, one of the authors clarified that outside interventions could go "only in the direction of *adding* free speech protections and the diversity of ideas, not of *restricting or inhibiting* any ideas or views."[47] He just assumed that expanding speech rights could never pose a threat to academic freedom. *Meriwether* stands as a correction and caution: adding the wrong speech protections, or speech protections in the wrong contexts, can actually undermine academic freedom just as thoroughly as limits on classroom speech do.

To be clear, however, the *Meriwether* opinion itself did not actually add the speech protection it is celebrated and vilified for. *Meriwether* did not establish a right to misgender students in class. Let me explain and make good on a promise made earlier.

As a reminder, step three of the government employee speech test requires courts to balance speech's value against its disruptiveness. I just described how the court of appeals piled its misguided praise of academic freedom on the expressive-value side of the scales. But that value still has to be weighed against any disruption the employee's speech causes at the workplace. And because the *Meriwether* case was decided at a point where Meriwether, but not his university, had alleged facts, and *no one* had presented actual evidence, the court was not yet looking at how Meriwether's misgendering might have disrupted Jane Doe's education, or how it might have exposed the university to liability under Title IX. The Sixth Circuit also simply ignored the question of whether Meriwether had violated the equal protection clause by misgendering his trans students. These were all questions left for later in the litigation. As a result, the *Meriwether* decision stands not for the idea that professors have a right to misgender their students in class; at best, it holds that professors have a free speech right to misgender *if* they can do so without disrupting students' education, exposing their universities to liability, or violating the equal protection clause. These are some pretty major ifs.

Normally, a case like this would go back to the trial court to find out whether any of these ifs actually prove true. Shawnee State and Jane Doe would present evidence to show how disruptive Meriwether's misgendering had been to her, to other trans students, and to the university. (The LGBTQ student group on campus has said, for example, that because Shawnee State is a small school, trans students who refuse to take classes with Meriwether struggle to fulfill their distribution requirements.) None of this ever happened, however. When the case returned to the trial court, Shawnee State settled with Professor Meriwether—much like every university has done after being sued by Speech First.[48]

Because evidence of disruption never became part of the case, *Meriwether*, like the *Speech First* cases, ended up getting decided on a purely hypothetical record, where those affected by offensive speech were never given a voice. The "right to misgender" allegedly upheld in *Meriwether* exists in reality only if it can be invoked without harming students' education or school operations. But those limits are all too easily forgotten.

Soon after *Meriwether* was decided, Tennessee passed a law saying that schools there can no longer require K–12 teachers to use their students' preferred pronouns. Arguing in favor of the law, one state senator claimed that since university professors have a right to misgender—which again, they don't—there is no reason why teachers in lower grades shouldn't be able to do so too. That's how easily misperceived precedent can become genuine law, and a misunderstanding of campus speech rules can set back transgender rights even beyond university campuses.

: : :

Meriwether and the *Speech First* cases have a lot in common. In both, courts stepped in to expand free speech rights at colleges and universities. In both, those courts operated with a conception of free speech that fails to recognize the differences among different spaces on campus, with their varying aims and needs. And in both, courts ended up limiting universities' ability to balance freedom of speech against other values that they see as crucial to their mission.

In the *Speech First* cases, those other values included equality and inclusion. Both those values were at stake in *Meriwether* as well, but so, too, were disciplinary expertise and quality teaching—two of the responsibilities that underlie academic freedom. Advocacy organizations like Speech First and FIRE don't always worry about these other values. Those groups focus solely on free speech, even bragging that they don't "hav[e] to deal with the tensions that may or may not exist with free speech and other values."[49] The trouble is, First Amendment law itself "deals with" these other values. As we have just seen, free speech protections for public university professors are supposed to hinge on how much disruption the speech causes. Not caring about things like trans rights or race and gender equity—the very things hostile speech often disrupts—leads to an overexpansive view of what the First Amendment protects on campus.

Unlike FIRE, Speech First, and the courts that they've persuaded, universities don't have the luxury of simply ignoring values like equality and inclusion, much less scholarly and pedagogical expertise. Deciding how to balance these values alongside universities' commitment to robust expression is unavoidable. And the balance that universities choose and enshrine in campus policy—to the extent courts still give them the breathing room do so—is a crucial expression of what they see their mission to be.

Coda

Who Should Decide a University's Opinions?

If a university can never be neutral about what values shape its mission, we're bound to ask what a school's values and mission should be—and who should get to decide.

This book has largely sidestepped the first of these questions: What should a university's mission be? Pushing instead for pluralism, each chapter of the book can be read as a response to something we're told the university, its mission, or its values allegedly *must* be. Diversity statements are something "other than merit" according to those who beg the question about what academic merit is, assuming that it can't be concerned with who benefits from academics' teaching and research. Student evaluations and university rankings both operate as homogenizing forces, imposing a common rubric on importantly different practices and institutions, and giving non-experts the power to decide what teachers and schools are best. When it comes to institutional statements, we're told that neutrality is a prerequisite for a university even to be a true university. And departments, too, must all stay quiet, no matter their mission or expertise. Universities can (perhaps) express empathy for students who experience harm, but they become recklessly political if they express a view on whatever in the world caused the harm in the first place. Freedom of speech, say some advocates and even courts, must everywhere take priority over values like equality and inclusion, perhaps even disciplinary expertise—unless and until that speech reaches a level of hostility defined (for a different purpose) in a 1999 Supreme Court opinion.

All of these are arguments for sameness across universities, no matter their character, context, or history. I've done my best to push back against them all, emphasizing instead the range of possibilities for how different universities might come to understand and balance the values that drive their distinctive missions. Which of these possibilities I would choose is, at least for the purposes of this book, beside the point. It's generally not my choice, after all.

But whose choice is it, then? If universities face unavoidable decisions about how to define their mission, someone has to make them. And if, as I've argued, the debates engaged in this book—on diversity statements, institutional neutrality, and campus speech regulations—all end up turning on a university's mission, how that mission gets defined becomes perhaps the most important decision of all.

No one understands this better than the red state governors and legislators who, in recent years, have taken it on themselves to redefine the mission of their states' universities. Take Florida. An extensive report published in December 2023 by a special committee of the AAUP detailed the barrage waged against public schools by Florida's governor Ron DeSantis and the Republican supermajority in the state legislature.[1] The law widely known as the Stop WOKE Act of 2022 prohibited instruction promoting any of a long list of ideas, including that certain races are morally superior to others (though the idea that some are *intellectually* superior was allowed); that someone, based on their race or sex, should be burdened "to achieve diversity, equity, or inclusion"; that virtues such as merit and color-blindness are racist; or that someone should feel "psychological distress" because of past actions by others of their race or sex.[2] All this despite a law from a year earlier that *prohibited* universities from "shielding" students from "ideas and opinions that they may find uncomfortable, unwelcome, disagreeable, or offensive."[3]

A law proposed in 2023 would have barred general education courses at Florida's public universities from including material or even "pedagogical methodology associated with" "Critical Race Theory," "Queer Theory," "Radical Feminist Theory," or "Intersectionality."[4] The bill that became law removed these specific topics, and instead dictated more generally that "courses with a curriculum based on unproven, speculative, or exploratory content are best suited as elective[s]," whereas required general education courses in Florida should "promote and preserve the constitutional republic" by providing "instruction on the historical background and philosophical foundation of Western civilization and this nation's historical documents."[5] Importantly, the 2023 law instructed the Board of Governors—fifteen out of seventeen of whom the governor appoints—to "periodically review the mission of each constituent university and make updates or revisions as needed," before then "review[ing] existing academic programs for alignment with the mission." In particular, the board was told to review Florida's public universities for any classes advancing ideas banned under the Stop WOKE Act, or those "based on theories that systemic racism, sexism, oppression, and privilege are inherent in the institutions of the United States." In 2024, after Florida's education commissioner said that "sociology has been hijacked by left-wing activists," the board voted to remove Principles of Sociology from the list of core classes throughout the state university system.[6] Other state laws passed in Florida have instituted a post-tenure review process that faculty have to navigate every five years, added burdens on membership in the faculty union, banned DEI offices and the use of diversity statements in faculty hiring, and prohibited trans people from using school bathrooms that match their gender identity.[7]

The most targeted attack on a school and its mission, however, occurred at New College of Florida, once the designated honors college of the state university system.[8] In January 2023, Governor DeSantis and allies appointed seven new trustees, including Christopher Rufo, whose earlier appearances in this book have included his campaigns to bring down former President Claudine Gay of Harvard and to attack DEI statements and programming, in part through the Manhattan Institute's model legislation, which he coauthored. Rufo's tweets from the time of the New College takeover warned that "public universities, which have been corrupted by woke nihilism, can be recaptured, restructured, and reformed." With the new board members at New College, Rufo bragged, "We are now over the walls and ready to transform higher education from within." Within months, the new board at New College fired the college's president and replaced her with a DeSantis ally at twice the pay, voted to deny five professors tenure, and received a vote of censure, with 80% of faculty voting in favor.[9] The following academic year, New College, which had been known as a liberal arts college with a small "quirky" student body, was rebranded in several ways. Its gender studies program was shut down (and its books thrown away);[10] a new classical curriculum was announced, modeled after that of Hillsdale College, a small Christian liberal arts school in Michigan; a "classical and Christian exam alternative to the SAT" was accepted for admission; and an unusually large class of 328 students was selected, including seventy freshman baseball players, all on scholarship. (The AAUP's report notes that the University of Florida has only thirty-seven scholarship baseball players in a student body that is ninety times larger.) Meanwhile, 27% of New College's students transferred away, and 40% of the faculty left. One person untroubled by the departures was Rufo, who'd earlier tweeted that "any faculty that prefer the old system of unfettered left-wing activism and a rubber-stamp board are free to self-select out." He was happy to drive away those not choosing to leave. In Rufo's words, quoted in the AAUP report:

> Despite recent shibboleths about "academic freedom," state legislators and boards of trustees have the right—the duty—to redirect, curtail, or close down academic programs in public universities that do not align with the mandate of the taxpayers who generously support them. . . . Yes, public university professors, such as those at New College, have a First Amendment right to promote gender pseudo-science—but they are not entitled to an unlimited state subsidy for that speech.[11]

The troubles in Florida—which have been a harbinger of things to come in other states and, more recently, in the second Trump administration—give a sharper edge to a question that's been hovering throughout this book. If I'm really a pluralist about university missions, am I bound to accept the new mission Governor DeSantis and Christopher Rufo have imposed at New College? And assuming the new mission is to be what DeSantis and Rufo might describe as an anti-woke college offering a classical education, should it not follow that DEI programs should be dismantled there, the curriculum and even department structure must change, admissions priorities need to shift, and faculty's inability or unwillingness to contribute to the mission should be considered in hiring, tenure, and advancement decisions?

Not exactly.

We need to accept that if a school's mission changes over time, corresponding changes in the curriculum, the budget, admissions priorities, and even, gradually, the composition of the faculty might also be necessary. In fact, since a university's mission is something deeper than its "mission statement," these actions and policies are much of what actually *constitute* a university's mission. It's not enough for the board to declare that New College is dedicated to providing a classical education if it then goes on to add few such classes, admit a wildly disproportionate number of baseball recruits, and establish "new majors in finance, communications, and sports psychology," which the new president said "will appeal to many of our newly admitted athletes."[12] Given its actions, it seems at this point that New College does not actually have an identifiable mission at all. Its institutional identity has been decimated, not transformed. And perhaps that was the goal.

Given all my talk of pluralism, it's worth repeating Stanley Fish's claim, quoted near the beginning of this book: "A university would still be one if all it contained were classrooms, a library, and facilities for research. A university would not be one if all it contained was a quad with some tables on it, a student union with a food court, an auditorium and a bowling alley, a gymnasium with a swimming pool and some climbing walls."[13] Being a pluralist about university missions doesn't require us to deny that universities are institutions dedicated to teaching and research. Eliminate either and we're no longer talking about a university. To say this, however, is to speak at an extraordinarily high level of generality. The pluralism appears when we zoom in and start focusing on the specific ways that teaching and research can be advanced, and on different views about what in the end makes teaching and research successful or valuable. This point is worth underscoring, because it provides a check on what kinds of mission-related decisions are appropriate at a university. Let's say, hypothetically, that DeSantis targeted New College not because he had better ideas for how it could successfully teach its students, but because attacking a school perceived as progressive would win him votes or gain him favor with a certain set of donors. Since, in this hypothetical, the reasons justifying the changes at New College would have nothing to do with improved teaching and research, those changes would be illegitimate.

Arguments against indoctrination at institutions of higher education take a similar form. If DeSantis's purpose in transforming New College were, say, to create a school that will produce more Republican voters, that would not be a transformation guided by a desire to improve teaching or research. Of course the same thing would be true for a school where the curriculum was chosen because of its potential to turn students into reliable voters for the Democrats. By contrast, producing an engaged citizenry might well be seen by some universities as part of their mission, and curricular reforms might be made to advance that teaching-related goal. (This would be a view about the *purpose* of teaching at the university level.)

Something meaningful follows from the weak limit just offered: if decisions about a university's mission should have a justification tied to teaching and research, it makes sense that people with expertise in teaching and research should be involved in those decisions.[14] This is the biggest reason why pluralism about university missions doesn't require us simply to accept DeSantis and Rufo's takeover of a school like New College—much less the censorship they've worked to impose on the rest of Florida's schools. When politicians unilaterally impose their vision of education from above, without the involvement of faculty or others who have expertise in teaching and research, they are flouting the core principles of academic freedom.

To put the same point positively rather than negatively, the answer to the question about how a university's opinions—the commitments and values that make up its mission—should be decided turns out to be: *through shared governance*. Shared governance doesn't mean that the faculty gets to make all the decisions. It's *shared* governance after all. As the AAUP described the concept decades ago, the basic idea behind shared governance is that the running of a university should be a joint effort among the governing board, administration, faculty, and, to a more limited extent, students and other members of the community.[15] The priority given to each of these groups should vary based on the kind of decision being made. So, for example, decisions about curriculum, appointments, and tenure should remain the primary responsibility of the faculty. Approval by the university's president or board may be required for decisions like tenure, but that approval should be made with great deference to the academic judgment of the faculty experts who were primarily responsible for judging the merits of the work. By contrast, budgetary decisions and fundraising are the primary responsibility of the board and administration, though consultation with faculty to get input on the university's needs and goals is still important. The point is that even when some group, such as the governing board, has formal authority over some matter like tenure or institutional policies, collaboration and sometimes deference is needed to respect the distinctive capacities of the different groups that make up a university. It's a process that's messy, slow, and purposefully (or at least productively) inefficient.[16] As a result, it's a lowercase-*c* conservative force in American universities, where the collaboration and dialogue necessary for big decisions ensures that tradition won't be abandoned rashly.

The AAUP's 1966 governance statement—itself a joint effort with the American Council on Education and the Association of Governing Boards of Universities and Colleges—claims that "the objectives of an institution and the nature, range, and pace of its efforts"—what I would call the university's *mission*—"is shaped by the institutional charter or by law, by tradition and historical development, by the present needs of the community of the institution, and by the professional aspirations and standards of those directly involved in its work." The coordination of faculty, board, and administration is needed to determine the school's educational goals, since "unilateral effort can lead to confusion or conflict." Once those goals are set, the statement says, "it becomes the responsibility primarily of the faculty to determine the appropriate curriculum and procedures of student instruction."[17]

The division of labor, the overlapping responsibilities, and the voluntary deference that characterize shared governance when it comes to setting a university's objectives, then deciding what actions best advance them, also offer lessons about who should be responsible for what universities *say*—a topic that wasn't fully addressed in chapter 3. Given that institutional statements are often meant to respond to issues of the moment, universities will generally speak through their presidents. There may be little time or desire for faculty meetings and consultation before something is said about a tragedy in the local community, a controversy that is causing disruption on campus, or many of the other things, internal and external, that are most likely to provoke institutional statements. A university president may also have a uniquely broad vantage point from which to decide whether speaking out on a particular topic is wise. Only the president has responsibility for faculty, staff, and students; for relationships with trustees, alums, donors, and political officials; and for facilities, the budget, and the endowment. Since institutional statements can affect all of these, it makes sense that a university's president generally would be expected to take the lead in speaking for the institution.

But as with most choices made through shared governance, taking the lead doesn't mean acting alone. When there is time for consultation—whether with the faculty, trustees, or others with expertise or a unique perspective on the subject at hand—there is little reason for the administration not to engage. And when that *doesn't* happen, when mutual respect breaks down and shared governance gets ignored, there should be mechanisms in place for groups like the faculty to speak on their own behalf. This is one of the reasons why departmental statements are potentially so important. Although ideally the faculty would be consulted to help shape institutional statements, there are times when the views of the faculty, or of a department or school, will diverge from that of the president, who is entrusted to speak on the university's behalf. Sometimes faculty might even want to use their collective voice to say that the university's president has lost their confidence. Doing so, even the threat of doing so, provides a powerful incentive for administrators to recommit to shared governance going forward.[18]

Aspirational as it may be, shared governance is the best answer we have to the question of how a university's opinions should be formed. It's a major part of what's been lacking in the governmental meddling with university affairs that has grown so pervasive in recent years.[19] Shared governance is what helps ensure that a university's mission reflects the aspirations of its particular community, which is largely what makes universities' varied missions worthy of respect in the first place.

This emphasis on shared governance underscores a communal side of academic freedom that often gets lost in the individualist accounts of academic freedom that we hear most loudly these days. The Kalven Report's focus on the freedom of individual scholars disregards the collective voice of the faculty, and the University of Chicago is hardly known for its faculty governance.[20] Similarly, FIRE's focus on expanding what can be said on university campuses does little to ensure that universities as we've known them will continue to exist. The freedom of faculty to say or research anything they choose doesn't do much good if their administration or legislature decides, without faculty input, to shut down their entire department or school.[21] Decisions like these have to be made with the benefit of the collective faculty's expertise, or else the promise of academic freedom will prove hollow.

Even accepting the need for shared governance in our universities, several challenges remain. I'll end by mentioning three.

First is the problem of dealing with the government. The AAUP's 1966 statement argues that shared governance is needed not just for internal deliberation about a university's mission, but also for successfully responding to and integrating *outside* "voices and forces." Shared governance helps universities present a united front to "governmental authorities, at all levels, [who] play a part in the making of important decisions in academic policy."[22] For all my talk of academic freedom as a freedom from external constraint, we have seen example after example—from gubernatorial board appointments and funding conditions to antidiscrimination laws and judicial orders—of state actors putting a thumb on the balance of values that make up a university's mission. Some of these interventions are simply wrong as a legal matter. The judicial opinions I described in chapter 5 fall into this category, as do many of the laws, just mentioned, that certain states have passed to control what gets taught in university classrooms. But other forms of government intervention aren't as obviously illegal—even if some are extremely bad ideas.

The toughest contemporary examples are the choices made by state politicians, and more recent attempts by federal officials, to cut off university funding or to fund specific new programs of their own choosing. To date, many of the funding cuts have been unconstitutionally retaliatory and viewpoint discriminatory, and the Trump administration has repeatedly violated the procedural protections federal law provides universities before certain forms of funding can be cut.[23] Assuming that universities stand up for themselves and sue, courts are likely to overturn these cuts, just as they've struck down the censorship laws that some states have passed to skew what individual professors can teach. Adding programs may prove more secure than cutting them. Even I have to admit that funding new schools and centers can potentially expand the variety of educational opportunities that a pluralist account of universities would seem to endorse. But these additions can also skew the content of what gets taught and thereby count as a threat to academic freedom. When Florida pours money into something like the Hamilton Center for Classical and Civic Education at the University of Florida[24] or the board at the University of North Carolina creates a School of Civic Life there,[25] the overall mission of those universities is being changed without the kind of meaningful faculty input that shared governance would require. A *legal* challenge to this kind of meddling by politicians may prove difficult, but that just means that a political fight is needed instead. Universities and their faculties will need a voice if they're to succeed in that fight.

This first challenge I've described for shared governance is external: the challenge of working with political officials and other funding providers outside the university, whose goals for higher education might differ from those of experts in the field. The second and third challenges come from within.

Shared governance is expensive. This is the second challenge. It's costly in the sense that I described a moment ago: inefficiency is a built-in feature, finding consensus or compromise takes time, and change is purposefully made difficult. But those are not its only costs. Truly shared governance requires faculty who are both invested in the future of their institution and secure enough to push back against the administrators and board members who share in the institution's governance. This requires significant material commitments. Chapter 2 briefly raised the issue of adjunctification—the turn from a mostly tenured or tenure-track professoriate to an increasing reliance on scholars who don't have permanent appointments. According to the AAUP, "In fall 2022 less than one-third of faculty in US colleges and universities were on tenure lines, and 68 percent of faculty held contingent appointments, compared with about 47 percent in fall 1987. Nearly half (49 percent) of US faculty members were employed part time in fall 2022."[26] Aside from not often having the economic security or time to participate in shared governance, contingent faculty have less incentive to devote their energy to shaping institutions that could end their employment at any time. Speaking boldly against the people responsible for renewing contracts is hardly in the best interest of most adjunct professors. Robust shared governance thus becomes one of the many casualties of the casualization of the academic workforce. The joint effort of faculty, board, and administration necessarily gets weakened when "the faculty" consists of only a third of the people who are actually carrying out a university's teaching mission.

The point here is that shared governance requires tangible support from the institution. To work as it should, it requires investment in full-time faculty, and it requires employment protections for teachers and researchers when they engage in intramural speech, even when trustees or administrators find it inconvenient.[27] If those investments and protections aren't given, they need to be demanded. The unionization of faculty and graduate workers and the unprecedented size and effectiveness of their recent strikes point to what will be an increasingly necessary path going forward.[28]

This gets us to the third and final challenge: this one for those of us privileged to have one of the permanent positions still available in the academy. Shared governance requires our effort and bravery. To some, this may sound silly. How much courage does it take for some of the only workers in America who enjoy security of employment—the protections of tenure—to speak their mind about the direction their institution should take? Yet even tenured faculty have reasons to be timid. They may have kept their heads down as they navigated the tenure process and never raised them afterward. They may fear, reasonably or not, the effect that dissent could have on their advancement or salary. They may just not want to devote their time to service work and shared governance, when teaching and, especially, research are more likely to get rewarded. But if shared governance is the best answer to the question of how a university's opinions should be formed, faculty's willingness to participate bravely in that process is essential. If faculty don't step up to help determine their institution's mission, recent history makes clear that others surely will. Faculty participation is what best ensures that expertise in teaching and research will guide the inevitably opinionated decisions that ultimately get made about what our universities are to be.

: : :

To return one more time, then, to neutrality, the myth at the heart of this book:

Kalvenism—the leading argument for institutional neutrality in higher education—rests on a snowflake account of academic freedom. Institutional silence is necessary, it's said, because faculty dissent will necessarily melt in the face of a university that expresses any opinions of its own. Were faculty truly so fragile, there would be little hope for shared governance, depending as it does on faculty pushback against administrators and board members who might otherwise run universities little differently than any other corporation.

To reject the view of faculty as snowflakes is to expect that they'll be hardy enough to persevere in their work even when their institution expresses a view they don't share. And happily, it's that very hardiness—the willingness to dissent, to organize, and to do the sometimes hard work of shared governance—that opens the possibility that faculty might help *determine* the opinions their university ends up expressing, whether in what it says or, just as importantly, in what it chooses to do.

Acknowledgments

Countless people have shared their knowledge and experience with me, shaping the way I think about the topics covered in this book. Many of them have tried to convince me that the way I think about these topics is wrong. A couple dozen people were generous enough to read chunks or even all of this book and offer comments. I'm incredibly grateful to them. Other people might actually be surprised to find themselves mentioned here; we don't always know the influence we've had. I'm grateful to them too.

Here, then, is a list of people who have influenced this book in one way or another. It's offered without comment about the nature of their influence, so that none can be held responsible for how the book turned out:

Raquel Aldana, Musa al-Gharbi, Ty Alper, Vik Amar, Will Beekman, Sigal Ben-Porath, Ash Bhagwat, Marc Blitz, Paul Brest, Alan Brownstein, Suzanne Buffam, Guido Calabresi, Susan Carlson, Ryan Chen, Jack Chin, Jessica Clarke, Carlos Cortes, Ryan Davis, Michelle Deutchman, Erin DeWitt, Elizabeth Branch Dyson, Chris Elmendorf, Katie Eyer, Tom Ginsburg, Jonathan Glater, Lydia Goehr, Ralph Hexter, Rana Jaleel, Courtney Joslin, Anil Kalhan, Ari Kelman, Chimène Keitner, Randall Kennedy, Amna Khalid, Matt Lane, Carlton Larson, Brian Leiter, Emily Levine, Shen-yi Liao, Risa Lieberwitz, Erich Hatala Matthes, Robert May, Mollie McFee, Jonathan and Josh Meltzer, Michael Meranze, Jacqueline Pfeffer Merrill, Shannon Minter, Jonathan Neufeld, Beth Niehaus, Julius Oatts, Chris Odinet, Tom O'Donnell, Liesl Olson, Robert Post, Lisa Pruitt, Gali Racabi, Daniel Rauch, Jonathan Rauch, Eric Rauchway, Chicu Reddy, Hank Reichman, Judith Resnik, Maura Roessner, Darren Rosenblum,

Jeffrey Sachs, Leticia Saucedo, Joan Wallach Scott, Amanda Shanor, Darien Shanske, Robert Shibley, Rick Shweder, Jeff Snyder, Mike Sweeney, Emerson Sykes, Aaron Tang, Eugene Volokh, Barbara Wilson, and John K. Wilson.

I also learned a great deal from audiences at the Freedom of Expression Scholars Conference at Yale Law School (twice), the UC Davis Forum on the Public University and the Social Good, Stanford's Restoring Inclusive Critical Discourse Workshop, the Executive Symposium on Institutional Speech and the Collegiate Mission run by the Bipartisan Policy Center and the UC National Center for Free Speech and Civic Engagement, *Drexel Law Review*'s 2023 symposium, the Civil Procedure Workshop at Northwestern Pritzker School of Law, the UC Center Sacramento, the University of Washington, the Medical College of Wisconsin, and from debates sponsored by FIRE, the Federalist Society, Open to Debate, and Heterodox Academy. My original work on diversity statements was supported by a fellowship from the UC National Center for Free Speech and Civic Engagement.

Several generations of research assistants helped me write this book, either by working on it directly or by providing research for one of the articles that preceded it. Thanks and happy futures to Noa Batlan, Dillon Beckett, Jacob Chabot, Oscar Contreras, Emily Dennis, Chester Dubov, Cobi Soda Furdek, Nicolas Mak-Wasek, Jack Mensik, Sydney Simon, Linda Tauscher, Tycho Toothaker, Cree Townsend, and Kelli Ward. My deans and senior associate deans at UC Davis School of Law—Kevin Johnson and Jessica Berg, Afra Afsharipour and Donna Shestowsky—could not have been more supportive of me and my work.

: : :

My husband, Matt Lane, has worked to make higher education better for many years longer than I have. When I finished my dissertation two decades ago, he wondered where his dedication was. I said he'd have to wait until I wrote something that made me proud enough to dedicate to him. This is for you, Matty.

Notes

Introduction

1. Representative Lisa McClain of Michigan said during the hearing that "talk is cheap, and we really need action . . . , not lip service." One person who *was* interested in what universities had said was Representative Kevin Kiley of California, who accused Harvard's President Claudine Gay of catering to "the forces of antisemitism . . . from your silence, from the carefully parsed statements[, and] from the Orwellian passive voice, and unfortunately that message was heard loud and clear by the forces of antisemitism on your campus and has reverberated across American higher education and seeped into our broader culture." US Congress, House of Representatives, Committee on Education and the Workforce, *Holding Campus Leaders Accountable and Confronting Antisemitism*, 118th Cong., 1st sess., December 5, 2023, 103, https://docs.house.gov/Committee/Calendar/ByEvent.aspx?EventId=116625.

2. US Congress, House of Representatives, Committee on Education and the Workforce, *Holding Campus Leaders Accountable and Confronting Antisemitism*, 49. For a description of responses to the hearing, see Adam Wren, "'Bud Light Moment': Stefanik Forces a Reckoning on the Left," *Politico*, December 11, 2023, https://www.politico.com/news/2023/12/11/stefanik-democrats-higher-education-00131193.

3. See US Congress, House of Representatives, Committee on Education and the Workforce, *Holding Campus Leaders Accountable and Confronting Antisemitism*, 67–68.

4. Noah Rothman, "Harvard Chooses DEI Over Academics," *National Review*, December 12, 2023, https://www.nationalreview.com/corner/harvard-choose-dei-over-academics/.

5. On the day of the hearing, Harvard donor Bill Ackman wrote on social media that the selection committee that chose Gay "would not consider a candidate who did not meet the DEI office's criteria." This, he wrote, "is not the right approach to identifying the best leaders for our most prestigious

universities. And it is also not good for those awarded the office of president who find themselves in a role that they would likely not have obtained were it not for a fat finger on the scale." Ackman concluded: "We are all shortly going to realize that the DEI era is the McCarthy era Part II." Bill Ackman (@BillAckman), "I learned from someone with first person knowledge of the @Harvard president search that the committee would not consider a candidate who did not meet the DEI office's criteria," X post, December 6, 2023, https://x.com/BillAckman/status/1732632488227303784. Christopher Rufo of the Manhattan Institute, who later took credit for bringing down President Gay, described her in the *Wall Street Journal* as "a scholar of not much distinction who climbed the ladder of diversity politics [and] built a DEI empire as a Harvard Dean." Christopher F. Rufo, "How We Squeezed Harvard to Push Claudine Gay Out," *Wall Street Journal: Opinion*, January 3, 2024, https://www.wsj.com/articles/how-we-squeezed-harvard-claudine-gay-firing-dei-antisemitism-culture-war-a6843c4c.

6. Jeffrey Flier, "Now Is the Time for Administrators to Embrace Neutrality," *Chronicle of Higher Education*, October 13, 2023, https://www.chronicle.com/article/now-is-the-time-for-administrators-to-embrace-neutrality; Steven Pinker, "A Five-Point Plan to Save Harvard from Itself," *Boston Globe: Opinion*, December 11, 2023, https://www.bostonglobe.com/2023/12/11/opinion/steven-pinker-how-to-save-universities-harvard-claudine-gay/ (pairing institutional neutrality with what he calls "DEI disempowerment"); Tom Ginsburg, "The Case for University Silence," *Persuasion*, October 25, 2023, https://www.persuasion.community/p/the-case-for-university-silence; Editorial Board, "Opinion: For Universities, the Less Said About Controversial Issues, the Better," *Washington Post: Opinion*, November 10, 2023, https://www.washingtonpost.com/opinions/2023/11/10/campus-israel-gaza-free-speech/.

7. Kalven Committee, *Report on the University's Role in Political and Social Action* (University of Chicago, 1967), https://provost.uchicago.edu/sites/default/files/documents/reports/KalvenRprt_0.pdf.

8. Christopher F. Rufo, Ilya Shapiro, and Matt Beienburg, *Abolish DEI Bureaucracies and Restore Colorblind Equality in Public Universities* (Manhattan Institute, 2023), https://media4.manhattan-institute.org/sites/default/files/model_dei_legislation013023.pdf; "Joint Statement: College and University Trustees and Regents Must Join Peers in Committing to Institutional Neutrality," Academic Freedom Alliance, Heterodox Academy, and Foundation for Individual Rights and Expression, last updated July 11, 2024, https://institutionalneutrality.org/.

9. For a list of examples, see Alex Arnold, *The Rising Tide of Statement Neutrality in Higher Education: How Universities Are Rethinking Institutional Speech* (Heterodox Academy, 2025), https://content.heterodoxacademy.org/uploads/HxA_Statement-Neutrality-Report_FINAL.pdf.

10. Stanley Fish, *Save the World on Your Own Time* (Oxford University Press, 2008), 17.

11. Obeying the First Amendment might seem like a tempting path to neutrality here, but this also fails. For one thing, the free speech clause only applies to public schools, so any private institutions that hew to its constraints do so by choice (at least outside California, which has its own rules). And even at public schools, the actual requirements of the Constitution in most concrete cases are so deeply underdetermined and seldom tested that judgment calls—which is to say, non-neutral choices—about how unfettered speech should be on campus will nearly always be necessary. Chapter 5 takes up this issue in more detail.

12. Exec. Order No. 13950, 3 C.F.R. 60683 (2020), https://www.federalregister.gov/documents/2020/09/28/2020-21534/combating-race-and-sex-stereotyping. See also Eesha Pendharkar, "Legal Challenges to 'Divisive Concepts' Laws: An Update," *Education Week*, October 17, 2022, https://www.edweek.org/policy-politics/legal-challenges-to-divisive-concepts-laws-an-update/2022/10.

13. Valerie Strauss, "More Than 160 Law Deans Denounce Attempted Insurrection and Effort to Decertify Election—but Don't Name Names," *Washington Post*, January 12, 2021, https://www.washingtonpost.com/education/2021/01/12/157-law-deans-denounce-attempted-insurrection-effort-decertify-election-dont-name-names/.

14. My pluralism about universities' missions—the varying commitments that both religious *and* secular universities might make alongside their commitment to academic and expressive freedom—owes a great deal to the work of my favorite colleague, Alan Brownstein, who once asked:

> Is it permissible to have a private secular university committed to moral principles that justify constraints on speech and belief? May a secular private university contend that its commitments to full racial and gender equality, reproductive autonomy, and the humanity and rights of members of the LGBTQ community are just as foundational and essential to its identity and purpose as religious orthodoxy is to a religious college? Is the goal of creating a nurturing and supportive environment grounded in these secular values less worthy of respect than the goal of creating a religiously supportive environment?

Alan Brownstein, "Making Sense of 'Orthodoxy' at Secular and Religious Colleges," *The Hill*, November 11, 2020, https://thehill.com/opinion/education/525463-making-sense-of-orthodoxy-at-secular-and-religious-colleges/.

15. David Labaree details how colleges and universities in the United States emerged not under the direction of a centralized authority as in Europe, but in response to market forces, which meant they had "to attract and retain students, position themselves in relation to competitors, adapt to changes in consumer demand and social conditions, and creatively pursue other forms

of outside revenue." David F. Labaree, *A Perfect Mess: The Unlikely Ascendancy of American Higher Education* (University of Chicago Press, 2017), 8. This led to a stratified system of different types of colleges, from Ivy League research institutions to community colleges to religious schools. Instead of following some master plan, American universities have often stumbled upon their distinctive organization and purpose(s), Labaree argues. American higher education has been "rigid in its focus on the need to survive, while being quite flexible over the years about how to justify its existence in the face of changing contexts and constituencies" (182).

16. Stanley Fish, "Free Speech Is Not an Academic Value," *Chronicle of Higher Education*, March 20, 2017, https://www.chronicle.com/article/Free-Speech-Is-Not-an-Academic/239536.

17. For a subtle and spirited defense of this variation, see Judith Jarvis Thomson, "Ideology and Faculty Selection," *Law and Contemporary Problems* 53, no. 3 (Summer 1990): 165:

> Reasonable people both on and off campus will disagree with the conclusions we reach at Such and Such College, whether about assessments of fields or educational mission. And different schools—even different schools that hope to attract similar student bodies—will therefore offer different programs. But that can hardly be regarded as ground for complaint; quite to the contrary, it is a sign of health in the nation's educational system that it allows for these differences. I may think your views on such matters grossly mistaken, idiotic in fact, and you may think the same of mine; we should both welcome the variety in institutional programs that grows out of our differences.

18. "DEI Legislation Tracker," *Chronicle of Higher Education*, last updated June 27, 2025, https://www.chronicle.com/article/here-are-the-states-where-lawmakers-are-seeking-to-ban-colleges-dei-efforts.

19. Brian Soucek, "Diversity Statements," *UC Davis Law Review* 55, no. 4 (2022): 2041–48; Brian Soucek, "How to Protect DEI Requirements from Legal Peril," *Chronicle of Higher Education*, May 24, 2022, https://www.chronicle.com/article/how-to-protect-dei-requirements-from-legal-peril.

20. Robert Maranto and James D. Paul, *Other Than Merit: The Prevalence of Diversity, Equity, and Inclusion Statements in University Hiring* (American Enterprise Institute, 2021), https://www.aei.org/wp-content/uploads/2021/11/Other-than-merit-The-prevalence-of-diversity-equity-and-inclusion-statements-in-university-hiring.pdf?x85095.

21. John W. Boyer, *Academic Freedom and the Modern University: The Experience of the University of Chicago* (The College of the University of Chicago, 2016), 4, https://news.uchicago.edu/sites/default/files/attachments/Academic_Freedom_V1.pdf: "The University of Chicago functions as a bellwether for

these debates [over academic freedom in the United States] because 'academic freedom is part of the DNA' of our institution" (quoting Jonathan R. Cole, "The Central Dogma of a Great University," in *Toward a More Perfect University* [Public Affairs, 2016]); Boyer, 4: referring to the University of Chicago's "uniqueness in this regard"; Boyer, 5: claiming that the committee's report outlining the so-called Chicago Principles both "underscores Chicago's historical commitments, [and] it has also been an important intervention in higher education generally, with the faculties of other major institutions of higher education, including Princeton University, Purdue University, and the University of Minnesota, deciding to associate with our statement." FIRE, "Adopting the Chicago Statement," Foundation for Individual Rights and Expression, https://www.thefire.org/research-learn/adopting-chicago-statement.

22. "If there be time to expose through discussion the falsehood and fallacies, to avert the evil by the processes of education, the remedy to be applied is more speech, not enforced silence." Whitney v. California, 274 U.S. 357, 377 (1927) (Brandeis, J., concurring).

23. Musa al-Gharbi describes these episodic events, plus an even older iteration from the 1930s, in chapter 2 of *We Have Never Been Woke: The Cultural Contradictions of a New Elite* (Princeton University Press, 2024).

24. AAUP, *Report of a Special Committee: Political Interference and Academic Freedom in Florida's Public Higher Education System* (AAUP, 2023), https://www.aaup.org/file/AAUP_Florida_final.pdf.

Chapter One

The slogan is adapted from an essay by law professor Stacy Hawkins, "DEI Statements Are Not About Ideology. They're About Accountability," *Chronicle of Higher Education*, April 19, 2024, https://www.chronicle.com/article/dei-statements-are-not-about-ideology-theyre-about-accountability: "DEI accountability should be no more suspect than these other measures of operational effectiveness. If . . . 'facilitating a more open and welcoming environment for everyone' is the aim, measuring faculty commitment to that aim is not a political litmus test. It is a performance evaluation."

1. Heather Mac Donald, "Op-Ed: UCLA's Infatuation with Diversity Is a Costly Diversion from Its True Mission," *Los Angeles Times: Opinion*, September 2, 2018, https://www.latimes.com/opinion/op-ed/la-oe-mac-donald-diversity-ucla-20180902-story.html.

2. Christopher F. Rufo, Ilya Shapiro, and Matt Beienburg, *Abolish DEI Bureaucracies and Restore Colorblind Equality in Public Universities* (Manhattan Institute, 2023), https://media4.manhattan-institute.org/sites/default/files/model_dei_legislation013023.pdf.

3. Christopher F. Rufo (@realchrisrufo), "We have successfully frozen their brand—'critical race theory'—into the public conversation and are steadily driving up negative perceptions," X post, March 15, 2021, https://x.com/realchrisrufo/status/1371540368714428416; Benjamin Wallace-Wells, "How a Conservative Activist Invented the Conflict Over Critical Race Theory," *New Yorker*, June 18, 2021, https://www.newyorker.com/news/annals-of-inquiry/how-a-conservative-activist-invented-the-conflict-over-critical-race-theory; Michael Kruse, "DeSantis' Culture Warrior: 'We Are Now Over the Walls,'" *Politico: Magazine*, March 24, 2023, https://www.politico.com/news/magazine/2023/03/24/chris-rufo-desantis-anti-woke-00088578; Ian Ward, "Q & A: We Sat Down with the Conservative Mastermind Behind Claudine Gay's Ouster," *Politico: Magazine*, January 3, 2024, https://www.politico.com/news/magazine/2024/01/03/christopher-rufo-claudine-gay-harvard-resignation-00133618.

4. Lauren Lumpkin, "Incoming Georgetown Law Administrator Apologizes After Tweets Dean Called 'Appalling,'" *Washington Post*, January 27, 2022, https://www.washingtonpost.com/education/2022/01/27/georgetown-law-ilya-shapiro-tweets/.

5. "DEI Legislation Tracker," *Chronicle of Higher Education*, last updated June 27, 2025, https://www.chronicle.com/article/here-are-the-states-where-lawmakers-are-seeking-to-ban-colleges-dei-efforts.

6. Ryan Quinn, "MIT Will Stop Asking Faculty Applicants for Diversity Statements," *Inside Higher Ed*, May 8, 2024, https://www.insidehighered.com/news/quick-takes/2024/05/08/mit-stops-asking-faculty-applicants-diversity-statements.

7. Jeremy W. Peters, "Is This the End for Mandatory D.E.I. Statements?" *New York Times*, June 6, 2024, https://www.nytimes.com/2024/06/06/us/politics/dei-statements-harvard-massachusetts-institute-of-technology.html.

8. "Academic Freedom Alliance DEI Statement," Academic Freedom Alliance, August 22, 2022, https://academicfreedom.org/wp-content/uploads/2022/08/AFA-DEI-Statement-081822.pdf.

9. For a study of the overlapping funding sources of many of the advocacy groups discussed below, see Ralph Wilson and Isaac Kamola, *Free Speech and Koch Money: Manufacturing a Campus Culture War* (Pluto Press, 2021); and Isaac Kamola, *Manufacturing Backlash: Right-Wing Think Tanks and Legislative Attacks on Higher Education, 2021–2023* (American Association of University Professors and Center for the Defense of Academic Freedom, 2024), https://www.aaup.org/file/Manufacturing_Backlash_final_1.pdf.

10. FIRE, "Letter to Bucks County Community College," Foundation for Individual Rights and Expression, February 22, 2001, https://www.thefire.org/research-learn/letter-bucks-county-community-college.

11. "FIRE Letter to Virginia Polytechnic Institute and State University Board of Visitors," Foundation for Individual Rights and Expression, September 14,

2009, https://www.thefire.org/research-learn/fire-letter-virginia-polytechnic-institute-and-state-university-board-visitors. For a more recent version of the argument, see "FIRE Statement on the Use of Diversity, Equity, and Inclusion Criteria in Faculty Hiring and Evaluation," Foundation for Individual Rights and Expression, https://www.thefire.org/research-learn/fire-statement-use-diversity-equity-and-inclusion-criteria-faculty-hiring-and. First Amendment scholar Eugene Volokh offers a slightly different version of this thought experiment, imagining universities in a wartime United States asking faculty about their contributions to the war effort. Eugene Volokh, "Do University Diversity Statement Requirements Violate the Constitution?" *The Volokh Conspiracy*, August 30, 2022, https://reason.com/volokh/2022/08/30/do-university-diversity-statement-requirements-violate-the-constitution/.

12. FIRE, "Letter to Bucks County Community College" (quoting AAUP, *1940 Statement of Principles on Academic Freedom and Tenure* [American Association of University Professors, 1940], https://www.aaup.org/report/1940-statement-principles-academic-freedom-and-tenure).

13. Abigail Thompson, "The University's New Loyalty Oath: Required 'Diversity and Inclusion' Statements Amount to a Political Litmus Test for Hiring," *Wall Street Journal*, December 19, 2019, https://www.wsj.com/articles/the-universitys-new-loyalty-oath-11576799749.

14. S.B. 958, 2023 Leg., Reg. Sess. (Fla. 2023), https://legiscan.com/FL/text/S0958/id/2757960:

> A political loyalty test includes compelling, requiring, or soliciting a person to identify commitment to or to make a statement of personal belief in support of: a. Any ideology or movement that promotes the differential treatment of a person or a group of persons based on race or ethnicity, including an initiative or a formulation of diversity, equity, and inclusion beyond upholding the equal protection of the laws guaranteed by the Fourteenth Amendment to the United States Constitution or a theory or practice that holds that systems or institutions upholding the equal protection of the laws guaranteed by the Fourteenth Amendment of the United States Constitution are racist, oppressive, or otherwise unjust; or b. A specific partisan, political, or ideological set of beliefs.

H.B. 5127, 88th Leg., R.S. (Tex. 2023), https://legiscan.com/TX/bill/HB5127/2023.

15. Goldwater Institute and James G. Martin Center for Academic Renewal, "Model Legislation: End Political Litmus Tests in Education Act," James G. Martin Center for Academic Renewal, February 8, 2022, https://www.jamesgmartin.center/2022/02/model-legislation-end-political-litmus-tests-in-education-act/.

The Goldwater/Martin legislation would prohibit public universities from basing admission or promotion on "political tests," defined to include a compelled or solicited "statement of personal belief in support of any ideology or movement . . . [t]hat promotes the differential treatment of any individual or groups of individuals based on race or ethnicity." This in turn includes "any initiative or formulation of diversity, equity and inclusion beyond upholding the equal protection of the laws guaranteed by the Fourteenth Amendment of the United States Constitution."

16. John O. McGinnis, "The University of California's New Loyalty Oath," *Law & Liberty*, October 30, 2018, https://lawliberty.org/the-university-of-californias-new-loyalty-oath/.

17. Richard A. Epstein, "The Civil Rights Juggernaut," *University of Illinois Law Review* 2020, no. 5 (2020): 1541–70.

18. Brian Leiter, "The Legal Problem with Diversity Statements," *Chronicle of Higher Education*, March 13, 2020, https://www.chronicle.com/article/the-legal-problem-with-diversity-statements/.

19. Brian Leiter, "Berkeley 'Diversity Statements' in Action in a Life Sciences Search," *Leiter Reports: A Philosophy Blog*, December 31, 2019, https://leiterreports.typepad.com/blog/2019/12/berkeley-diversity-statements-in-action-in-a-life-sciences-search.html; Brian Leiter, "How Does Berkeley Evaluate 'Diversity' Statements from Faculty Candidates?," *Leiter Reports: A Philosophy Blog*, December 1, 2019, https://leiterreports.typepad.com/blog/2019/12/how-does-berkeley-evaluate-diversity-statements-from-faculty-candidates.html; Brian Leiter, "Were You Rejected in One of the University of California Job Searches Utilizing the Unlawful 'Diversity Statements'?," *Leiter Reports: A Philosophy Blog*, January 28, 2020, https://leiterreports.typepad.com/blog/2020/01/were-you-rejected-in-one-of-the-university-of-california-job-searches-utilizing-the-unlawful-diversi.html; Brian Leiter, "While 'Diversity Statements' Are Being Used System-Wide in the University of California . . . ," *Leiter Reports: A Philosophy Blog*, January 7, 2020, https://leiterreports.typepad.com/blog/2020/01/while-diversity-statements-are-being-used-system-wide-in-the-university-of-california.html.

20. Second Am. Compl., *Haltigan v. Drake*, No. 5:23-cv-2437-NC (N.D. Cal. 2024); J. D. Haltigan, "My Diversity, Equity, & Inclusion (DEI) Statement for a Recent Academic Job Posting," *Multilevel Mailer*, February 23, 2023, https://www.jdhaltigan.com/p/my-diversity-equity-and-inclusion. Haltigan also brought a second constitutional claim based on the so-called "unconstitutional conditions doctrine." For reasons that are too wonky to explore in detail, this amounts to the same thing as the viewpoint discrimination claim. Briefly: the government puts "unconstitutional conditions" on a benefit like a job when it uses the job as leverage to coerce people to speak or act in ways the government wants them to *outside* of the job. But as I'll explain later in this chapter, whether or not diversity contributions are part of the job ends up

being the crux of viewpoint discrimination claims as well. The two claims should stand or fall together.

21. Jeffrey Flier (@jflier): "As a dean of a major academic institution, I could not have said this. But I will now. Requiring such statements in applications for appointments and promotions is an affront to academic freedom, and diminishes the true value of diversity, equity of inclusion by trivializing it." X post, November 10, 2018, https://x.com/jflier/status/1061400170515054593.

22. Robert Shibley, "UCLA Diversity Requirement Threatens Academic Freedom, Trust in Academia," Foundation for Individual Rights and Expression, November 9, 2018, https://www.thefire.org/news/ucla-diversity-requirement-threatens-academic-freedom-trust-academia; AAUP, *1915 Declaration of Principles on Academic Freedom and Academic Tenure* (American Association of University Professors, 1915), https://www.aaup.org/NR/rdonlyres/A6520A9D-0A9A-47B3-B550-C006B5B224E7/0/1915Declaration.pdf:

> To the degree that professional scholars, in the formation and promulgation of their opinions, are, or by the character of their tenure appear to be, subject to any motive other than their own scientific conscience and a desire for the respect of their fellow experts, to that degree the university teaching profession is corrupted; its proper influence upon public opinion is diminished and vitiated; and society at large fails to get from its scholars, in an unadulterated form, the peculiar and necessary service which it is the office of the professional scholar to furnish.

23. "Solidarity in Pursuit of Truth," Academic Freedom Alliance, https://academicfreedom.org/; Stuart Taylor Jr., "Academic Freedom Alliance: Q&A with Keith Whittington," Princetonians for Free Speech, March 8, 2021, https://princetoniansforfreespeech.org/blogs/news/academic-freedom-alliance-q-a-with-keith-whittington?_pos=1&_sid=f73f92bf4&_ss=r.

24. Taylor, "Academic Freedom Alliance: Q&A with Keith Whittington."

25. "Academic Freedom Alliance DEI Statement."

26. Douglas Haynes, "UCI Inclusive Excellence Career Eco-System: A Pilot Program," UC Irvine, Irvine, CA, April 26, 2019, https://drive.google.com/file/d/1ZLzYNm4HC5Q66YE4WEE5U92C6r7n8IeE/view; "UCI Office of Inclusive Excellence," University of California, Irvine, https://inclusion.uci.edu/.

27. Bob Blauner, *Resisting McCarthyism: To Sign or Not to Sign California's Loyalty Oath* (Stanford University Press, 2009), xiii. For background on the loyalty oath era, see AAUP, "Academic Freedom and Tenure in the Quest for National Security: Report of a Special Committee of the American Association of University Professors," *AAUP Bulletin* 42, no. 1 (Spring 1956): 49–107; and Ellen W. Schrecker, *No Ivory Tower: McCarthyism and the Universities* (Oxford University Press, 1986).

28. University of California Board of Regents, Bylaw 40.3(a), September 27, 2018, https://regents.universityofcalifornia.edu/governance/bylaws/bl40.html#bl40.3; see also Brian Soucek, "Diversity Statements," *UC Davis Law Review* 55, no. 4 (2022): 2043.

29. Vogel v. County of Los Angeles, 68 Cal.2d 18, 23 (1967) (citing Elfbrandt v. Russell, 384 U.S. 11, 17–19 (1966) and Keyishian v. Bd. of Regents of Univ. of State of N.Y., 385 U.S. 589, 589 (1967)).

30. The Academic Senate at the University of California—after collaborative efforts by the faculty's Committee on Academic Freedom and its Committee on Affirmative Action, Diversity, and Equity—emphasized exactly this when it revised its official recommendations on the use of diversity statements in 2022: "DEI statements should focus on actions, not beliefs. . . . DEI statements should provide faculty and faculty applicants the opportunity to describe how they have advanced, or sincerely plan to advance, the University's commitment to diversity and equal opportunity, regardless of their own views about that commitment." University of California Academic Senate, "The Use of Contributions to Diversity, Equity, and Inclusion (DEI) Statements for Academic Positions at the University of California," April 27, 2022, https://senate.universityofcalifornia.edu/_files/reports/rh-division-chairs-recommendations-dei-statements.pdf. Seldom do critics or reporters talking about UC's use of DEI statements note the actual content of the university's official policies and guidance documents on the subject. For one prominent example, see Michael Powell, "D.E.I. Statements Stir Debate on College Campuses," *New York Times*, September 12, 2023, https://www.nytimes.com/2023/09/08/us/ucla-dei-statement.html.

31. PBS Utah, "Governor's Monthly News Conference | December 2023," YouTube, December 20, 2023, video, 1:08:20, https://www.youtube.com/watch?v=mpX6ZKxl2NY, 32:43. Even the *New Yorker* has taken up Governor Cox's framing: a 2025 article incorrectly summed up diversity statements as "essentially a pledge from job candidates to promote diversity, equity, and inclusion." Emma Green, "What Comes After D.E.I.?," *New Yorker*, April 14, 2025, https://www.newyorker.com/magazine/2025/04/21/what-comes-after-dei.

32. John Tomasi, "Just Like MIT, Every University Should Reject Political 'Diversity Statements,'" Minding the Campus, July 2, 2024, https://www.mindingthecampus.org/2024/07/02/just-like-mit-every-university-should-reject-political-diversity-statements/.

33. Rosenberger v. Rector and Visitors of the University of Virginia, 515 U.S. 819 (1995); Matal v. Tam, 528 U.S. 218 (2017).

34. Erica Goldberg, "Good Orthodoxy and the Legacy of *Barnette*," *FIU Law Review* 13, no. 4 (2019): 653: "At public universities, viewpoint discrimination in hiring violates the First Amendment." Leiter, "The Legal Problem with Diversity Statements": "Government cannot, excluding a few exceptions such as political appointments, base a hiring decision on the speaker's political viewpoint."

35. University of California, "Appointment Procedures for Tenure Staff Changed; Political Test Barred," *University Bulletin* 17, no. 1 (1969): 159, https://babel.hathitrust.org/cgi/pt?id=uc1.31378008229687&seq=177; see also University of California Board of Regents, Standing Order 101.1(d), July 21, 2016, https://regents.universityofcalifornia.edu/regmeet/july21/g7attach8.pdf; University of California Board of Regents, Bylaw 40.3(a), September 27, 2018, https://regents.universityofcalifornia.edu/governance/bylaws/bl40.html#bl40.3; Soucek, "Diversity Statements," 2041–48.

36. Robert C. Post, "Subsidized Speech," *Yale Law Journal* 106, no. 1 (1996): 167 (emphasis added). Judith Jarvis Thomson makes a similar point, also about a chemistry department, though she imagines one that's considering a faculty candidate who denies the Holocaust. Judith Jarvis Thomson, "Ideology and Faculty Selection," *Law and Contemporary Problems* 53, no. 3 (Summer 1990): 171.

37. Robert Maranto and James D. Paul, *Other Than Merit: The Prevalence of Diversity, Equity, and Inclusion Statements in University Hiring* (American Enterprise Institute, 2021), https://www.aei.org/wp-content/uploads/2021/11/Other-than-merit-The-prevalence-of-diversity-equity-and-inclusion-statements-in-university-hiring.pdf?x85095.

38. George F. Will, "Higher Education's Mandatory Political Participation," *Washington Post*, March 11, 2020, https://www.washingtonpost.com/opinions/higher-educations-mandatory-political-participation/2020/03/10/7a119cf8-62fe-11ea-845d-e35b0234b136_story.html.

39. Daniel M. Ortner, "In the Name of Diversity: Why Mandatory Diversity Statements Violate the First Amendment and Reduce Intellectual Diversity in Academia," *Catholic University Law Review* 70, no. 4 (Fall 2021): 549.

40. Carrie Johnson, "New Research Could Help Nurses, Police Detect Bruises on People with Dark Skin," NPR, February 21, 2023, https://www.npr.org/2023/02/21/1158334975/new-research-could-help-nurses-police-detect-bruises-on-people-with-dark-skin.

41. Nicholas Alden Riggle, "Street Art: The Transfiguration of the Commonplaces," *Journal of Aesthetics and Art Criticism* 68, no. 3 (Summer 2010): 243–57; C. Thi Nguyen, *Games: Agency as Art* (Oxford University Press, 2020); Paul C. Taylor, *Black Is Beautiful: A Philosophy of Black Aesthetics* (Wiley Blackwell, 2016); Lydia Goehr, "Street Signs of Libation and Liberation," in *Red Sea, Red Square, Red Thread: A Philosophical Detective Story* (Oxford University Press, 2022), 514–45; Luvell Anderson, "Why So Serious? An Inquiry on Racist Jokes," *Journal of Social Philosophy* 54, no. 3 (2020): 370–84, https://doi.org/10.1111/josp.12384; Ted Cohen, *Jokes: Philosophical Thoughts on Joking Matters* (University of Chicago Press, 1999); Sherri Irvin, ed., *Body Aesthetics* (Oxford University Press, 2016); Dominic McIver Lopes, *Aesthetic Injustice* (Oxford University Press, 2024); "Cultural Appropriation," special issue, *British Journal of Aesthetics* 61, no. 3 (July 2021).

42. "Diversity Curriculum Grants," American Society for Aesthetics, https://aesthetics-online.org/page/CurriculumGrants.

43. "Rutgers Summer Institute for Diversity in Philosophy," Rutgers University Department of Philosophy, https://www.philosophy.rutgers.edu/summer-institute.

44. The Supreme Court, for example, has noted that the Virginia Military Institute's mission is "to produce educated and honorable men, prepared for the varied work of civil life, imbued with love of learning, confident in the functions and attitudes of leadership, possessing a high sense of public service, advocates of the American democracy and free enterprise system, and ready as citizen-soldiers to defend their country in time of national peril." United States v. Virginia, 518 U.S. 515, 521–22 (1996) (hereinafter VMI). Incredibly, Justice Scalia, dissenting to the court's insistence that women be included in this mission, claimed that *no public college* in Virginia would be worth funding "if they did *not* aim to create individuals 'imbued with love of learning, etc.,' right down to being ready 'to defend their country in time of national peril.'" VMI, 518 U.S. at 587 (Scalia, J., dissenting). Part of Scalia's "etc."—one of the aims he finds necessarily to justify public funding—is producing "advocates of the American democracy and free enterprise system." VMI, 518 U.S. at 586.

45. "Regents Policy 4400: Policy on University of California Diversity Statement," University of California Board of Regents, September 16, 2010, https://regents.universityofcalifornia.edu/governance/policies/4400.html.

46. AAUP, *1915 Declaration of Principles*." For excellent further reading on the AAUP's academic freedom policies, see Matthew W. Finkin and Robert C. Post, *For the Common Good: Principles of American Academic Freedom* (Yale University Press, 2009); Henry Reichman, *Understanding Academic Freedom* (Johns Hopkins University Press, 2025); and Joan Wallach Scott, *Knowledge, Power, and Academic Freedom* (Columbia University Press, 2019). For the historical context in which the 1915 Declaration came about, see Emily J. Levine, *Allies and Rivals: German-American Exchange and the Rise of the Modern University* (University of Chicago Press, 2021): 151–71; Walter Metzger, *Academic Freedom in the Age of the University* (Columbia University Press, 1961); and Hans-Joerg Tiede, *University Reform: The Founding of the American Association of University Professors* (Johns Hopkins University Press, 2015).

47. Keyishian v. Board of Regents of University of State of N.Y., 385 U.S. 589, 603 (1967).

48. For a magisterial review of the case law, and a valiant effort to derive from it a comprehensive constitutional theory of academic freedom, see David M. Rabban, *Academic Freedom: From Professional Norm to First Amendment Right* (Harvard University Press, 2024).

49. The University of California describes the academic freedom of faculty in Academic Personnel Manual (APM) section 010, University of California, "APM - 010: Academic Freedom," September 29, 2003, https://www.ucop.edu/academic-personnel-programs/_files/apm/apm-010.pdf; its extension to "non-faculty academic appointees" in APM section 011, University of

California, "APM - 011: Academic Freedom, Protection of Professional Standards, and Responsibilities of Non-Faculty Academic Appointees," February 1, 2020, https://www.ucop.edu/academic-personnel-programs/_files/apm/amp-011-issuance/apm-011.pdf; and corresponding academic responsibilities in APM section 015, University of California, "APM - 015: The Faculty Code of Conduct," September 23, 2020, https://www.ucop.edu/academic-personnel-programs/_files/apm/apm-015.pdf. The corresponding "freedom of scholarly inquiry" enjoyed by students is described in APM section 010, Appendix B, University of California, "APM - 010, Appendix B: Student Freedom of Scholarly Inquiry," September 14, 2009, https://www.ucop.edu/academic-personnel-programs/_files/apm/apm-010.pdf.

50. Conor Friedersdorf, in a thoughtful response to my earlier work on this topic, has objected that chemistry professors are the best of our options for evaluating chemistry research, but not necessarily for judging ideas about advancing diversity. Insofar as he's right, I think this is one area where seeking help from outside experts who study these issues more directly may be advisable. (We could imagine a similar dynamic when it comes to teaching, which very few university professors have been specifically trained to do.) Friedersdorf, like others, may also be imagining (and generalizing from) a subset of chemistry professors who haven't given DEI issues much thought, at least in comparison to colleagues of theirs who come from underrepresented or less traditional backgrounds. Conor Friedersdorf, "The Hypocrisy of Mandatory Diversity Statements," *Atlantic*, July 3, 2023, https://www.theatlantic.com/ideas/archive/2023/07/hypocrisy-mandatory-diversity-statements/674611/.

51. John Donvan, moderator, "Are DEI Mandates for University Faculties a Bad Idea?," debate between Randall Kennedy and Brian Soucek, Open to Debate, November 3, 2023, audio recording, 49:26, https://opentodebate.org/debate/are-dei-mandates-for-university-faculties-a-bad-idea/, at 17:12; Jeffrey Flier, "Against Diversity Statements," *Chronicle of Higher Education*, January 3, 2019, https://www.chronicle.com/article/against-diversity-statements/.

52. According to John Tomasi of Heterodox Academy, "'Diversity' is a hotly contested concept, and 'DEI' even more so. Asking for a commitment to such values, while leaving them undefined, has an inevitable chilling effect. Clearly there is a 'right' answer, so applicants on Left and Right must consider what it is—and how willing they are to parrot it back." Tomasi, "Just Like MIT, Every University Should Reject Political 'Diversity Statements.'"

53. John Cochrane, "Wokeademia," *Grumpy Economist: John Cochrane's Blog*, January 30, 2020, https://johnhcochrane.blogspot.com/2020/01/wokeademia.html.

54. US Congress, House of Representatives, Committee on Education and the Workforce, *Holding Campus Leaders Accountable and Confronting Antisemitism*, 118th Cong., 1st sess., 2023, 26–28, 43–44, 108–9, https://docs.house.gov/Committee/Calendar/ByEvent.aspx?EventId=116625.

55. Gertz v. Robert Welch, Inc., 418 U.S. 323, 339 (1974); see also Robert C. Post, *Democracy, Expertise, Academic Freedom: A First Amendment Jurisprudence for the Modern State* (Yale University Press, 2012).

56. Musa al-Gharbi, "Why Should We Care About Ideological Diversity in the Academy?" *Heterodox Academy*, May 23, 2018, https://heterodoxacademy.org/blog/why-should-we-care-about-ideological-diversity-in-the-academy-the-definitive-response/.

57. Steven M. Teles, "Beyond Academic Sectarianism," *National Affairs* 60 (Summer 2024), https://www.nationalaffairs.com/publications/detail/beyond-academic-sectarianism.

58. Kenji Yoshino, *Covering: The Hidden Assault on Our Civil Rights* (Random House, 2006).

59. In his surveys of nearly 5,000 US faculty on DEI statements, Nathan Honeycutt found: "The median number of times participants reported having served on a search committee to hire at the assistant professor rank was five (M=7.26, SD=7.39). But, very few reported evaluating a DEI statement as a part of serving on an assistant professor search committee (Median=1, M=2.61, SD=4.51), or when serving on a promotion committee (Median=0, M=2.21, SD=6.04)." Nathan Honeycutt, "Faculty Evaluations of DEI Statements for Academic Hiring," *PsyArXiv Preprints*, 2024, 34, https://doi.org/10.31234/osf.io/mwt5r.

60. For a stunning account of how reading a bunch of actual DEI statements can change someone's opinion about their worth, see Suzanne Penuel, "Why I'm a Convert to Diversity Statements," *Inside Higher Ed*, April 10, 2024, https://www.insidehighered.com/opinion/views/2024/04/10/why-im-convert-diversity-statements-opinion.

61. Plessy v. Ferguson, 163 U.S. 537 (1896). Contemporary equal protection law can be framed as a fight over how to read Justice Harlan's dissent in *Plessy*, the case that blessed the state-imposed race segregation that the Supreme Court finally overturned in *Brown v. Board of Education* in 1954. Conservatives focus on Justice Harlan's color-blindness language and would end nearly all explicit racial classification, while liberals, who tend to support race-conscious efforts to undo centuries of race-based subordination, focus on Harlan's previous two sentences: "In view of the Constitution, in the eye of the law, there is in this country no superior, dominant, ruling class of citizens. There is no caste here." For the most prominent recent example, compare the majority opinion and Justice Thomas's concurrence with Justice Sotomayor's dissenting opinion (joined by her two liberal colleagues) in Students for Fair Admissions, Inc. v. President & Fellows of Harvard Coll., 600 U.S. 181 (2023). First, Chief Justice Roberts, writing for the court: "Lost in the false pretense of judicial humility that the dissent espouses is a claim to power so radical, so destructive, that it required a Second Founding to undo. 'Justice Harlan knew better,' one of the dissents decrees. Indeed he did: [quoting *Plessy*]." Students

for Fair Admissions, 600 U.S. at 230. Second, Justice Thomas, endorsing the court's judgment: "All citizens of the United States, regardless of skin color, are equal before the law. . . . This was Justice Harlan's view in his lone dissent in *Plessy*, where he observed that '[o]ur Constitution is color-blind.' It was the view of the Court in *Brown*, which rejected 'any authority . . . to use race as a factor in affording educational opportunities.' And, it is the view adopted in the Court's opinion today, requiring 'the absolute equality of all citizens' under the law." Students for Fair Admissions, 600 U.S. at 233 (Thomas, J., concurring). Finally, Justice Sotomayor, with the counterargument: "It distorts the dissent in *Plessy* to advance a colorblindness theory." Students for Fair Admissions, 600 U.S. at 330 (Sotomayor, J., dissenting). "Justice Harlan explained in *Plessy* that the Louisiana law perpetuated a 'caste' system. . . . [A]ll knew that the law's purpose was not 'to exclude white persons from railroad cars occupied by blacks,' but 'to exclude colored people from coaches occupied by or assigned to white persons.'" Students for Fair Admissions, 600 U.S. at 326–27 (Sotomayor, J., dissenting).

62. Discrimination—Public Entities—Initiative Constitutional Amendment, 1996 Cal. Legis. Serv. Prop. 209 (codified as Cal. Const. art. I, § 31); Allows Diversity as a Factor in Public Employment, Education, and Contracting Decisions—Legislative Constitutional Amendment, 2020 Cal. Legis. Serv. Prop. 16 (rejected by voters, in general election of Nov. 3, 2020).

63. Ortner, "In the Name of Diversity," 552–53 (citing Heather Mac Donald, *The Diversity Delusion: How Race and Gender Pandering Corrupt the University and Undermine Our Culture* [St. Martin's Press, 2018], 35, 39).

64. Leiter, "Berkeley 'Diversity Statements' in Action in a Life Sciences Search."

65. University of California Office of the President, *Final Report on the 2016–17 Use of One-Time Funds to Support Best Practices in Equal Employment Opportunity in Faculty Employment: Report to the State Legislature Submitted by UC Office of the President*, November 22, 2017, 4, https://www.ucop.edu/operating-budget/_files/legreports/17-18/Final_2016-17UseofOne-timefundstoSupportBestPracticesinFacultyEmployment-Nov-15-17.docx.pdf; see also Susan Carlson, *The Art of Diversity: A Chronicle of Advancing the University of California Faculty Through Efforts in Diversity, Equity, and Inclusion, 2010–2022* (eScholarship Publishing, University of California, 2024), 73–76, https://doi.org/10.6074/D4159V.

66. Rebecca Heald and Mary Wildermuth, *Initiative to Advance Faculty Diversity, Equity and Inclusion in the Life Science at UC Berkeley Year End Summary Report: 2018–2019* (University of California, 2019), 3, https://math.berkeley.edu/~lott/lifesciences.pdf.

67. Matt Burgess, "It's Time to Stop the Double Talk Around Diversity Hiring," *Chronicle of Higher Education*, June 5, 2024, https://www.chronicle.com/article/its-time-to-stop-the-double-talk-around-diversity-hiring; Wilson Freeman, "For University of California Faculty, It's DEI or Die," *National Review*,

July 14, 2023, https://www.nationalreview.com/2023/07/for-university-of-california-faculty-its-dei-or-die/.

68. Gratz v. Bollinger, 539 U.S. 244, 305 (2003) (Ginsburg, J., dissenting): "If honesty is the best policy, surely Michigan's accurately described, fully disclosed College affirmative action program is preferable to achieving similar numbers through winks, nods, and disguises."

69. Adarand Constructors, Inc. v. Pena, 515 U.S. 200 (1995); City of Richmond v. J.A. Croson Co., 488 U.S. 469 (1989); Gratz v. Bollinger, 539 U.S. 244 (2003); Students for Fair Admissions, Inc. v. President & Fellows of Harvard Coll., 600 U.S. 181 (2023).

70. Parents Involved in Community Schools v. Seattle School District No. 1, 551 U.S. 701, 789 (2007) (Kennedy, J., concurring in part).

71. Fisher v. University of Texas at Austin, 579 U.S. 365 (2016).

72. Sonja Starr, "The Magnet School Wars and the History of Color Blindness," *Stanford Law Review* 76, no. 1 (January 2024), https://www.stanfordlawreview.org/print/article/the-magnet-school-wars-and-the-future-of-colorblindness/.

73. Students for Fair Admissions, Inc. v. President & Fellows of Harvard Coll., 600 U.S. 181, 230 (2023).

74. "A benefit to a student who overcame racial discrimination, for example, must be tied to that student's courage and determination. Or a benefit to a student whose heritage or culture motivated him or her to assume a leadership role or attain a particular goal must be tied to that student's unique ability to contribute to the university. In other words, the student must be treated based on his or her experiences as an individual—not on the basis of race." Students for Fair Admissions, Inc. v. President & Fellows of Harvard Coll., 600 U.S. 181, 230–31 (2023).

75. Susan Carlson, UC's former vice provost of Academic Personnel and Programs, tells this history in *The Art of Diversity*.

76. "Regents Policy 4400: Policy on University of California Diversity Statement," University of California Board of Regents, September 16, 2010, https://regents.universityofcalifornia.edu/governance/policies/4400.html. Importantly, the policy talks of diversity both in a broad sense—as referring to "the variety of personal experiences, values, and worldviews that arise from differences of culture and circumstance[, including] race, ethnicity, gender, age, religion, language, abilities/disabilities, sexual orientation, gender identity, socioeconomic status, and geographic region, and more"—as well as a more focused one: "The University particularly acknowledges the acute need to remove barriers to the recruitment, retention, and advancement of talented students, faculty, and staff from historically excluded populations who are currently underrepresented."

77. University of California, "APM 210-1 (d): Criteria for Appointment, Promotion, and Appraisal," in "Appointment and Promotion: APM - 210,"

March 25, 2024, https://www.ucop.edu/academic-personnel-programs/_files/apm/apm-210.pdf.

78. Katherine S. Newman, "Re: Diversity Statements at the University of California," Office of the Provost and Executive Vice President for Academic Affairs, March 20, 2025, https://ucop.edu/communications/_files/2025-03-20-provost-ltr-re-diversity-statements.pdf; Vimal Patel, "The University of California Will Stop Requiring Diversity Statements in Hiring," *New York Times*, March 20, 2025, https://www.nytimes.com/2025/03/20/us/diversity-statements-university-of-california.html.

79. "Regents Policy 4400."

Chapter Two

1. The social psychologist Wolfgang Stroebe reports that while only 29% of colleges used student teaching evaluations in 1973, that number rose to 68% in 1983, 86% in 1993, and 94% in 2010. The 2010 survey found that "nearly all deans declared that classroom teaching was a major part of the performance evaluation of their faculty." Wolfgang Stroebe, "Student Evaluations of Teaching Encourages Poor Teaching and Contributes to Grade Inflation: A Theoretical and Empirical Analysis," *Basic and Applied Social Psychology* 42, no. 4 (2020): 276 (citing J. Elizabeth Miller and Peter Seldin, "Changing Practices in Faculty Evaluation: Can Better Evaluation Make a Difference?," *Academe* 100, no. 3 [May–June 2014]: https://www.aaup.org/article/changing-practices-faculty-evaluation).

2. Wendy Nelson Espeland and Michael Sauder, *Engines of Anxiety: Academic Rankings, Reputation, and Accountability* (Russell Sage Foundation, 2016), 28.

3. Ryerson University v. Ryerson Faculty Association, 2018 CanLII 58446 (ON LA) (Kaplan, Arb.), https://mcliu.ca/wp-content/uploads/2018/08/Student_evaluation_arbitration.pdf.

4. Ryerson University v. Ryerson Faculty Association, 2018 CanLII 58446, at 3, https://mcliu.ca/wp-content/uploads/2018/08/Student_evaluation_arbitration.pdf ("the results were actually skewed by bias and their use quite possibly contravened the *Human Rights Code*"); see also Dan Cavanagh et al., "Does the Use of SET Results in Faculty Employment Decisions Violate Anti-Discrimination Laws?," May 22, 2023, available at https://papers.ssrn.com/sol3/papers.cfm?abstract_id=4455833; and Troy Heffernan and Paul Harpur, "Discrimination Against Academics and Career Implications of Student Evaluations: University Policy Versus Legal Compliance," *Assessment & Evaluation in Higher Education* 48, no. 8 (2023): 1283–94, https://doi.org/10.1080/02602938.2023.2225806.

5. Title VII of the Civil Rights Act of 1964, 42 U.S.C. §§ 2000e–2000e17 (as amended), https://www.eeoc.gov/statutes/title-vii-civil-rights-act-1964.

6. Bob Uttl, Carmela A. White, and Daniela Wong Gonzalez, "Meta-Analysis of Faculty's Teaching Effectiveness: State Evaluation of Teaching Ratings and Student Learning Are Not Related," *Studies in Educational Evaluation* 54 (2017): 22, 40.

7. Bob Uttl and Dylan Smibert, "Student Evaluations of Teaching: Teaching Quantitative Courses Can Be Hazardous to One's Career," *PeerJ* (2017): 5, https://pubmed.ncbi.nlm.nih.gov/28503380/.

8. John A. Centra, *Differences in Responses to the Student Instructional Report: Is It Bias?* (Educational Testing Service, 2009), https://www.ets.org/research/policy_research_reports/publications/report/2009/jwuf.html; James Felton et al., "Attractiveness, Easiness and Other Issues: Student Evaluations of Professors on Ratemyprofessors.com," *Assessment & Evaluation in Higher Education* 33, no. 1 (2008): 45–61.

9. Usha Chowdhary, "Instructor's Attire as a Biasing Factor in Students' Ratings of an Instructor," *Clothing and Textiles Research Journal* 4, no. 2 (1988): 17–22.

10. Landon D. Reid, "The Role of Perceived Race and Gender in the Evaluation of College Teaching on RateMyProfessors.com," *Journal of Diversity in Higher Education* 3, no. 3 (2010): 137–52.

11. Felton et al., "Attractiveness, Easiness and Other Issues"; Andrew S. Rosen, "Correlations, Trends and Potential Biases Among Publicly Accessible Web-Based Student Evaluations of Teaching: A Large-Scale Study of RateMyProfessors.com Data," *Assessment & Evaluation in Higher Education* 43, no. 1 (2018): 31–44.

12. Yanan Fan et al., "Gender and Cultural Bias in Student Evaluations: Why Representation Matters," *PLoS ONE* 14, no. 2 (2019): 1–16, https://doi.org/10.1371/journal.pone.0209749.

13. Friederike Mengel, Jan Sauermann, and Ulf Zolitz, "Gender Bias in Teaching Evaluations," *Journal of the European Economic Association* 17, no. 2 (2019): 535–66.

14. Lillian MacNell, Adam Driscoll, and Andrea N. Hunt, "What's in a Name: Exposing Gender Bias in Student Ratings of Teaching," *Innovations Higher Education* 40 (2015): 291–303.

15. Lauren A. Rivera and Andras Tilcsik, "Scaling Down Inequality: Rating Scales, Gender Bias, and the Architecture of Evaluation," *American Sociological Review* 84, no. 2 (2019): 248–74.

16. Whitney Buser, Cassondra L. Batz-Barbarich, and Jill Kearns Hayter, "Evaluation of Women in Economics: Evidence of Gender Bias Following Behavioral Role Violations," *Sex Roles* 86 (2022): 699. Professor Buser's study was discussed in Colleen Flaherty, "Ratings and Gender Bias Over Time," *Inside Higher Ed*, October 30, 2022, https://www.insidehighered.com/news/2022/10/31/ratings-and-bias-against-women-over-time, which is where I first encountered it.

17. Stroebe, "Student Evaluations of Teaching," 283–89; Wolfgang Stroebe, "Why Good Teaching Evaluations May Reward Bad Teaching: On Grade Inflation and Other Unintended Consequences of Student Evaluations," *Perspectives on Psychological Science* 11, no. 6 (2016): 800. The sources in the following notes, and many others, are collected and described in Professor Stroebe's articles. It's worth noting that the promise of high grades is not the only "bribe" that works to inflate student teaching evaluation scores. Studies have found that chocolate bars and cookies work too, even when they weren't given by the instructor being rated. Stroebe, "Student Evaluations of Teaching," 285; Robert J. Youmans and Benjamin D. Jee, "Fudging the Numbers: Distributing Chocolate Influences Student Evaluations of an Undergraduate Course," *Teaching of Psychology* 34, no. 4 (2007): 245–47; Michael Hessler et al., "Availability of Cookies During an Academic Course Session Affects Evaluation of Teaching," *Medical Education* 52, no. 10 (2018): 1064–72.

18. Kristin F. Butcher, Patrick J. McEwan, and Akila Weerapana, "The Effects of an Anti-Grade-Inflation Policy at Wellesley College," *Journal of Economic Perspectives* 28, no. 3 (Summer 2014): 200, https://doi.org/10.1257/jep.28.3.189.

19. In fact, as Dennis E. Clayson has observed, even if students didn't base their evaluations on expected good grades and lighter rigor, professors' perceptions that they did would be enough to lead to changes in their grades and class content. See Dennis E. Clayson, *A Comprehensive Critique of Student Evaluation of Teaching: Critical Perspectives on Validity, Reliability, and Impartiality* (Routledge, 2021), 58.

20. Michael H. Birnbaum, "A Survey of Faculty Opinions Concerning Student Evaluations of Teaching," California State University, Fullerton (2000): http://psych.fullerton.edu/mbirnbaum/faculty3.htm.

21. Melanie Moore and Richard Trahan, "Tenure Status and Grading Practices," *Sociological Perspectives* 41 no. 4 (1998): 778, https://doi.org/10.2307/1389669.

22. Stroebe, "Student Evaluations of Teaching," 288.

23. Stuart Rojstaczer, "Grade Inflation at American Colleges and Universities," GradeInflation.com, last updated March 29, 2016, https://www.gradeinflation.com/.

24. Stanley Rothman, April Kelly-Woessner, and Matthew Woessner, *The Still Divided Academy: How Competing Visions of Power, Politics, and Diversity Complicate the Mission of Higher Education* (Rowman & Littlefield, 2010), 182.

25. April Kelly-Woessner and Matthew C. Woessner, "My Professor Is a Partisan Hack: How Perceptions of a Professor's Political Views Affect Student Course Evaluations," *PS: Political Science and Politics* 39, no. 3 (2006): 499.

26. Eric Kaufmann, *Academic Freedom in Crisis: Punishment, Political Discrimination, and Self-Censorship*, Center for the Study of Partisanship and Ideology, CSPI Report No. 2 (March 1, 2021): 132–33, https://www.cspicenter.com/p/academic-freedom-in-crisis-punishment.

27. Jeannie Suk Gersen, "The Trouble with Teaching Rape Law," *New Yorker*, December 15, 2014, https://www.newyorker.com/news/news-desk/trouble-teaching-rape-law. Gersen's colleague Alan Dershowitz, whose approach to teaching of rape law has been particularly controversial over the years, has written publicly about a student telling him he "should expect to be 'savaged'" in his reviews because of his approach to teaching rape law. Dershowitz claimed that at the end of the semester, "a small group of students used the power of the evaluations in an attempt to exact their political revenge." Although Dershowitz didn't change what he taught, the moral he drew from the experience was that untenured professors are surely "being coerced into changing their teaching by the fear of negative evaluations." Connie Bruck, "Alan Dershowitz, Devil's Advocate," *New Yorker*, July 29, 2019, https://www.newyorker.com/magazine/2019/08/05/alan-dershowitz-devils-advocate; Alan M. Dershowitz, "Political Correctness Cops Strike on Campus," in *Contrary to Popular Opinion* (Pharos Books, 1992), 117.

28. Khiara M. Bridges, "Evaluating Pressures on Academic Freedom," *Houston Law Review* 59, no. 4 (2022), https://houstonlawreview.org/article/35601-evaluating-pressures-on-academic-freedom.

29. For notable exceptions, see William Arthur Wines and Terence J. Lau, "Observations on the Folly of Using Student Evaluations of College Teaching for Faculty Evaluation, Pay, and Retention Decisions and Its Implications for Academic Freedom," *William & Mary Journal of Race, Gender, and Social Justice* 13, no. 4 (2006): 167–202; Jason Rodriguez, "The Weaponization of Student Evaluations of Teaching: Bullying and the Undermining of Academic Freedom," *AAUP Journal of Academic Freedom* 10 (2019): 1–16; Stanley Rothman, April Kelly-Woessner, and Matthew Woessner, "Academic Freedom, Tenure, and the Free Exchange of Ideas," in *The Still Divided Academy*, 166:

> As student satisfaction and retention become more important to the bottom line, institutions place greater emphasis on student evaluations of professors. . . . [P]eer evaluation is one of the key processes that secure academic freedom. The principle that academics are best able to judge the competency of their peers is the justification for faculty committees on tenure and promotion. Yet colleges and universities appear to place increased emphasis on students' evaluations of faculty.

Robert E. Haskell, "Academic Freedom, Tenure, and Student Evaluation of Faculty: Galloping Polls in the 21st Century," ERIC Clearinghouse on Assessment and Evaluation, August 1998, https://eric.ed.gov/?id=ED426114.

30. S.B. 83, 2024 Gen. Assemb., 2024 Sess. (Ohio 2024), https://www.legislature.ohio.gov/legislation/135/sb83.

31. Sweezy v. New Hampshire, 354 U.S. 234, 263 (1957) (Frankfurter, J., concurring) (quoting University of Cape Town and University of the

Witwatersrand, *The Open Universities in South Africa* [Witwatersrand University Press, 1957], 10–12).

32. Robert Morse and Eric Brooks, "How U.S. News Calculated the 2025 Best Colleges Rankings," *U.S. News & World Report*, September 23, 2024, https://www.usnews.com/education/best-colleges/articles/how-us-news-calculated-the-rankings.

33. AAUP, *Contingent Appointments and the Academic Profession* (American Association of University Professors, 2003, revised 2023, updated 2024), https://www.aaup.org/report/contingent-appointments-and-academic-profession.

34. American Federation of Teachers, *An Army of Temps: AFT Contingent Faculty Quality of Work/Life Report, 2022* (American Federation of Teachers, 2022), https://www.aft.org/sites/default/files/media/documents/2023/Contingent_Faculty_Survey_2022_interactive.pdf.

35. For work by those who do have the relevant expertise, see Adrianna Kezar, Tom DePaola, and Daniel T. Scott, *The Gig Academy: Mapping Labor in the Neoliberal University* (Johns Hopkins University Press, 2019); Herb Childress, *The Adjunct Underclass: How America's Colleges Betrayed Their Faculty, Their Students, and Their Mission* (University of Chicago Press, 2019); Joe Berry and Helena Worthen, *Power Despite Precarity: Strategies for the Contingent Faculty Movement in Higher Education* (Pluto Press, 2021); Henry Reichman, "Introduction: Academic Capitalism and the Crisis of the Professoriate," *Journal of the Early Republic* 42, no. 4 (Winter 2022): 543–55; Eric Fure-Slocum and Claire Goldstene, eds., *Contingent Faculty and the Remaking of Higher Education: A Labor History* (University of Illinois Press, 2024).

36. Espeland and Sauder, *Engines of Anxiety*, 38–39. Equally essential is Colin Diver's book on the effect of rankings at the undergraduate level. As Diver says of *U.S. News* rankings, "by far their most consequential impact has been their distortion of institutional priorities and programs." Colin Diver, *Breaking Ranks: How the Rankings Industry Rules Higher Education and What to Do About It* (Johns Hopkins University Press, 2022), 60.

37. Colin Diver tells part of this story as well in *Breaking Ranks*, quoting a retired University of Chicago professor as having "recently accused Chicago of succumbing to 'the false coin of academic glory doled out by the U.S. News and World Report.'" Diver, *Breaking Ranks*, 21–22.

38. "Academics," The University of Chicago, accessed July 14, 2024, https://collegeadmissions.uchicago.edu/academics.

39. Tyler Warner, "U of C Jumps to Tie for Eighth in Latest U.S. News Ranking," *Chicago Maroon*, September 22, 2008, https://chicagomaroon.com/9439/news/u-of-c-jumps-to-tie-for-eighth-in-latest-us-news-ranking/.

40. Ted O'Neill, "The Brief and Wondrous Life of the Uncommon Application," *Noodle*, September 29, 2015, https://www.noodle.com/articles/the-brief-and-wondrous-life-of-the-uncommon-application (available as a drop-down page under the "College Application" heading).

41. Dean O'Neill's successor, James Nondorf, has said something similar about the pressures from above. "'Don't kid yourselves, the presidents and trustees want you to have more applications,' he said. 'If you don't think that's the case, I don't know what schools you're working at, but it's true.'" Eric Hoover, "Application Inflation," *Chronicle of Higher Education*, November 5, 2010, https://www.chronicle.com/article/application-inflation/.

42. Al Gaspari, "Acceptance Rate Falls with Common Application," *Chicago Maroon*, April 7, 2009, https://chicagomaroon.com/10084/news/acceptance-rate-falls-with-common-application/.

43. "Graphing Tool for US News Rankings (1984–2024)," Aron Frishberg, https://www.aronfrishberg.com/projects/usnews.

44. O'Neill, "Brief and Wondrous Life."

45. See Diver, *Breaking Ranks*, 17.

46. Apologies to Mark 8:36, Matthew 16:26, and Luke 9:25.

Chapter Three

1. Kalven Committee, *Report on the University's Role in Political and Social Action* (University of Chicago, 1967), https://provost.uchicago.edu/reports/report-universitys-role-political-and-social-action. A particularly clear argument for why other schools should follow Chicago comes from the founding director of the University of Chicago's Forum on Free Inquiry and Expression, law professor Tom Ginsburg: "The Case for University Silence," *Persuasion*, October 25, 2023, https://www.persuasion.community/p/the-case-for-university-silence.

2. Stanley Fish, *Save the World on Your Own Time* (Oxford University Press, 2008), 17.

3. "FIRE Launches Campaign in Support of University of Chicago Free Speech Statement," Foundation for Individual Rights in Education, September 28, 2015, https://www.thefire.org/news/fire-launches-campaign-support-university-chicago-free-speech-statement. "The Chicago Principles: Report of the Committee on Freedom of Expression," American Council of Trustees and Alumni, accessed August 21, 2024, https://www.goacta.org/the-chicago-principles/: "ACTA has long recognized the value of this statement and has worked tirelessly to ensure other institutions enact the Chicago Principles or similar policies."

4. End Woke Higher Education Act, H.R. 3724, 118th Congress, 2nd Session (2024), https://www.congress.gov/bill/118th-congress/house-bill/3724/text.

5. Geoffrey R. Stone et al., *Report of the Committee on Freedom of Expression* (2014), 2, http://provost.uchicago.edu/FOECommitteeReport.pdf (emphasis added).

6. "An Open Letter to College and University Trustees and Regents: It's Time to Adopt Institutional Neutrality," Academic Freedom Alliance,

Heterodox Academy, and Foundation for Individual Rights and Expression, last updated July 11, 2024, https://institutionalneutrality.org/.

7. Michael Vasquez, "Is Institutional Neutrality Catching On?" *Chronicle of Higher Education*, February 8, 2024, https://www.chronicle.com/article/is-institutional-neutrality-catching-on.

8. Heterodox Academy reports that by the end of 2024, 148 colleges and universities had adopted something akin to an institutional neutrality statement, most in the previous year. Alex Arnold, *The Rising Tide of Statement Neutrality in Higher Education: How Universities Are Rethinking Institutional Speech* (Heterodox Academy, 2025), https://content.heterodoxacademy.org/uploads/HxA_Statement-Neutrality-Report_FINAL.pdf.

9. The American Council of Trustees and Alumni keeps a running list on its website. "Adopt a Policy of Institutional Neutrality," American Council of Trustees and Alumni, https://www.goacta.org/kalven-report/.

10. Columbia University Senate, "Resolution Reconfirming Our Commitment to the Principles of Academic Freedom and Shared Governance," in University Senate Plenary, February 2, 2024, 39–40, https://senate.columbia.edu/sites/default/files/content/Plenary%20Binders%202023-24/US_Plenary%20Binder_20240202.pdf. By requiring a "compelling institutional interest" akin to a legal obligation for institutional speech, the resolution of the University Senate—passed without dissent—would be even more restrictive than the Kalven Report. For a pointed description of the powerlessness of Columbia's Senate ("the most broadly representative body on campus . . . seem[s] to become less relevant with every passing year") in an era of "presidentialization," see David Pozen, "Seeing the University More Clearly," *Balkinization*, May 6, 2024, https://balkin.blogspot.com/2024/05/seeing-university-more-clearly.html.

11. "Our Statement on Statements," College of the Holy Cross, https://www.holycross.edu/our-statement-statements#:~:text=Institutional%20statements%20are%20not%20opinion,are%20welcome%20at%20Holy%20Cross. The board of regents of the University of Texas, the chancellor of Vanderbilt University, and the presidents of Johns Hopkins, Northwestern University, Stanford University, Williams College, and USC have stated similar commitments. Kate McGee, "UT System Prohibits Its Universities from Making Political or Social Statements," *Texas Tribune*, August 23, 2024, https://www.texastribune.org/2024/08/23/ut-system-free-speech-policy/; August 21–22, 2024, Meeting of the UT System Board of Regents, "U.T. System: Discussion and Appropriate Action Related to Updates to the University of Texas System Commitment to Freedom of Speech and Expression," August 22, 2024, University of Texas Systems, https://www.utsystem.edu/board-of-regents/meetings/board-meeting-2024-08-21; Daniel Diermeier, "'Principled Neutrality,'" *Inside Higher Ed*, May 4, 2022, https://www.insidehighered.com/views/2022/05/05/academic-leaders-shouldnt-take-political-stances-opinion; Ron Daniels

et al., "On Institutional Statements from the University," Johns Hopkins University, August 15, 2024, https://president.jhu.edu/messages/2024/08/15/on-institutional-statements-from-the-university/; Michael Schill, "Message from President Schill to Senior Leadership," Northwestern University, October 12, 2023, https://www.northwestern.edu/leadership-notes/2023/message-from-president-schill-to-senior-leadership.html; Richard Seller and Jenny Martinez, "An Update for the Stanford Community," *Stanford Report*, October 11, 2023, https://news.stanford.edu/report/2023/10/11/update-stanford-community/; Maud S. Mandel, "Campus Vigil on Israel and Gaza, and the College President's Role in the Wake of World Crises," Office of the President, Williams College, October 12, 2023, https://president.williams.edu/writings-and-remarks/letters-from-the-president/campus-vigil-on-israel-and-gaza-and-the-college-presidents-role-in-the-wake-of-world-crises/; Carol L. Folt, Andrew Guzman, and Steven Shapiro, "Welcome to a New Year at USC," University of Southern California, August 20, 2024, https://we-are.usc.edu/2024/08/20/welcome-to-a-new-year-at-usc/.

12. The Ohio State University Board of Trustees, "Adoption of Ohio State Philosophy on Institutional and Leadership Statements in Support of the Chicago Principles," Ohio State University, August 16, 2023, https://www.goacta.org/wp-content/uploads/2023/08/Resolution-Public-Statements.pdf; CMC Board of Trustees, "CMC Policy on Institutional Nonpartisanship," Claremont McKenna College, December 6, 2018, https://www.cmc.edu/free-expression/institutional-nonpartisanship. Utah's Board of Higher Education has required the sixteen institutions it oversees to make policies clarifying that they, "as governmental entities, or employees acting in their official capacities as representatives of the institution must refrain from taking public positions on political, social, or unsettled issues that do not directly relate to the institution's mission, role, or pedagogical objectives." Amanda Covington and Geoffrey Landward, "Resolution Establishing Expectations for Implementing Principles of Free Expression on Campus," Utah System of Higher Education, December 1, 2023, https://www.documentcloud.org/documents/24180310-resolution-on-freedom-of-expression-on-university-campuses.

13. S.B. 195, 2023 Gen, Assemb., 2023–2024 Sess. (N.C. 2023), https://www.ncleg.gov/BillLookup/2023/S195; S.B. 202, 2024 Gen. Assemb., 2024 Sess. (Ind. 2024), https://iga.in.gov/legislative/2024/bills/senate/202/actions.

14. John W. Boyer, *Annual Report to the Faculty: The University of Chicago in the 1960s and 1970s* (The College of the University of Chicago, 1999), 20–21, https://college.uchicago.edu/sites/default/files/documents/Boyer_OccasionalPapers_V4.pdf.

15. John W. Boyer, *Academic Freedom and the Modern University: The Experience of the University of Chicago* (The College of the University of Chicago, 2016),

88–89, https://news.uchicago.edu/sites/default/files/attachments/Academic_Freedom_V1.pdf.

16. Boyer, *Annual Report to the Faculty*, 21.

17. Boyer, *Academic Freedom and the Modern University*, 88.

18. This and the quotes that follow from the Kalven Report can all be found at Kalven Committee, *Report on the University's Role in Political and Social Action*, https://provost.uchicago.edu/sites/default/files/documents/reports/KalvenRprt_0.pdf. The Kalven Report is also collected alongside other University of Chicago policies and speeches on free speech and academic freedom in Tony Banout and Tom Ginsburg, eds., *The Chicago Canon on Free Inquiry and Expression* (University of Chicago Press, 2024).

19. William Rainey Harper, "The Thirty-Sixth Quarterly Statement of the President of the University," *University Record* 5, no. 42 (January 18, 1901): 376, https://campub.lib.uchicago.edu/view/?docId=mvol-0007-0005-0042#page/8/mode/1up. Longtime UChicago dean and historian John Boyer notes that Chicago's then-provost Edward Levi sent the 1899 statement to Kalven while he was drafting the committee's report. Boyer, *Academic Freedom and the Modern University*, 94.

20. For an especially wide-ranging critique, see Ben Medeiros, "The Ideological Significance of 'Institutional Neutrality' Mandates in State-Level Campus Speech Legislation," *First Amendment Studies* 53, nos. 1–2 (2019): 22–40.

21. Peter C. Herman, "Institutional Neutrality Doesn't Go Far Enough," *Inside Higher Ed*, October 1, 2024, https://www.insidehighered.com/opinion/views/2024/10/01/institutional-neutrality-doesnt-go-far-enough-opinion; Daniel Diermeier, "Scholarly Associations Aren't Entitled to Their Opinions," *Wall Street Journal: Opinion*, September 6, 2024, https://www.wsj.com/opinion/scholarly-associations-arent-entitled-to-their-opinions-it-chills-debate-harms-young-faculty-2584c09c?mod=e2two.

22. Harry Kalven's son, Jamie Kalven, has written of his father that "as a legal scholar, he appreciated a strong dissent in which a judge gives full-voiced expression to his own views, but he was, above all, moved to celebrate what he called 'judicial statesmanship'—the personal qualities and craftsmanship required to locate common ground and build consensus in support of an institutional statement." Jamie Kalven, "Unfinished Business of the Kalven Report," *Chicago Maroon*, November 28, 2006, https://chicagomaroon.com/7464/viewpoints/op-ed/unfinished-business-of-the-kalven-report/.

23. Robert Post, "The Kalven Report, Institutional Neutrality, and Academic Freedom," in *Revisiting the Kalven Report: The University's Role in Social and Political Action*, ed. Keith E. Whittington and John Tomasi (John Hopkins University Press, forthcoming), available at https://papers.ssrn.com/sol3/papers.cfm?abstract_id=4516235, *5n14 (hereinafter Post, "Kalven Report"). Emphasis is added in the quotation from the Kalven Report.

24. Post, "Kalven Report," *5–6.

25. Post, "Kalven Report," *10; Richard Knight, "Sanctions, Divestment, and U.S. Corporations in South Africa," in *Sanctioning Apartheid*, ed. Robert E. Edgar (Africa World Press, 1990), 69.

26. Professor Stone wrote this after the University of Chicago, invoking the Kalven Report, declined calls in 2007 to divest from Sudan after the genocide in Darfur. Geoffrey Stone, "Darfur and the Kalven Report: A Personal Journey," *The University of Chicago Law School Faculty Blog*, February 9, 2007, https://uchicagolaw.typepad.com/faculty/2007/02/darfur_and_the_.html.

27. Post, "Kalven Report," *6–7, *6n17.

28. AAUP, "A Statement of the Association's Council: The Question of Institutional Neutrality," *AAUP Bulletin* 55, no. 4 (December 1969): 488, https://www.jstor.org/stable/40223872; Post, "Kalven Report," *6n17; Peter Wood, *The Illusion of Institutional Neutrality* (National Association of Scholars, 2024), 6, https://www.nas.org/storage/app/media/Reports/Illusion_of_Institutional_Neutrality/Wood_The_Illusion_of_Institutional_Neutrality.pdf.

29. AAUP, "A Statement of the Association's Council," 488.

30. Donald N. Koster and Winton U. Solberg, "On Institutional Neutrality," *AAUP Bulletin* 56, no. 1 (March 1970): 11, https://www.aaup.org/sites/default/files/On_Institutional_Neutrality.pdf; see also Carl Landauer et al., "Further Comments on Institutional Neutrality," *AAUP Bulletin* 56, no. 2 (June 1970): 123: "I wish to state my opinion that institutional neutrality is an indispensable condition of academic freedom, that all arguments for the opposite position are spurious, and that our Association [the AAUP] would destroy its own foundation if it were to countenance institutional partisanship."

31. Stanley Kurtz, James Manley, and Jonathan Butcher, *Campus Free Speech: A Legislative Proposal* (Goldwater Institute, 2017), 5, https://goldwaterinstitute.org/wp-content/uploads/2019/03/Campus-Free-Speech-A-Legislative-Proposal_Web.pdf.

32. As the AAUP has argued, "Institutional neutrality is neither a necessary condition for academic freedom nor categorically incompatible with it." AAUP, *On Institutional Neutrality* (AAUP, 2025), https://www.aaup.org/report/institutional-neutrality. I was a coauthor of the AAUP's statement, which explains its overlap with some of the arguments to come in this chapter.

33. Robert Paul Wolff, *The Ideal of the University* (Routledge, 2017), 77.

34. Both Heterodox Academy's proposed neutrality policy and Harvard's Institutional Voice report—both discussed in the following section—explicitly set actions such as divestment aside without any explanation of how they are relevantly distinguished from statements. Heterodox Academy, *Extraordinary U: The Heterodox Academy Model of Statement Neutrality in College and University Speech on Contested Social Issues* (Heterodox Academy, 2024), https://content.heterodoxacademy.org/uploads/Extraordinary-U-The-Heterodox-Academy-Model-of-Statement-Neutrality.pdf; Harvard University Institutional Voice

Working Group, *Report on Institutional Voice in the University* (Harvard University, 2024), 1, https://provost.harvard.edu/sites/hwpi.harvard.edu/files/provost/files/institutional_voice_may_2024.pdf.

35. Stone, "Darfur and the Kalven Report."

36. "In its building names and its campus symbols, the University communicates values, confers honor, and expresses gratitude to those who have contributed to its mission. In other words, the University itself speaks through its building names." Committee to Establish Principles on Renaming, "Letter of the Committee to Establish Principles on Renaming," Yale University, November 21, 2016, 3, https://president.yale.edu/sites/default/files/files/CEPR_FINAL_12-2-16.pdf.

37. "A Time for Change: Contextualizing the Removal of 'Boalt Hall' from the Law School's Identity," UC Berkeley Law, https://www.law.berkeley.edu/atimeforchange/.

38. "Chancellor & Dean David Faigman: Board of Directors Votes on New Name for the College," University of California College of the Law, San Francisco, July 27, 2022, https://www.uclawsf.edu/2022/07/27/chancellor-dean-david-faigman-board-of-directors-votes-on-new-name-for-the-college/. Changing the name of UC Hastings required the school both to get state legislation passed and to survive litigation seeking to stop the name change. See A.B. 1936, 2021–2022, Reg. Sess. (Cal. 2022); Karen Sloan, "Lawsuit Over UC Hastings Name Change Is Tossed," Reuters, February 7, 2024, https://www.reuters.com/legal/government/lawsuit-over-uc-hastings-name-change-is-tossed-2024-02-07/.

39. For example, Harmeet Dhillon—the attorney who represented the descendants of Serranus Hastings in opposing the UC Hastings name change in court—framed the law school's decision as another "woke issue du jour." Sergio Quintara, "Legal Fight Over Renaming San Francisco Law School," NBC Bay Area, October 4, 2022, https://www.nbcbayarea.com/news/local/san-francisco/legal-fight-renaming-san-francisco-law-school/3021281/. Dhillon now leads the Civil Rights Division at the US Department of Justice.

40. "Commemoration expresses values. . . . [A] change in the way a community memorializes its past offers a way to recognize important alterations in the community's values. . . . [A] great university will rightly decide what to commemorate and what to honor, subject always to the obligation not to efface the history that informs the world in which we live." "Letter of the Committee to Establish Principles on Renaming," 3. Yale University's Witt Report from 2016 very helpfully recommends a presumption against renaming, made stronger when the name honors someone who made major contributions to the university. This presumption can be overcome, however, if the namesake's principal legacy is "fundamentally at odds with the mission of the University," especially if that legacy was problematic even at the time the namesake lived, if it was part of the reason why the university

honored the namesake, and if the name marks something (like a building or residential college) that is meant to build community. "Letter of the Committee to Establish Principles on Renaming."

41. "Letter of the Committee to Establish Principles on Renaming."

42. Stone, "Darfur and the Kalven Report."

43. Neive Rodriguez, "Oriental Institute Renamed Institute for the Study of Ancient Cultures," *Chicago Maroon*, April 4, 2023, https://chicagomaroon.com/38707/news/oriental-institute-renamed-institute-for-the-study-of-ancient-cultures/; Andrew Ferry and Rory Nevins, "Millennia of History in 100 Years," *Chicago Maroon*, January 14, 2020, https://chicagomaroon.com/27413/grey-city/millennia-history-100-years/.

44. Robert Michaelson, "Should UChicago Rename the 'Robert A. Millikan Professorship'?," *Chicago Maroon*, March 4, 2021, https://chicagomaroon.com/28355/viewpoints/letter/uchicago-rename-robert-millikan-professorship/. Compare "Twenty-Three UChicago Faculty Receive Named, Distinguished Service Professorships in 2019," *UChicago News*, December 30, 2019, https://news.uchicago.edu/story/twenty-three-uchicago-faculty-receive-named-distinguished-service-professorships-2019, with "Seventeen UChicago Faculty Members Receive Named, Distinguished Service Professorships," *UChicago News*, January 3, 2023, https://news.uchicago.edu/story/seventeen-uchicago-faculty-members-receive-named-distinguished-service-professorships.

45. Edward Nik-Khan, "Chicago Neoliberalism and the Genesis of the Milton Friedman Institute (2006–2009)," in *Building Chicago Economics: New Perspectives on the History of America's Most Powerful Economics Program*, ed. Robert Van Horn, Philip Mirowski, and Thomas A. Stapleford (Cambridge University Press, 2011), 382; Michael Lipkin, "Faculty Senate to Weigh Future of New Friedman Institute," *Chicago Maroon*, September 22, 2008, https://chicagomaroon.com/9433/news/faculty-senate-to-weigh-future-of-new-friedman-institute/; Adam Kissel, "Divesting from Milton Friedman," Foundation for Individual Rights and Expression, June 19, 2008, https://www.thefire.org/news/divesting-milton-friedman; Hussein Agrama et al., "University of Chicago Faculty Letter on the Milton Friedman Institute," *The Shock Doctrine*, June 6, 2008, https://web.archive.org/web/20120119054047/naomiklein.org/shock-doctrine/resources/faculty-letter-mfi; David Glenn, "At U. of Chicago, Dispute over Friedman Center Continues to Simmer," *Chronicle of Higher Education*, October 31, 2008, https://www.chronicle.com/article/at-u-of-chicago-dispute-over-friedman-center-continues-to-simmer.

46. Qi Xu, "Law School Project Pushes for Portraits of Females," *Yale News*, November 19, 2015, https://yaledailynews.com/blog/2015/11/19/law-school-project-pushes-for-portraits-of-females/.

47. Judith Resnik and Denny Curtis have traced in colorful detail the shift in the iconography of justice from figurative to increasingly abstract. Significant commissions for contemporary art in courthouses built in the

last few decades has tended to go toward artists like Ellsworth Kelly, whose monochromes fill the Moakley Federal Courthouse in Boston. Brian Soucek, "Not Representing Justice: Ellsworth Kelly's Abstraction in the Boston Courthouse," *Yale Journal of Law & the Humanities* 24, no. 1 (2012): 287–304; Judith Resnik and Dennis Curtis, *Representing Justice: Invention, Controversy, and Rights in City-States and Democratic Courtrooms* (Yale University Press, 2011).

48. Xu, "Law School Project Pushes for Portraits of Females."

49. Tom Ginsburg, "A Constitutional Perspective on Institutional Neutrality," in *Revisiting the Kalven Report*, ed. Whittington and Tomasi.

50. According to historian and longtime UChicago dean John Boyer, these two sentences were Kalven's response to another member of his committee, education scholar Jacob Getzels, who "thought it necessary to include some reference to the University's willingness to defend a basic social milieu of tolerance and individual freedom, invoking the precedent of the German universities under Hitler." Boyer, *Academic Freedom and the Modern University*, 91n149. The report goes on to discuss cases of actions—like owning property, accepting gifts, awarding honors—where choices are unavoidable. "In the exceptional instance, these corporate activities of the university may appear so incompatible with paramount social values as to require careful assessment of the consequences." But the report insists on a "heavy presumption against the university . . . modifying its corporate activities to foster social or political values, however compelling and appealing they may be."

51. Covington and Landward, "Resolution Establishing Expectations for Implementing Principles of Free Expression on Campus."

52. Kurtz, Manley, and Butcher, *Campus Free Speech*, 22.

53. This criticism has come both from inside and outside the University of Chicago, and from both the left and the right. See, for example, Wood, *The Illusion of Institutional Neutrality*, 22, 29; Anton Ford, "The Cynicism of Institutional Neutrality," *Chronicle of Higher Education*, May 29, 2024, https://www.chronicle.com/article/the-cynicism-of-institutional-neutrality; Max Servetar, "The University of Chicago Is Not Neutral," *Chicago Maroon*, October 12, 2020, https://chicagomaroon.com/28025/viewpoints/op-ed/university-chicago-neutral/; Eli Nova Rose, "Kalven Report and Chicago Academic Politics," *Decasia*, November 30, 2008, https://decasia.org/academic_culture/2008/11/kalven-report-and-chicago-academic-politics/index.html.

54. Brief of Amici Curiae Brown University et al. in Support of Respondents, Students for Fair Admissions, Inc. v. President & Fellows of Harvard Coll., 600 U.S. 181 (2023) (Nos. 20-1199 & 21-707); Brief for Amici Curiae Nineteen Colleges and Universities in Support of Respondents, Dep't of Homeland Sec. v. Regents of the Univ. of California, 140 S. Ct. 1891 (2020) (Nos. 18-587, 18-588, and 18-589); Brief of Amici Curiae Colleges and Universities in Support of Respondents, Trump v. Hawaii, 585 U.S. 667 (2018) (No. 17-965); Paul Alivisatos and Katherine Baicker, "Upholding the Value of

Diversity," University of Chicago Office of the Provost, June 29, 2023, https://provost.uchicago.edu/announcements/upholding-value-diversity; Robert J. Zimmer and Daniel Diermeier, "Message Regarding Immigration," *UChicago News*, January 29, 2017, https://news.uchicago.edu/story/message-regarding-immigration.

55. Zimmer and Diermeier, "Message Regarding Immigration."

56. Brief of Brown University et al. as Amici Curiae in Support of the Relief Sought by Petitioners and Intervenor-Plaintiff, 1, Darweesh v. Trump, No. 17 CIV. 480 (AMD), 2017 WL 388504 (E.D.N.Y. Jan. 28, 2017) (1:17-cv-00480).

57. "UChicago Launches Scholarships and Comprehensive Support for Students and Scholars Impacted by War in Ukraine," *UChicago News*, March 15, 2022, https://news.uchicago.edu/story/uchicago-launches-scholarships-comprehensive-support-students-scholars-ukraine-war.

58. Dobbs v. Jackson Women's Health Org., 597 U.S. 215 (2022).

59. "Reproductive Services Through the University of Chicago Medicine," UChicago Medicine, June 24, 2022, https://www.uchicagomedicine.org/forefront/news/2022/june/reproductive-services-through-the-university-of-chicago-medicine.

60. Michael V. Drake, "UC Statement on Dobbs v. Jackson Women's Health Organization Decision," UC Office of the President, June 24, 2022, https://www.universityofcalifornia.edu/press-room/uc-statement-dobbs-v-jackson-womens-health-organization-decision.

61. "Challenges to Trump Administration 'Denial of Care' Rule," Americans United for the Separation of Church and State, last modified January 11, 2024, https://www.au.org/how-we-protect-religious-freedom/legal-cases/cases/challenges-to-trump-administration-denial-of-care-rule/.

62. John Garvey, "On Dobbs: Let's Build a Civilization of Love," Catholic University of America, June 24, 2022, https://garvey.catholic.edu/communications/letters/on-dobbs-lets-build-a-civilization-of-love.html.

63. This is what makes my claim about Kalven's illusory promise of neutrality meaningfully different from those that Tony Banout, the executive director of the University of Chicago Forum for Free Inquiry and Expression, has written to refute. Tony Banout, "Institutional Neutrality Has Never Been About Politics," *Chronicle of Higher Education*, April 29, 2024, https://www.chronicle.com/article/institutional-neutrality-has-never-been-about-politics.

64. Ginsburg, "A Constitutional Perspective on Institutional Neutrality," 2.

65. Anthony J. Casey and Tom Ginsburg, "Kalven for Corporations: Should For-Profit Corporations Adopt Public Statement Policies?" *University of Chicago Business Law Review* 3 (2024): 303–22.

66. Heterodox Academy, *Extraordinary U*, 2. The short version of Heterodox's proposal is this:

> When a contested social issue arises that does not directly concern the academic mission of our college or university, institutional leadership

> will not issue a position statement on that issue. On rare occasions when a public issue arises that directly affects the mission of this college or university, institutional leaders may issue statements that articulate the significance of that issue to our campus community. (1)

67. Heterodox Academy, *Extraordinary U*, 7.

68. Harvard University Institutional Voice Working Group, *Report on Institutional Voice in the University* 1.

69. Michael Della Rocca et al., *Report of the Committee on Institutional Voice* (Yale University, 2024), 4, https://president.yale.edu/sites/default/files/files/Committee-on-Institutional-Voice-Report-Oct_27_2024.pdf.

70. According to Harvard's Institutional Voice report, university leaders have no business speaking beyond "their area of institutional expertise and responsibility: the running of a university." UCLA's report claims that its "recommendation to restrict the use of institutional voice aligns with the skills and responsibilities of university leaders. . . . University leaders may not—indeed likely will not—have enough expertise in a relevant subject to weigh in on societal, political and public matters." UCLA Office of the Executive Vice Chancellor and Provost, "UCLA Statement on Statements," working group report, September 12, 2024, https://evcp.ucla.edu/plans-and-reports/detail/statement-on-statements-working-group-report/.

71. Christopher L. Eisgruber, "Princeton's Tradition of Institutional Restraint," *Princeton Alumni Weekly*, November 7, 2022, https://paw.princeton.edu/article/princeton-president-christopher-eisgruber-tradition-institutional-restraint.

72. Della Rocca et al., "Report of the Committee on Institutional Voice."

73. UCLA Office of the Executive Vice Chancellor and Provost, "UCLA Statement on Statements."

74. Sam Haselby (@samhaselby), "Not sure what to think of the war, waiting for a statement from the Cornell Department of Comparative Literatures to help me sort things," X post, October 10, 2023, https://x.com/samhaselby/status/1711691167039971452.

75. The AAUP's *1915 Declaration of Principles on Academic Freedom and Academic Tenure* argued that just as presidents can't control the decisions of judges they put on the bench, trustees can't direct what conclusions professors will reach. "For the same reason, trustees are no more to be held responsible for, or to be presumed to agree with, the opinions or utterances of professors, than the president can be assumed to approve of all the legal reasonings of the courts." AAUP, *1915 Declaration of Principles on Academic Freedom and Academic Tenure* (AAUP, 1915), 4, https://www.aaup.org/NR/rdonlyres/A6520A9D-0A9A-47B3-B550-C006B5B224E7/0/1915Declaration.pdf. Around the same time, President Lowell of Harvard argued similarly that "if a university or college censors what its professors may say, if it restrains them from uttering something that is does not approve, it thereby assumes responsibility for that which it permits

them to say." Abbott Lawrence Lowell, "President's Report," *Official Register of Harvard University* 15, no. 6 (1918): 20, https://iiif.lib.harvard.edu/manifests/view/drs:427018586$22i.

76. For an argument to this effect, see Joel Hass et al., "Davis Faculty for Israel letter to UC Davis Campus Counsel," Steering Committee of Davis Faculty for Israel, July 2021, https://academicengagement.org/wp-content/uploads/2021/07/Davis-Faculty-for-Israel_July-2021.pdf?fbclid=IwAR3dGIAzH1C8EVqsdXn1YM7Ns23aFRmXbThjAZS9vRunAT29DZJbnBb-PcM. Section 92000 of the California Education Code prohibits use of UC's name in support of any "political, religious, sociological, or economic movement, activity, or program." Cal. Educ. Code § 92000.

77. Lanham Act of 1946, 15 U.S.C. §§ 1051 (confusion), 1052 (tarnishment); see also Jack Daniel's Properties, Inc. v. VIP Prod. LLC, 599 U.S. 140 (2023).

78. "If individual units on campus can easily go rogue and engage in institutional speech on their own initiative, it is the university that will suffer the political consequences. An individual department posting controversial political statements on its official website invites political retaliation not only against itself but against the university as a whole. Self-preservation dictates that the university be able to control its own institutional speech." Keith E. Whittington, "Political Solidarity Statements Threaten Academic Freedom," *Chronicle of Higher Education*, January 26, 2024, https://www.chronicle.com/article/political-solidarity-statements-threaten-academic-freedom.

79. J. Sellers Hill and Nia L. Orakwue, "Harvard Student Groups Face Intense Backlash for Statement Calling Israel 'Entirely Responsible' for Hamas Attack," *Harvard Crimson*, October 10, 2023, https://www.thecrimson.com/article/2023/10/10/psc-statement-backlash/.

80. "Defenders of departmental statements argue that junior faculty have tough skins and are not intimidated by collective statements. This is an empirical question, but my intuition is that anyone who makes such a claim either agrees with the dominant, mainly left-wing views expressed in departmental statements, or has not been a junior faculty member for a very long time." Ginsburg, "A Constitutional Perspective on Institutional Neutrality," 4.

81. "The smaller the number of individuals composing a majority, and the smaller the compass within which they are placed, the more easily will they concert and execute their plan of oppression. Extend the sphere and you take in a greater variety of parties and interests; you make it less probable that a majority of the whole will have a common motive to invade the rights of other citizens; or if such a common motive exists, it will be more difficult for all who feel it to discover their own strength and to act in unison with each other." James Madison, *The Federalist*, no. 10.

82. Brian Leiter, "Some Thoughts About the 'Encampment' at the University of Chicago (and Its End)," *Leiter Reports: A Philosophy Blog*, May 7,

2024, https://leiterreports.typepad.com/blog/2024/05/the-encampment-at-the-university-of-chicago.html.

83. This limit is even more directly related to that found in Harvard's recent Institutional Voice policy, discussed above, which argues that university leaders "should restrict themselves to matters within their area of institutional expertise and responsibility: the running of a university." Harvard University Institutional Voice Working Group, "Report on Institutional Voice in the University," 1.

84. "UCSF Principles of Community in Response to COVID-19," University of California San Francisco, August 18, 2020, https://coronavirus.ucsf.edu/principles-community; Valerie Strauss, "More than 160 Law Deans Denounce Attempted Insurrection and Effort to Decertify Election—but Don't Name Names," *Washington Post*, January 12, 2021, https://www.washingtonpost.com/education/2021/01/12/157-law-deans-denounce-attempted-insurrection-effort-decertify-election-dont-name-names/.

85. American Association of University Professors, American Council on Education, and Association of Governing Boards of Universities and Colleges, *Statement on Government of Colleges and Universities* (American Association of University Professors, 1966), https://www.aaup.org/report/statement-government-colleges-and-universities.

86. The remainder of this section is in part adapted from material originally published in the spring 2022 issue of *Academe*, the magazine of the American Association of University Professors. Brian Soucek, "Academic Freedom and Departmental Speech," *Academe* 108, no. 2 (Spring 2022: Beyond Town and Gown), https://www.aaup.org/article/academic-freedom-and-departmental-speech.

87. "Gender Studies Departments in Solidarity with Palestinian Feminist Collective," Palestinian Feminist Collective, May 15, 2021, https://genderstudiespalestinesolidarity.weebly.com/.

88. "UPDATED UCD Faculty Statement of Solidarity with Palestinians," UC Davis Department of Asian American Studies, May 27, 2021, https://asa.ucdavis.edu/faculty-public-statements.

89. Hass et al., "Davis Faculty for Israel Letter to UC Davis Campus Counsel."

90. Cal. Educ. Code § 92000.

91. This became the official position of the University of California in July 2024, when the Board of Regents voted to make previous Academic Senate recommendations on departmental statements, including disclaimers, mandatory systemwide. Michael Burke, "UC Approves Policy to Limit Faculty Speech on Websites," EdSource, July 17, 2024, https://edsource.org/2024/uc-approves-less-restrictive-policy-to-limit-faculty-speech-on-websites/715825. "Regents Policy 4408: Policy on Public and Discretionary Statements by Academic Units," University of California Board of Regents, July 18, 2024,

https://regents.universityofcalifornia.edu/governance/policies/4408.html: "In particular, the Policy requires the following: . . . That Discretionary Statements be accompanied by a disclaimer expressly stating that the statement should not be taken as a position of the University, or the campus, as a whole."

92. Kevin R. Johnson, "Statement Regarding Military Recruitment," Office of the Dean, UC Davis School of Law, September 28, 2017, https://law.ucdavis.edu/sites/g/files/dgvnsk10866/files/media/documents/Statement%20regarding%20Military%20Recruitment1.pdf.

93. Natalie M. Batalha et al., "Black Lives Matter: A Statement from Our Department," UC Santa Cruz Astronomy and Astrophysics, June 24, 2020, https://www.astro.ucsc.edu/news-events/news/blm-statement.html.

94. "Recommendations for Department Political Statements," University of California, Academic Senate, June 2, 2022, https://senate.universityofcalifornia.edu/_files/reports/rh-senate-divs-recs-for-dept-statements.pdf. These recommendations were subsequently turned into mandates when the UC Regents incorporated them into its own policy in July 2024. "Regents Policy 4408." UC Board of Regents.

95. Hari M. Osofsky, "Open Letter Against Racism," Office of the Dean, Penn State Law and the School of International Affairs, June 9, 2020, https://pennstatelaw.psu.edu/sites/default/files/documents/pdfs/Penn%20State%20Law%20and%20SIA%20Open%20Letter%20Against%20Racism%20for%20Signature_6.9.20.pdf; Brian Leiter, "The Northwestern Law Dean Search," *Brian Leiter's Law School Reports*, May 10, 2021, https://leiterlawschool.typepad.com/leiter/2021/05/the-northwestern-law-dean-search.html#more.

96. University of California, "APM - 011: Academic Freedom, Protection of Professional Standards, and Responsibilities of Non-Faculty Academic Appointees," February 1, 2020, 1n2, https://www.ucop.edu/academic-personnel-programs/_files/apm/amp-011-issuance/apm-011.pdf.

97. Mark Gabbart, *Report on the Implications for Academic Freedom in the Case of Andrew Potter at McGill University* (Ottawa: Canadian Association of University Teachers, 2018), https://www.caut.ca/sites/default/files/caut_report_-andrew_potter_-_mcgill_university_2018-11.pdf.

98. "Law Deans Antiracist Clearinghouse," Association of American Law Schools, https://www.aals.org/antiracist-clearinghouse/.

99. Colin A. Webster, "BLM Solidarity Statement," UC Davis Classics, July 20, 2020, https://classics.ucdavis.edu/news/blm-solidarity-statement.

100. Robert J. Zimmer, "Reinforcing the Chicago Principles and the Kalven Report," University of Chicago, Office of the President, October 5, 2020, https://web.archive.org/web/20211001214546/https://president.uchicago.edu/from-the-president/announcements/100520-kalven-report.

101. Keith E. Whittington, "On Institutional Neutrality and the Purpose of a University," April 20, 2024, 30, available at https://papers.ssrn.com/sol3/papers.cfm?abstract_id=4801896: "If the expression of political opinions is

no longer merely an extramural, private matter but is instead an aspect of the professional speech and conduct of a member of the faculty acting on institutional business, then political opinions can no longer be reasonably ruled out of bounds in hiring and promotion decisions." To be clear, Whittington offers this as a reason why institutional and departmental statements should be generally disfavored, whereas I draw from his work a reason for limiting the topics on which departments choose to speak.

102. Robert Post, "The Unfortunate Consequences of a Misguided Free Speech Principle," *Daedalus: Journal of the American Academy of Arts & Sciences* 153, no. 3 (Summer 2024: The Future of Free Speech): 136–37, https://www.amacad.org/daedalus/future-of-free-speech.

Chapter Four

"The remedy for speech that is false is speech that is true. This is the ordinary course in a free society. The response to the unreasoned is the rational; to the uninformed, the enlightened; to the straight-out lie, the simple truth." United States v. Alvarez, 567 U.S. 709, 727 (2012), citing Whitney v. California, 274 U.S. 357, 377 (1927) (Brandeis, J., concurring): "If there be time to expose through discussion the falsehood and fallacies, to avert the evil by the processes of education, the remedy to be applied is more speech, not enforced silence."

1. Solomon Amendment, 10 U.S.C. § 983.

2. Rumsfeld v. F. for Acad. & Institutional Rts., Inc., 547 U.S. 47, 60 (2006).

3. Rumsfeld v. F. for Acad. & Institutional Rts., Inc., 547 U.S. 47, 65 (2006).

4. I discuss this history and the legal issues surrounding the FDA's former blood donation policies in Brian Soucek, "The Case of the Religious Gay Blood Donor," *William & Mary Law Review* 60, no. 5 (2019): 1893–942, https://scholarship.law.wm.edu/cgi/viewcontent.cgi?article=3812&context=wmlr.

5. Ruthann Richter, "Stanford Blood Center Officials Say SJSU Ban on Blood Drives Could Hurt Supply," Stanford Medicine, February 5, 2008, https://med.stanford.edu/news/all-news/2008/02/stanford-blood-center-officials-say-sjsu-ban-on-blood-drives-could-hurt-supply.

6. "Chancellor's Statement on Donating Blood," UC Davis, April 2, 2020, https://www.ucdavis.edu/news/chancellors-statement-on-donating-blood.

7. Soucek, "The Case of the Religious Gay Blood Donor," 1902; see also Jennifer Scharpf, *Summary of Responses to FDA Docket Opened July 26, 2016: Blood Donor Deferral Policy for Reducing the Risk of HIV Transmission by Blood and Blood Products* (US Food & Drug Administration, 2017), 14, https://fda.report/media/104972/BPAC-04.04.17-04.05.17-Meeting-Presentation-Summary-of-Responses-to-FDA-Docket-Opened-July-26-2016-Blood-Donor-Deferral-Policy-for-Reducing-the-Risk-of-HIV-Trans.pdf (noting that nearly half

of the comments received that were against changes to the deferral policy "appear[ed] linked to a single write-in campaign").

8. Heterodox Academy, *Extraordinary U: The Heterodox Academy Model of Statement Neutrality in College and University Speech on Contested Social Issues* (Heterodox Academy, February 2024), 6, https://content.heterodoxacademy.org/uploads/Extraordinary-U-The-Heterodox-Academy-Model-of-Statement-Neutrality.pdf.

9. Sydney Amestoy, "Students React to Violence Outside of Turning Point USA Event," *California Aggie*, November 3, 2022, https://theaggie.org/2022/11/03/students-react-to-violence-outside-of-turning-point-usa-event/.

10. Erin Reed (@ErinInTheMorn), "Charlie Kirk, CEO of Turning Point USA, is openly calling for the lynching of transgender individuals," X post, February 17, 2023, https://x.com/ErinInTheMorn/status/1626747081275715585.

11. Kevin R. Johnson, "UC Davis Stands Against Hate," UC Davis School of Law, March 14, 2023, https://law.ucdavis.edu/deans-blog/uc-davis-stands-against-hate (linking to Chancellor May's video).

12. Charlie Kirk (@charliekirk11), "UC Davis Chancellor Gary S. May took the time to record a bizarre video and slander me and our amazing students at TPUSA ahead of our event tonight, so I took the time to respond," X post, March 14, 2023, https://x.com/charliekirk11/status/1635751427883814912.

13. NTD News, "LIVE: Conservative Activist Charlie Kirk Speaks About American Values at UC Davis," YouTube, streamed live on March 14, 2023, video, 1:40:56, https://www.youtube.com/watch?v=tuUMxAJFFAo.

14. Here my account finds an ally in Kristine Bowman and Sigal Ben-Porath's New Democratic Model of Free Speech, under which "institutions at times use their voices to engage in counterspeech, expressing their commitment to core values of equality and inclusion, and speaking out against speech that is harmful or dehumanizing toward groups of members of the campus community." Kristine L. Bowman and Sigal R. Ben-Porath, "Institutional Neutrality, Fairness, and the New Democratic Model of Free Speech," in *Revisiting the Kalven Report: The University's Role in Social and Political Action*, ed. Keith E. Whittington and John Tomasi (John Hopkins University Press, forthcoming), 9. Bowman and Ben-Porath argue for a fairness principle to guide universities in deciding when to speak in order to ensure "epistemic equality": an atmosphere where speakers of all backgrounds feel welcome and can expect to be heard. This may be a more interventionist approach than mine turns out to be, but we certainly share an emphasis on the potential for university speech to advance the equality and inclusion values that many universities see as part of their mission.

15. Kristine L. Bowman and Katharine Gelber, "Responding to Hate Speech: Counterspeech and the University," *Virginia Journal of Social Policy & the Law* 28, no. 3 (2021): 248–74. Bowman and Gelber develop their argument by drawing on a long line of philosophical work on speech act theory and the potential

uses of counterspeech to defuse the power of hate speech. See Rae Langton, "Blocking as Counter-Speech," in *New Work on Speech Acts*, ed. Daniel Fogal, Daniel W. Harris, and Matt Moss (Oxford University Press, 2018); Maxime Lepoutre, "Can 'More Speech' Counter Ignorant Speech?," *Journal of Ethics & Social Philosophy* 16, no. 3 (2019); Mary Kate McGowan, "Responding to Harmful Speech: The More Speech Response, Counter Speech, and the Complexity of Language Use," in *Voicing Dissent: The Ethics and Epistemology of Making Disagreement Public*, ed. Casey Rebecca Johnson (Routledge, 2018).

16. Gertz v. Robert Welch, Inc., 418 U.S. 323, 339 (1974); see also Robert C. Post, *Democracy, Expertise, Academic Freedom: A First Amendment Jurisprudence for the Modern State* (Yale University Press, 2012).

17. "Administrators who claim to defend academic freedom and then condemn the content of faculty and student speech and expression that it should protect risk chilling speech and expression and eroding the very academic freedom that they claim to protect." "Polarizing Times Demand Robust Academic Freedom," AAUP, November 15, 2023, https://www.aaup.org/news/polarizing-times-demand-robust-academic-freedom.

Chapter Five

1. For a broader argument against "more speech is better speech" conceptions of the First Amendment, see Mary Anne Franks, *Fearless Speech: Breaking Free from the First Amendment* (Bold Type Books, 2024).

2. Sigal R. Ben-Porath, *Free Speech on Campus* (University of Pennsylvania Press, 2017); Erwin Chemerinsky and Howard Gillman, *Free Speech on Campus* (Yale University Press, 2017); Keith E. Whittington, *Speak Freely: Why Universities Must Defend Free Speech* (Princeton University Press, 2018); Vikram David Amar and Alan E. Brownstein, "A Close-Up, Modern Look at First Amendment Academic Freedom Rights of Public College Students and Faculty," *Minnesota Law Review* 101 (2017): 1943–85; Charles R. Lawrence III, "If He Hollers Let Him Go: Regulating Racist Speech on Campus," *Duke Law Journal* 39, no. 3 (1990): 431–83; Mary-Rose Papandrea, "The Free Speech Rights of University Students," *Minnesota Law Review* 101 (2017): 1801–61; Robert Post, "Theorizing Student Expression: A Constitutional Account of Student Free Speech Rights," *Stanford Law Review* 76, Symposium Issue (2024): 1643–73.

3. For those looking for a deeper dive into the legal landscape here, see Brian Soucek, "Speech First, Equality Last," *Arizona State Law Journal* 55 (2023): 681–732; Todd E. Pettys, "Hostile Learning Environments, the First Amendment and Public Higher Education," *Connecticut Law Review* 54, no. 1 (2022): 1–55.

4. Catherine E. Lhamon, "Dear Colleague Letter on Shared Ancestry," US Department of Education, Office for Civil Rights, November 7, 2023,

https://www2.ed.gov/about/offices/list/ocr/letters/colleague-202311-discrimination-harassment-shared-ancestry.pdf:

> Schools that receive federal financial assistance have a responsibility to address discrimination against Jewish, Muslim, Sikh, Hindu, Christian, and Buddhist students, or those of another religious group, when the discrimination involves racial, ethnic, or ancestral slurs or stereotypes; when the discrimination is based on a student's skin color, physical features, or style of dress that reflects both ethnic and religious traditions; and when the discrimination is based on where a student came from or is perceived to have come from, including discrimination based on a student's foreign accent; a student's foreign name, including names commonly associated with particular shared ancestry or ethnic characteristics; or a student speaking a foreign language.

See also Catherine E. Lhamon, "Dear Colleague Letter: Protecting Students from Discrimination, Such as Harassment, Based on Race, Color, or National Origin, Including Shared Ancestry or Ethnic Characteristics," US Department of Education, Office for Civil Rights, May 7, 2024, https://www2.ed.gov/about/offices/list/ocr/letters/colleague-202405-shared-ancestry.pdf.

5. "U.S. Department of Education Releases Final Title IX Regulations, Providing Vital Protections Against Sex Discrimination," press release, US Department of Education, April 19, 2024, https://www.ed.gov/news/press-releases/us-department-education-releases-final-title-ix-regulations-providing-vital-protections-against-sex-discrimination; Katherine Knott and Johanna Alonso, "A New Title IX Era Brings Confusion and Frustration," *Inside Higher Ed*, August 1, 2024, https://www.insidehighered.com/news/students/safety/2024/08/01/enforcement-bidens-title-ix-rule-complicated-lawsuits.

6. Davis v. Monroe Cnty. Bd. of Educ., 526 U.S. 629, 650 (1999).

7. Espinoza v. Montana Dep't of Revenue, 591 U.S. 464, 520 (2020) (Breyer, J., dissenting) (cleaned up); Walz v. Tax Comm'n of City of New York, 397 U.S. 664, 669 (1970).

8. As the Office of Civil Rights in the Department of Education puts it, "[A] hostile environment may take the form of a single victim and multiple offenders." Lhamon, "Dear Colleague Letter: Protecting Students from Discrimination."

9. For an example of one such complaint, filed against my own university, see StandWithUs Center for Legal Justice, "Letter of Complaint Pursuant to Title VI of the Civil Rights Act of 1964," April 1, 2024, https://swulegaljustice.org/legal-actions/uc-davis-title-vi-complaint/. UC Davis, along with four other UC campuses, voluntarily resolved the cases filed against them in a December 2024 agreement with the Department of Education. Anamaria Loya, "University of California Resolution Letter," US Department of Education

Office for Civil Rights, December 20, 2024, https://ocrcas.ed.gov/sites/default/files/ocr-letters-and-agreements/09222257-a.pdf.

10. Brian Gnandt, "University of Michigan Resolution Letter," US Department of Education Office for Civil Rights, June 17, 2024, 10, https://www2.ed.gov/about/offices/list/ocr/docs/investigations/more/15242066-a.pdf (emphasis added).

11. University of Michigan, "University of Michigan Resolution Agreement to OCR Complaint Number 15-24-2066 and 15-24-2128," US Department of Education Office for Civil Rights, June 14, 2024, 4, 1, https://www2.ed.gov/about/offices/list/ocr/docs/investigations/more/15242066-b.pdf (emphasis added).

12. "Feds' New 'Anti-Harassment' Mandate to Universities: Violate the First Amendment," Foundation for Individual Rights and Expression, June 27, 2024, https://www.thefire.org/news/feds-new-anti-harassment-mandate-universities-violate-first-amendment.

13. Alex Morey (@1AMorey), "It's the biggest campus story flying under the radar right now," X post, June 27, 2024, https://x.com/1AMorey/status/1806356604775764236.

14. Lhamon, "Dear Colleague Letter: Protecting Students from Discrimination," 3.

15. Lhamon, "Dear Colleague Letter: Protecting Students from Discrimination," 12.

16. Ralph Wilson and Isaac Kamola, *Free Speech and Koch Money: Manufacturing a Campus Culture War* (Pluto Press, 2021), 92–94.

17. Compl., ¶39, Speech First, Inc. v. Schlissel, 333 F. Supp. 3d 700 (E.D. Mich. 2018), vacated and remanded, 939 F.3d 756 (6th Cir. 2019).

18. Speech First, Inc. v. Sands, 144 S. Ct. 675 (2024).

19. Soucek, "Speech First, Equality Last," 709.

20. Speech First, Inc. v. Schlissel, 939 F.3d 756, 774 (6th Cir. 2019) (White, J., dissenting) (describing university officials' testimony, not mentioned in the majority opinion, swearing that no students have been or would be disciplined for speaking in the way Students A, B, and C desired). Sworn assurances from university leaders that students would not be disciplined for such speech was deemed irrelevant, since the mere existence of a vague policy by itself "causes self-censorship." Speech First, Inc. v. Fenves, 979 F.3d 319, 337 (5th Cir. 2020).

21. For more on how narratives surrounding so-called cancel culture on college campuses have been deliberately crafted to serve conservative political ends, see Mary Anne Franks, "The Lost Cause of Free Speech," 2 *Journal of Free Speech Law* 337 (2022): 337–58, https://www.journaloffreespeechlaw.org/franks.pdf; Isaac Kamola, *Manufacturing Backlash: Right-Wing Think Tanks and Legislative Attacks on Higher Education, 2021–2023* (Center for the Defense of Academic Freedom, AAUP, 2024), https://www.aaup.org/file/Manufacturing_Backlash_final_1.pdf.

22. Soucek, "Speech First, Equality Last," 720–21.

23. Speech First, Inc. v. Schlissel, 939 F.3d 756, 766 (6th Cir. 2019).

24. Speech First, Inc. v. Fenves, 979 F.3d 319, 332, 337, 334 n.12 (5th Cir. 2020), as revised (Oct. 30, 2020).

25. Speech First, Inc. v. Cartwright, 32 F.4th 1110, 1115, 1118, 1118 n.2, 1121 (11th Cir. 2022).

26. Speech First, *Free Speech in the Crosshairs: Bias Reporting on College Campuses* (2022), 3, https://speechfirst.org/wp-content/uploads/2023/04/SF-2022_Bias-Response-team-and-Reporting-System-Report_Final.pdf.

27. Speech First, Inc. v. Schlissel, 939 F.3d 756, 763, 765 (6th Cir. 2019).

28. Speech First, Inc. v. Schlissel, 939 F.3d 756, 765 (6th Cir. 2019); Speech First, Inc. v. Fenves, 979 F.3d 319, 338 (5th Cir. 2020).

29. Speech First, Inc. v. Fenves, 979 F.3d 319, 338 (5th Cir. 2020).

30. Speech First, Inc. v. Cartwright, 32 F.4th 1110, 1124 (11th Cir. 2022).

31. Pete Grieve, "University to Freshmen: Don't Expect Safe Spaces or Trigger Warnings," *Chicago Maroon*, August 23, 2016, https://chicagomaroon.com/22405/news/university-to-freshmen-dont-expect-safe-spaces-or-trigger-warnings/ (quoting a letter to incoming students at the University of Chicago sent by its dean of students, Jay Ellison).

32. For an especially subtle account of how universities' truth-seeking mission and their social and civic missions can be mutually reinforcing, even if they may seem to give rise to conflicting demands regarding speech, see Sigal R. Ben-Porath, *Cancel Wars: How Universities Can Foster Free Speech, Promote Inclusion, and Renew Democracy* (University of Chicago Press, 2023).

33. "FIRE Letter to Medical College of Wisconsin, May 8, 2023," Foundation for Individual Rights in Education, May 8, 2023, https://www.thefire.org/research-learn/fire-letter-medical-college-wisconsin-may-8-2023.

34. Robert Post has contested the idea that university quads should be treated the same way that the First Amendment treats public parks. Robert Post, "The Classic First Amendment Tradition Under Stress: Freedom of Speech and the University," in *The Free Speech Century*, ed. Lee C. Bollinger and Geoffrey R. Stone (Oxford University Press, 2019), 121. Post argues that "public universities are not public parks. State institutions of higher education exist to educate students. The appropriate First Amendment inquiry for a court is therefore whether student demonstrations . . . seriously interfere with the educational mission of a public university." Post's view might be more aspirational than descriptive, however. Other free speech scholars largely do equate public universities, or at least the quad-like spaces at public universities, with public parks. See, for example, Whittington, *Speak Freely*, 124: "State college campuses are generally recognized as designated public fora." For an especially rich if unconclusive discussion of the doctrinal possibilities, see Vikram David Amar and Alan E. Brownstein, "A Close-Up, Modern Look at

First Amendment Academic Freedom Rights of Public College Students and Faculty," *Minnesota Law Review* 101 (2017): 1963–70.

35. Ryan Chen and I have explained in detail why the holding of *Meriwether v. Hartop* is far narrower than it's generally taken to be, how a series of actions both by conservatives *and* liberals helped that misunderstanding take hold, and what consequences have followed. See Brian Soucek and Ryan Chen, "Misunderstanding Meriwether," *Fordham Law Review* 92, no. 1 (2023): 57–101. The opinion discussed in this section is Meriwether v. Hartop, 992 F.3d 492 (6th Cir. 2021).

36. AAUP, *1915 Declaration of Principles on Academic Freedom and Academic Tenure* (AAUP, 1915), https://www.aaup.org/NR/rdonlyres/A6520A9D-0A9A-47B3-B550-C006B5B224E7/0/1915Declaration.pdf.

37. Robert Post convincingly argues that the standard test for protecting government employee speech misses the point of academic freedom protections. The standard test serves a different value: roughly, protecting contributions to public opinion that are necessary for democratic legitimacy. Academic freedom, by contrast, exists to protect the development of expertise—what Post calls democratic competency. According to Post, "regulation of faculty research and publication should trigger First Amendment coverage whether or not faculty speech involves matters of public concern." Robert C. Post, *Democracy, Expertise, Academic Freedom: A First Amendment Jurisprudence for the Modern State* (Yale University Press, 2012), 85.

38. As the US Court of Appeals for the Ninth Circuit has said: "Recognizing our limitations as judges, we should hesitate before concluding that academic disagreements about what may appear to be esoteric topics are mere squabbles over jobs, turf, or ego." Demers v. Austin, 746 F.3d 402, 413 (9th Cir. 2014).

39. Meriwether v. Hartop, 992 F.3d 492, 505 (6th Cir. 2021) (internal quotations omitted) (quoting Keyishian v. Bd. of Regents of Univ. of State of N.Y., 385 U.S. 589, 603 (1967)). But see Post, *Democracy, Expertise, Academic Freedom*, 62, 66–67.

40. Meriwether v. Hartop, 992 F.3d 492, 509 (6th Cir. 2021) (quoting Keyishian v. Bd. of Regents of Univ. of State of N.Y., 385 U.S. 589, 603 (1967)).

41. Meriwether v. Hartop, 992 F.3d 492, 504 (6th Cir. 2021) (quoting Keyishian v. Bd. of Regents of Univ. of State of N.Y., 385 U.S. 589, 603 (1967)).

42. Meriwether v. Hartop, 992 F.3d 492, 505 (6th Cir. 2021) (quoting Sweezy v. State of N.H. by Wyman, 354 U.S. 234, 250 (1957)).

43. Amici Curiae Brief of Law Professors Darren Rosenblum and Brian Soucek et al. in Support of Petition for Panel Rehearing or Rehearing En Banc, 3, Meriwether v. Hartop, 992 F.3d 492 (6th Cir. 2021).

44. Joan Wallach Scott, *Knowledge, Power, and Academic Freedom* (Columbia University Press, 2019), 117.

45. Jeffrey M. Jones, "U.S. Confidence in Higher Education Now Closely Divided," Gallup, July 8, 2024, https://news.gallup.com/poll/646880/confidence-higher-education-closely-divided.aspx.

46. "Educational Gag Orders," PEN America, November 8, 2021, https://pen.org/report/educational-gag-orders/; "CRT Forward," UCLA School of Law Critical Race Studies Program, https://crtforward.law.ucla.edu/.

47. "Princeton Principles for a Campus Culture of Free Inquiry," James Madison Program in American Ideals and Institutions, Princeton University, https://jmp.princeton.edu/princeton-principles-campus-culture-free-inquiry; Donald A. Downs, "Reply to John Wilson's Critique of the Princeton Principles for a Campus Culture of Free Inquiry," *Academe Blog*, September 12, 2023, https://academeblog.org/2023/09/12/reply-to-john-wilsons-critique-of-the-princeton-principles-for-a-campus-culture-of-free-inquiry/.

48. The eventual settlement in the case can be found at Settlement Agreement and Release, Meriwether v. Hartop, 992 F.3d 492 (6th Cir. 2021), https://ohiocapitaljournal.com/wp-content/uploads/2022/04/Meriwether-Final-Settlement-w_Meriwether-signature.pdf. See also Susan Tebben, "Shawnee State Professor Settles Case, Won't Be Required to Use Identified Pronouns," *Ohio Capital Journal*, April 21, 2022, https://ohiocapitaljournal.com/2022/04/21/shawnee-state-professor-settles-case-wont-be-required-to-use-preferred-pronouns/.

49. As one of FIRE's leaders has said in the press, "We're not having to deal with the tensions that may or may not exist with free speech and other values. . . . [T]here's no other values that we have to defend, which makes our work a little bit easier and more focused" compared to that of organizations like the ACLU. Matt Taibbi, "Move over ACLU, FIRE Is the New Champion of Free Speech," *Racket News*, June 6, 2022, https://taibbi.substack.com/p/move-over-aclu-fire-is-the-new-champion.

Coda

1. AAUP, *Report of a Special Committee: Political Interference and Academic Freedom in Florida's Public Higher Education System* (AAUP, 2023), https://www.aaup.org/file/AAUP_Florida_final.pdf.

2. Stop W.O.K.E. Act, Fla. Stat. § 1000.05 (2022).

3. Fla. Stat. § 1004.097 (2022).

4. H.B. 999, 2023 Leg., Reg. Sess. (Fla. 2023).

5. Fla. Stat. § 1007.55 (2023).

6. Anemona Hartocollis, "Florida Eliminates Sociology as a Core Course at Its Universities," *New York Times*, January 24, 2024, https://www.nytimes.com/2024/01/24/us/florida-universities-sociology.html.

7. AAUP, *Report of a Special Committee: Political Interference and Academic Freedom in Florida's Public Higher Education System*, 22–24, 24, 26, 27–28.

8. The AAUP report describes the takeover in detail at AAUP, *Report of a Special Committee: Political Interference and Academic Freedom in Florida's Public Higher Education System*, 3–12. Unless otherwise noted, citations for quotations in the discussion that follows can all be found in the AAUP's report. Christopher Rufo has provided his own perspective on the takeover of New College in a YouTube video, available at Christopher F. Rufo, "The Conservative Counter-Revolution Begins in the Universities," YouTube, January 12, 2023, video, 17:38, https://www.youtube.com/watch?v=gOftsRQyHAg.

9. Jeremy Bauer-Wolf, "New College of Florida Approves Corcoran's President Contract—Doubling His Predecessor's Salary," *Higher Ed Dive*, October 20, 2023, https://www.highereddive.com/news/new-college-of-florida-approves-corcorans-president-contract-doubling-hi/697400/.

10. Liam Knox, "New College of Florida Trashes Library Books," *Inside Higher Ed*, August 16, 2024, https://www.insidehighered.com/news/quick-takes/2024/08/16/new-college-florida-throws-away-hundreds-library-books.

11. Christopher F. Rufo, "The Arc of Reform: New College of Florida Votes to Abolish Its Gender Studies Program," Christopher F. Rufo.com, August 10, 2023, https://christopherrufo.com/p/the-arc-of-reform; AAUP, *Report of a Special Committee: Political Interference and Academic Freedom in Florida's Public Higher Education System*, 9–10.

12. AAUP, *Report of a Special Committee: Political Interference and Academic Freedom in Florida's Public Higher Education System*, 9.

13. Stanley Fish, "Free Speech Is Not an Academic Value," *Chronicle of Higher Education*, March 20, 2017, https://www.chronicle.com/article/Free-Speech-Is-Not-an-Academic/239536.

14. "Teaching and research are the very purpose of an academic institution and the reason why the public values and supports it. This means that the faculty, who are responsible for carrying out those central tasks, should be viewed as having a special status within the institution." AAUP, *On the Relationship of Faculty Governance to Academic Freedom* (AAUP, 1994), https://www.aaup.org/report/relationship-faculty-governance-academic-freedom.

15. American Association of University Professors, American Council on Education, and Association of Governing Boards of Universities and Colleges, "Statement on Government of Colleges and Universities," AAUP, 1966, https://www.aaup.org/report/statement-government-colleges-and-universities; AAUP, *On the Relationship of Faculty Governance to Academic Freedom*. For a historical account of shared governance in the United States, see Larry G. Gerber, *The Rise and Decline of Faculty Governance: Professionalization and the Modern American University* (Johns Hopkins University Press, 2014). For a critique of the current state of university governance, see Timothy V. Kaufman-Osborn, *The Autocratic Academy: Reenvisioning Rule Within America's Universities* (Duke University Press, 2023).

16. David Labaree celebrates the "organizational complexity" of American universities, which on his account have come to combine three distinct forms

of authority—traditional, charismatic, and rational—and three different organizational structures: traditional departments, which provide stability; institutes and centers, which offer flexibility; and central administration, which acts as mediator between the university and the world beyond. David F. Labaree, *A Perfect Mess: The Unlikely Ascendancy of American Higher Education* (University of Chicago Press, 2017), 186–88.

17. AAUP, American Council on Education, and Association of Governing Boards of Universities and Colleges, "Statement on Government of Colleges and Universities."

18. A 2022 study by the *Chronicle of Higher Education* found that "about 51 percent of the time, a president on the receiving end of a no-confidence vote winds up leaving office within a year." The *Chronicle* also estimates that no-confidence votes led to 13% of presidential resignations between 2018 and 2023. Megan Zahneis, "The Past Month Has Seen a Flurry of No-Confidence Votes in College Presidents," *Chronicle of Higher Education*, May 9, 2024, https://www.chronicle.com/article/the-past-month-has-seen-a-flurry-of-no-confidence-votes-in-college-presidents.

19. "America's Censored Classrooms 2024," PEN America, https://pen.org/report/americas-censored-classrooms-2024/.

20. As Anton Ford, a philosopher at the University of Chicago, has asked of the Kalven Report, "Why should 'the instrument of dissent and criticism' be either the individual or the institution? Those are not the only two possibilities. Why shouldn't the instrument of dissent and criticism ever be, instead of the individual faculty member, the collective faculty, and instead of the individual student, the student body? This is not some radical idea. It is a basic principle of democratic governance." Anton Ford, "The Chicago Principles Are Undemocratic," *Chronicle of Higher Education*, May 6, 2024, https://www.chronicle.com/article/the-chicago-principles-are-undemocratic.

21. Liam Knox, "Shrinking Pains at West Virginia University," *Inside Higher Ed*, June 23, 2023, https://www.insidehighered.com/news/governance/executive-leadership/2023/06/23/distraught-west-virginia-u-faculty-push-back.

22. AAUP, American Council on Education, and Association of Governing Boards of Universities and Colleges, "Statement on Government of Colleges and Universities."

23. Harvard University's lawsuit against the Trump administration, the first to be filed by a university in response to attempted funding cuts, laid out the first amendment and procedural problems in detail. "Upholding Our Values, Defending Our University," Harvard University, April 21, 2025, https://www.harvard.edu/president/news/2025/upholding-our-values-defending-our-university/.

24. AAUP, *Report of a Special Committee: Political Interference and Academic Freedom in Florida's Public Higher Education System*, 16–17; Garrett Shanley, "'Oath of Fealty,'" *Chronicle of Higher Education*, November 4, 2024, https://www.chronicle.com/article/oath-of-fealty.

25. Ryan Quinn, "Has Chapel Hill's 'Civic Life' School Become a Conservative Center?" *Inside Higher Ed*, December 11, 2024, https://www.insidehighered.com/news/faculty-issues/curriculum/2024/12/11/chapel-hills-civic-life-school-conservative-center.

26. AAUP, *Contingent Appointments and the Academic Profession* (AAUP, 2024), https://www.aaup.org/file/2024Bulletin_ContingentAppts_0.pdf.

27. Henry Reichman, *Understanding Academic Freedom* (Johns Hopkins University Press, 2025), chap. 4; Keith E. Whittington, "What Can Professors Say on Campus? Intramural Speech and the First Amendment," Yale Law School, August 2, 2023, available at https://papers.ssrn.com/sol3/papers.cfm?abstract_id=4551168.

28. Ruth Milkman and William Herbert, "New Study Reveals Upsurge in Unionization and Strikes in Higher Education," Roosevelt House Public Policy Institute at Hunter College, August 31, 2023, https://www.roosevelthouse.hunter.cuny.edu/new-study-reveals-upsurge-unionization-strikes-higher-education/; Nelson Lichtenstein, "The Largest Strike in the History of American Higher Ed," *Dissent*, November 22, 2022, https://www.dissentmagazine.org/online_articles/largest-strike-higher-ed-uc/; Eleanor J. Bader, "Academic Labor Unions Are Key to Fighting Trump's Repressive Higher Ed Agenda," *Truthout*, December 5, 2024, https://truthout.org/articles/academic-labor-unions-are-key-to-fighting-trumps-repressive-higher-ed-agenda/.

Index